Doing a PhD in the Social Sciences

Covering the academic and operational aspects of PhD research degree programmes, this accessible yet comprehensive book is an essential guide to navigating through the PhD research journey.

Using a mixture of useful information, practical strategies and valuable advice, this book helps readers through the process of doing a PhD by providing essential hints and tips on key aspects such as the following:

- How to start, conduct and manage PhD research
- Working with your supervisor
- Writing your thesis
- Preparing for the viva

This is a crucial resource for anyone wanting to know about approaches to research, substantive theories, data analytical techniques, essential research tools and a range of other issues that affect the chances of PhD success and completion. With global case studies and examples, this invaluable guide is a must-read for anyone undertaking a PhD in the social sciences.

Francis Jegede is Associate Professor in International Relations and Diplomacy and Chair of College Research Committee at the University of Derby, UK.

T0399757

Doing a PhD in the Social Sciences

A Student's Guide to Post-Graduate Research and Writing

Francis Jegede

Routledge
Taylor & Francis Group

LONDON AND NEW YORK

First published 2021
by Routledge
2 Park Square, Milton Park, Abingdon, Oxon OX14 4RN

and by Routledge
605 Third Avenue, New York, NY 10158

Routledge is an imprint of the Taylor & Francis Group, an informa business

British Library Cataloguing-in-Publication Data
A catalogue record for this book is available from the British Library

Library of Congress Cataloging-in-Publication Data
Names: Jegede, Jola, author.
Title: Doing a PhD in the social sciences : a student's guide to post-graduate research and writing / Francis Jegede.
Identifiers: LCCN 2020056609 (print) | LCCN 2020056610 (ebook) | ISBN 9780367519407 (hardback) | ISBN 9780367519414 (paperback) | ISBN 9781003055761 (ebook)
Subjects: LCSH: Dissertations, Academic—Authorship. | Social sciences—Research—Methodology.
Classification: LCC LB2369 .J44 2021 (print) | LCC LB2369 (ebook) | DDC 808.02071—dc23
LC record available at https://lccn.loc.gov/2020056609
LC ebook record available at https://lccn.loc.gov/2020056610

ISBN: 978-0-367-51940-7 (hbk)
ISBN: 978-0-367-51941-4 (pbk)
ISBN: 978-1-003-05576-1 (ebk)

Typeset in Minion
by Apex CoVantage, LLC

This book is dedicated to Daisy, our precious little baby who brings lots of happiness and joy to me and my wife, Sylwia – a wonderful friend, companion and mother of my Daisy.

Shortly after the contract to write this book was signed, the world was hit with COVID-19 health emergency. The pandemic has not only taken many lives and devastated many families and communities around the world, but it has also caused major disruptions to our way of life. This book is also dedicated to the memories of those who lost their lives to COVID-19 pandemic and to the extraordinary work of health care workers around the world who are working hard to save people's lives in a very challenging and worrying time for everyone.

Contents

Figures and tables

Figures

Tables

Introduction

The idea of this book has developed from my experience of supervising and working with many PhD students over an academic career spanning three decades. In my role as a teacher, supervisor, researcher, viva voce examiner and chair of the College Research Committee of the University of Derby, I have gained considerable experience and insight into the challenges and issues that PhD students face. This experience has inspired me to write a book that all prospective PhD students could benefit from.

If you are currently doing your master's programme and thinking of doing a PhD or you are in a PhD programme already and need some support and guidance to get you through your PhD journey, if you ever wonder what a PhD is and where to begin the process of choosing the right institution to do your research, if you are thinking of how to make a success of your PhD thesis or Professional Doctorate or worried about how to face your viva voce examination or if you are a supervisor and have PhD students under your supervision that may benefit from reading a useful and handy tips to help them with their research or you are new to supervisory role, then *Doing a PhD in the Social Sciences: A Student's Guide to Post-Graduate Research and Writing* is the book for you.

Covering the academic and operational aspects of PhD research degree programmes, this book provides essential guide to help you with your PhD as you navigate through your PhD research journey. It offers essential tips and provides valuable information that could help you and your supervisor or director of studies to understand the processes and educational systems that underpin PhD research in UK universities.

Using this book, you will be able to navigate and ease your way through the entire journey, starting from when you start thinking or decide whether to or not to do a PhD, choosing your research topic and the university to study or conducting your research, writing a proposal, deciding on your research methodology, carrying out your research, writing up your thesis and doing your viva voce examination. The book will serve as a useful companion at every stage of your PhD from pre-enrolment through to the very final stage. It concludes with a chapter on how to make the most of your PhD.

By using a mixture of useful information, practical strategies and valuable advice, the book will help you through the process of doing a PhD, giving you essential hints and tips along the way on how to start, conduct and manage your PhD research and work with your director of studies or supervisor.

The book is not intended as, nor does it pretend to be, a research-focused text for those researching in the field of doctoral education. Researching doctoral education is acknowledged as a research field and enterprise in its own right, and there is a large and growing level of resources on the field of researching doctoral education.

This book, however, is about how to undertake doctoral studies in the context of the UK higher education sector. It is a practical handbook packed with proven advice based on real-life experiences of PhD students and supervisors in the UK institutions and other parts of the English-speaking world. It covers the personal, emotional, supervisory, regulatory and institutional environment that affect PhD students' research and offers useful advice and support towards progression and successful completion of doctoral programme.

It provides a wealth of information on active learning, further readings, case studies, examples and illustrations that you can use to good effect to make a success of your PhD project. The book makes the experience of doing a PhD less daunting and guides you through the common pitfalls and obstacles that most doctoral students face while doing their PhD research. It is a real companion and a valuable resource in a journey that can be quite lonely and frustrating to many who embark on doing a PhD.

The book will help experienced PhD supervisors and those new to the role of supervising PhD students to develop practical and effective ways to support their students through their PhD journey. It highlights the purpose, functions and role of supervisors and the responsibility of PhD students to own and drive their own success. Whether you are new to your PhD or you are at an advanced stage of your study, this book will offer you essential guide through the processes you need to go through to complete your PhD. It is an original book based on the experience of the author and of the PhD students he has supervised, managed, examined and directed.

PhD students using this book will find that each chapter contains useful information that could form the basis of discussion with their supervisors and directors of studies. Supervisors and directors of studies will find it useful to guide and provide advice and support for their PhD students. The tips and guidance provided throughout the book will help make your PhD journey less exasperating and the tasks less daunting. The book offers valuable information on the support system PhD students could draw on to deal with challenges relating to personal, emotional and practical issues they may face in the course of their PhD.

It provides practical advice for doing a PhD and offers prospective PhD students and their supervisors a way of understanding the processes involved and how to deal with any challenges they may face while doing their doctoral studies.

Preface

Doing a PhD either through the traditional route of on campus enrolment or via online distance learning is becoming an important and growing feature of higher education in many countries. The rising number of university graduates in the developed world and the improved access to education in low-income countries mean more and more people are venturing further into pursuing advanced post-graduate degrees leading to a PhD awards.

The rapid expansion and growth of undergraduate degree programme and access to higher education means that a large number of people who have completed their undergraduate study now venture further into pursuing a post-graduate research study.

In 2014, 25,020 PhDs were awarded in the UK across all subjects. The top ten countries with PhD awards in 2014 were the US (67,449), Germany (28,147), the UK (25,020), India (24,300), Japan (16,039), France (13,729), South Korea (12,931), Spain (10,889), Italy (10,675) and Australia (8,400). These countries also have the highest number of students currently doing research degree leading to PhD.

The rapid growth in the number of people enrolled in post-graduate research in the last decade suggests that possession of a PhD degree is no longer perceived or considered as the prerogative of those seeking a career in academia. Most people now seek to do a PhD for a variety of reasons.

However, the PhD completion given figures earlier hide the fact that a large number of students who started a PhD never complete their programme. Globally, about a quarter of students who start a PhD never complete it.

There are many reasons why PhD students drop out of post-graduate research study. These, amongst others, include factors such as personal issues, hardness and length of PhD programmes, poor or a lack of supervision/ support, poor research design, a lack of data or poor access to information, unrealistic expectations, financial difficulties, loneliness, depression/mental health issues and loss of motivation, among others. To compound these myriad of inhibiting factors, the general lack of resources and information on what it means to do a PhD means many students' dream of obtaining a PhD were never realised.

While the market is full of textbooks focusing on students doing their undergraduate studies. There are relatively few good textbooks and educational resources available to support PhD students. The vast resources available online are often lacking in structure and require sifting through to obtain necessary information.

Many students who dropped out of PhD programmes did so because of a general lack of support and guidance, especially at the initial stage of their research. The general focus on undergraduate students means that the need of PhD students in terms of academic resources in form of essential guides and textbooks available to support students doing PhD programmes remain largely unmet. Also, the available textbooks in this area are often very limited in focus and content. In general, they tend to concentrate on academic structure of PhD programmes rather than encompassing all the personal, emotional, supervisory and institutional environment that affect PhD students' progression and successful completion.

This book seeks to fill the gap by providing an essential textbook that covers every aspect of PhD journey. It is intended to serve as an invaluable guide and resource for anyone thinking of, currently undertaking or about to complete their PhD. It is also a useful resource for PhD supervisors and examiners.

The book aims to serve as a useful companion to anyone initiating, conducting and completing a PhD degree in the social science subject area.

The author seeks to fill a gap in the market by producing a textbook that has global appeal and offers support to PhD students at various stages of their research in the social sciences regardless of their institution of study and mode of study. Factors underlying the high dropout rates in PhD students compared to their undergraduate counterparts are addressed, using case studies and examples drawn from different parts of the world.

The book offers an important resource for the growing number of PhD students who want to know about the approaches to research, substantive theories, data analytical techniques and a range of other issues that affect their chances of success and completion. This book is an essential source of information for any PhD student aiming to enjoy their research experience and achieve their goals. Unlike the existing texts, the book demystifies doing a PhD by providing an easy and useful step-by-step guide for students who may find doing a PhD a daunting task.

The book aims to highlight the key stages in a doctoral journey. Starting from the question of deciding whether to do a PhD or not through to preparing a research proposal, choosing the right institution, deciding on the mode of study, conducting the research, writing a thesis and preparing for a viva examination, the book offers a comprehensive guide to students. It explores the important issue of research ethics; the relationship among PhD students, their directors of studies and supervisors; and the place of academic research in society.

The book uses examples and case studies to illustrate different forms of PhD research and suggest different methodological approaches to conducting research based on the ontological, epistemological, axiological or rhetorical focus of the study. It draws on different forms analytical techniques commonly used in PhD research involving quantitative and qualitative data.

As well as explaining the theoretical/conceptual frameworks on which most PhDs in the social sciences are based, the book highlights the essential research tools required for a successful PhD research. Specific issues facing international students doing their PhDs away from their home countries are also discussed.

As the title suggests, the book is not just about the processes of undertaking a PhD; it also offers practical guides on doing a PhD. It identifies common mistakes that students make and explains 'what to do' and 'what not to do' when doing a PhD. It offers both academic and practical guides that most PhD students will find useful in their journey. The book draws on the author's experience as an established academic with considerable experience in supervising and examining PhD students.

Given its contents, type of presentation and practical guide, the book is expected to be one that you may wish to use as a source book to enable you to respond to some of the frequent questions, concerns and practical issues you may encounter when doing your PhD and writing your thesis.

The book recognises that the 'journey' through the process of writing a successful thesis can be completed. So it offers a dependable resource and advice to help you start writing your thesis and offers you guidance along the way to the completion of your thesis to your viva examination.

It is hoped that this book will offer you some practical support along your PhD journey, and I welcome feedback from you on how I might be able to improve future editions of this book.

About the author

Dr Francis Jegede is Associate Professor in International Relations and Diplomacy in the College of Law, Humanities and Social Sciences and the Chair of College Research Committee at the University of Derby, UK. He has an extensive experience in supervising and managing doctoral students across many disciplines in the social sciences. He has nurtured, tutored and supported many UK and international students through their doctoral journeys. As Chair of the College Research Committee and a researcher, he has considerable experience in academic and operational matters relating to postgraduate research, including quality management and enhancement issues, regulations, student progression, examinations and monitoring. Dr Jegede has had a long service at the University of Derby as a leading academic. He has taught and supervised students across many social science disciplines, including geography, global development studies, political science, international relations and diplomacy.

His research interests include international politics, security, terrorism, diplomacy and international development. He has a well-developed research and educational links with international institutions such as the United Nations, European Union and international non-governmental organisations. He has an extensive experience of working with the Post Graduate Research Student Office, Directors of Studies and Supervisors across several Schools and Faculties in his university. He takes keen interest in any initiatives aimed at enhancing the research experience of all his post-graduate research students and works with PGR Students Wellbeing Department to support post-graduate research students and creating a stimulating research environment for PhD students. He has chaired many viva voce examinations and served as external examiner and consultant in post-graduate research programme validation for many institutions in the UK and overseas.

Acknowledgements

This book came about as a result of the author's experience with PhD and Professional Doctorate students in UK universities and was inspired by the need to share ideas that could help potential PhD students and those already doing their PhDs and their supervisors.

I would like to thank all my students from whom, through their experiences; I have learnt a great deal about their PhD journeys. The challenges and frustrations they faced along the way in their PhD journeys has spurred me and offered me insight and practical knowledge that enable me to write this book. Their experiences have made it possible to write a book that is relevant, practical and informative that other students can use to help them in their own journeys.

I would like to thank Sarah Tuckwell at Routledge for her patience and understanding for submitting manuscript later than scheduled due to the disruptions caused by the COVID-19 pandemic.

With all usual disclaimers, a special thanks to Dr John Stubbs for reading through the draft chapters and for offering some useful comments. Thanks are also due to him and all the reviewers of the manuscript proposal for their insights that fed into this book. I also recognise the editorial team at Routledge: Sarah Tuckwell and her colleagues who are always a pleasure to work with.

My biggest thanks goes to all the post-graduate research students whom I have had the privilege of supervising, nurturing and supporting along their PhD journeys. Their experiences have provided the incentive and motivation to write this book.

Acronyms

3MT – 3-Minute Thesis
AGO – Alternative Guide Online
ANOVA – Analysis of Variance
APA – American Psychological Association
BAMEs – Black, Asian and Minority Ethnic groups
CAE – Cambridge Advanced Certificate
COVID-19 – Coronavirus disease 2019
CCPE – Cambridge Certificate of Proficiency in English
DArch – Doctor of Architecture
DBA – Doctor of Business Administration
UK-DPA – UK Data Protection Act
DPA – Doctor of Public Administration
DProf – Doctor of Professional Studies
Dr – Doctor
DSA – Disabled Student's Allowance
DSc – Doctor of Science
EdD/D.Ed – Doctor of Education
EnD – Doctor of Engineering
ESRC – Economic and Social Research Council
GDPR – General Data Protection Regulations
HE – Higher Education

HEFCE – Higher Education Funding Council for England
HESA – Higher Education Statistics Agency
HMPPS – Her Majesty's Prison and Probation Service
IELTS – International English Language Testing System
ICO – Information Commissioners Office
IPA – Interpretative Phenomenological Analysis
IPR – Intellectual Property Rights
MA – Master of Arts
MBA – Master of Business Administration
MD – Doctor of Medicine
MPhil – Master of Philosophy
MPhil – Master of Philosophy with transfer opportunity to Doctor of Philosophy
MRes/ResM – Master's Research or Research Master's
MSc – Master of Science
NGO – Non-Governmental Organisation
NPS – National Probation Service
NRC – National Research Committee
OECD – Organisation for Economic Co-operation and Development
OfS – The Office for Students
OSCOLA – Oxford Standard for the Citation of Legal Authorities
PGR – Post-Graduate Research
PhD – Doctor of Philosophy
PRES – Postgraduate Research Experience Survey
PTE:A – Pearson Test of English (Academic)
QAA – Quality Assurance Agency
REF – Research Excellence Framework
SD – Standard Deviation
TEF – Teaching Excellence Framework
ThD – Doctor of Theology
UKRI – UK Research & Innovation
UKVI – UK Visas and Immigration

CHAPTER 1

What is and why do a PhD?

Introduction

A growing number of people around the world are studying for or aiming to undertake Doctor of Philosophy (PhD) – the highest academic degree awarded in academia. In Organisation for Economic Co-operation and Development (OECD) countries, 1.1% of adults within the age range of 25 to 64 years held a doctorate degree in 2018 (Education at a Glance, OECD, 2019). Between 2013 and 2017, there was an 8% growth across OECD countries in the number of people with doctorate degrees. In countries such as Mexico, Spain and the US, there has been a significant rise in doctorate holders. According to the OECD report, if the current rates of growth continue, 2.3% of young adults living in OECD countries will undertake doctoral study in their lifetime (OECD, 2019). The growing number of people aspiring to gain advanced qualification at doctorate level reflects the perceived benefits of doctoral studies. People with masters and doctorate degrees generally have the best employment prospects. In all OECD countries, except Greece, the Slovak Republic and the Russian Federation, at least 90% of doctorate holders are in employment (OECD, 2020).

This chapter explores the nature and purpose of PhD research degrees. Differences and similarities between traditional PhDs and Professional or Practice-Based Doctorates (DProf) are explained using examples from different institutions in the UK and overseas. Key issues prospective candidates need to know about and consider before deciding on doing a PhD are discussed. The chapter also explains why about a quarter of people who start a PhD globally never complete their research study. The challenges and opportunities of doing a PhD are examined with reference to personal professional development and career advancement.

By the end of the chapter, you will have a better understanding of

- the nature and purpose of PhD research degrees;
- what makes a PhD research degree different from all other degrees or research programmes;

- the importance of a PhD degree for your personal, professional and career development;
- reasons why about a quarter of students who started a PhD never complete it;
- factors to consider before you decide on doing a PhD; and
- how to prepare for your PhD journey.

What is a PhD?

A PhD is an advanced post-graduate study leading to the award of a doctorate degree of philosophy in a named subject or discipline or profession. A PhD is the highest degree a university or an academic awarding institution could confer on anyone after successfully completing a course of study, usually in the form of independent research. Generally, a PhD is a research-based course or programme that expands existing knowledge leading to the production of an original research report commonly known as a ***thesis***.

A post-graduate research (PGR) degree is awarded after fulfilling a set of requirements set out by the awarding university or institution. While the nature and requirements for a PhD may vary considerably across different subjects/disciplines and universities/institutions around the world, it is nonetheless possible to identify key features and characteristics of a PhD.

The history and evolution of PhDs

As an important element of the academic tradition, the PhD has developed and evolved over a long time. Opinions differ amongst academic historians as to the origin of PhD awards. While some scholars suggest that the PhD has its origins in the 9th-century schools of Muslim study, the PhD tradition was only formally adopted by European universities in the 19th century (Hall, 2019). Others, however, contend that the exact time the first PhD degree was awarded is unknown (Bogle, 2017).

Early medieval educational institutions were based on apprenticeships. The title of 'Master' was conferred on individuals who passed their apprenticeship training, and that qualified them to teach others. The notion of a university as a teaching institution came about when the 'Masters' joined together to form a legal corporation that was recognised by the pope or emperor (Bogle, 2017).

According to the historical account of the PhD in Europe, the first PhD degree was awarded in Paris in 1150 (Noble, 1994). The University of Paris was later followed in Germany by the Universities of Munich in 1474, Leiden in 1580 and Utrecht in 1644 (Bogle, 2017). However, the German universities were said to have had a variety of different features and patterns (Clark, 2006). From these medieval northern European universities, the tradition of a PhD degree spread to other parts of Europe, the US, Canada and across the world.

Since then, the PhD has evolved and developed into a prestigious and most desirable academic honour with different universities, countries and regions of the world adapting their PhDs to suit their needs. While the PhD was originally awarded in professions and disciplines relating to law, medicine and theology, the award of the PhD later spread to other subjects and has now become the highest academic award across all disciplines and professions.

Originally, the award of a PhD was based on the concept of disputation – a formal and insightful means of argument framed within theological assumptions. It then progressed from just an oral exercise to being a published work, and this led to the creation of modern theses or dissertations as being essential products of doctoral students' research (Clark, 2006). As academic research-based exercises, research doctorates began in the 1700s and became popular in Germany. The German state considered universities to be a national status symbol and a show of power resulting in the growth of PhD-awarding institutions there between the 16th and 18th centuries. In contrast, only two ancient universities – Oxford and Cambridge – were established in England, with Scotland having four. An overview of the UK institutions and the opportunities they provide for PGR and PhD are discussed in Chapter 2.

Key features of a PhD

While PhDs may vary greatly in scope, nature and requirements of different institutions in different parts of the world and across disciplines, it is possible to identify a number of key characteristics. A PhD usually requires the following:

1 A prolonged engagement with the chosen research topic lasting typically for about 3 years for full-time students and longer for part-time students
2 The researcher to determine the focus and direction of their own work through a written research proposal
3 Work to be conducted independently and on an individual basis – although usually with some support, direction or guidance from a supervisor, a mentor or a director of study
4 Extensive and substantial research into a specific issue or issues or problems clearly set out in a proposal
5 The research aim(s) and objectives to be made clear and usually stated as research questions that may involve testing the validity of hypotheses
6 An extensive review of literature and collection of primary data or use of existing/secondary data
7 The production of an original research report commonly known as a 'thesis' or 'dissertation'
8 A final oral examination commonly known as 'viva voce' in which a PhD candidate defends their work before a panel of experts

Types of PhD awards

There are different types of PhD degrees, and knowing about the basic features of each of these could help you in your decision as to which PhD is right for you, if any. Generally, a PhD can be divided into four main categories:

Academic PhDs – These are PhDs awarded purely on academic grounds following completion of original research and scholarship in traditional academic subjects such as politics, geography, sociology, criminology and others. As standard academic awards, academic doctorates focus mainly on a theoretical understanding of the subject of the PhD and not on the professional practice of the award holder (Find A PhD 2020).

Professional PhDs – Unlike the standard academic PhDs, professional doctorates focus mainly on specific professions or vocations, such as engineering, law, medicine and architecture, among others. These awards tend to reflect specific contribution the award holder has made directly to knowledge and practice in the profession. While professional PhDs still require evidence of research and analytical rigours expected in any standard academic PhDs, a greater premium is placed on the holder's practical training and experience in the field or profession (Find A PhD 2020).

Honorary PhDs – These are doctorates awarded to individuals in recognition of their achievements in a profession, vocation, business or any area of social, economic and political endeavour. Unlike both academic and professional doctorates, the award holders of honorary PhDs do not need to undertake any academic study or research as those awards are given purely at the discretion of the awarding institution (Find A PhD 2020).

Higher PhDs – Higher doctorates are usually awarded to distinguished individuals or highly esteemed researchers or practitioners. These are similar to honorary doctorates but are awarded at a much higher level of experience and career progression of the award holder. Like the honorary PhDs, award holders are not required to enrol in a university or an awarding institution for these doctorates (Find A PhD 2020).

Within these four broad types of PhDs, there are many different variants of PhDs in terms of titles of awards. These are summarised in Figure 1.1.

While PhD/DPhil are common doctorate titles awarded in most subjects, Doctor of Business Administration (DBA), Doctor of Public Administration (DPA), Doctor of Engineering (EnD), Doctor of Education (EdD/D. Ed), Doctor of Clinical Psychology (DClinPsy) Doctor of Social Sciences (DSocSci), Doctor of Professional Studies (DProf), Doctor of Architecture (DArch), Doctor of Medicine (MD) and others are professional doctorates

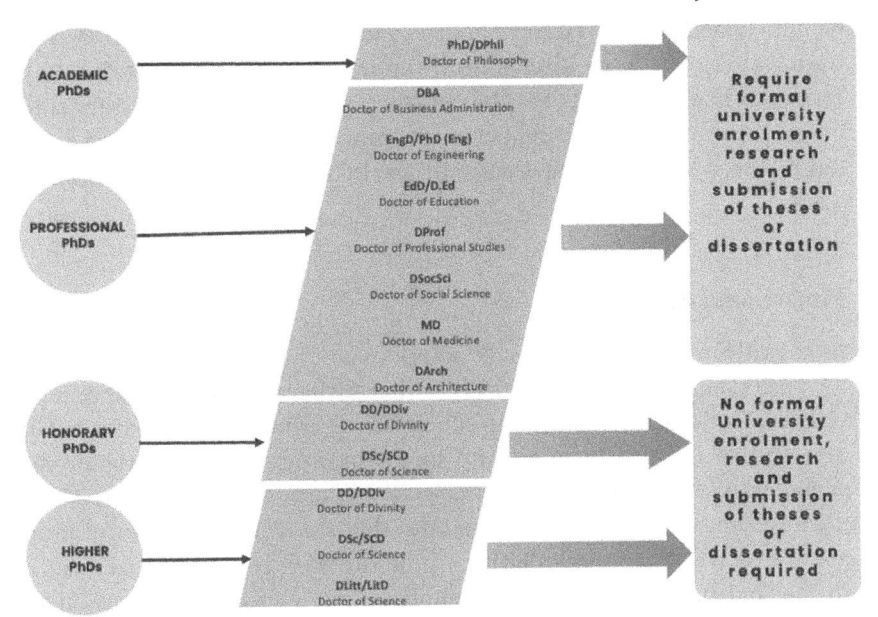

Figure 1.1 Types of PhDs

with letters prefixing or suffixing letter D (i.e. BA, En, ED, SocSci, prof, Arch, etc.), reflecting the specific profession or vocation relating to the award.

Different routes to a PhD

Depending on the university and region of the world where you are doing or thinking of doing your study, there are different routes to obtaining a PhD.

The traditional PhD

This route usually allows students who have already completed their master's degree or MPhil to launch straight into a PhD research programme. In most universities, students may be required to register first for MPhil and then go through a process of confirmation or transfer of registration, approval of PhD research proposal and ethical approval and the like before the student is able to commence their PhD research.

Integrated PhD

Some universities offer integrated PhD where students are enrolled in a master's degree programme such as an MRes which, if successfully completed, allows them to progress onto a PhD. The master's degree involves a taught element which lasts for about 12 months. This adds an extra year to the usual 3 to 4 years required for full-time study under the traditional PhD. Doing an integrated PhD has the benefit of giving you the necessary skills in research through the taught element from which you can develop essential research skills and experience to use in your advanced PhD research work.

Professional doctorate

As the title implies, professional doctorates are PhD programmes designed for professionals seeking to get PhDs that focus on their specific occupation or practice such as teaching, education, pharmacy, engineering, health care and social care, business and so on. In order to develop the professional, as well as the academic, aspects of the programme, professional doctorates usually have taught modules that students need to enrol in for about 2 years before transitioning to the full PhD research phase. Unlike in the traditional PhD, the main emphasis in a DProf is the focus on the development of professional or practice-based training alongside research skills. Hence, these types of PhDs tend to involve a significant taught element compared to the research-focused projects in a traditional PhD. It is conventional, but not always the case, for DProfs to be done on a part-time basis and are often subject to accreditation by a professional body (Higginbotham, 2018a).

PhD through published work

Some universities allow a PhD through a non-traditional route such as getting a PhD through published work. This involves submission and assessment of already-published research-informed work or other creative work by the candidate. These could be journal articles, books or chapters in books, amongst others, that show and demonstrate a significant contribution to the knowledge in a particular area or field of study (Higginbotham, 2018a). While this option is opened to everyone in some universities, others reserve this route for their alumni and existing academic staff. This is by no means an easy route to doing a PhD as publication can be quite tasking as evidence of extensive and sustained publications are often required together with a written statement that provides context and critical appraisal for the published work.

PhD and other post-graduate degrees – a clarification

It is necessary to make a distinction between a PhD and other post-graduate studies or degrees. While a PhD is a PGR study leading to the award of a doctorate, not all post-graduate studies lead to a PhD or a doctorate award. There are post-graduate taught modules with exit awards at a master's level, such as MA, MBA, MSc, MPhil and so on. Other post-graduate-taught programmes offer the opportunity for students to continue to do a dissertation or thesis stage or confirmation or transfer of registration leading to a PhD. This transition usually occurs after a student has completed the required credits or grades to qualify for a full PhD study.

It is equally important to note that while this book has been written with UK universities mostly in mind, there are a number of doctorates with different titles in different countries of the world that are equivalent or similar to the traditional PhD research degrees in the UK (Find A PhD 2020). Examples of these are the following:

- Doctor of Science (DSc) – commonly awarded in countries such as Japan, the US, Egypt and South Korea
- Doctor of Theology (ThD) – doctorates based on theology that are awarded in countries such as the US, Romania, Italy, Ireland, and Czech Republic
- Doctor of Juridical Science – doctorates based on the science of law and legal practice commonly available in countries such as the US, Canada and Australia
- Doctor of the Science of Law – doctorates based on the science of law and legal practice commonly available in countries such as the US, UK, Australia, Singapore and Canada
- Dr. rer. nat. or *Doctor rerum naturalium* ('Doctor of the things of nature') – doctorates based on the science of nature, available in Germany
- Doktor Nauk (Doctor of Science) – doctorates based on science and scientific investigations awarded in many countries including Russia and Poland, among others

Modes of study for a PhD

PhD study can be done through two main modes of study – full-time or part-time. Depending on your personal circumstances, there are advantages and disadvantages in doing a PhD through each of these modes (Figure 1.2). Changes in personal circumstances often require some full-time students to change their study mode to part-time, especially toward the latter part of their study.

PhD by distance learning is a relatively less common mode of study. This mode of study is based essentially on independent research with very limited face-to-face interactions with supervisors and the university staff. Regular contacts are, however, maintained with the university through communication media to access essential resources and training (Higginbotham, 2018b).

PhD through distance learning is the norm in the Open University which has considerable history and experience in remote teaching and learning.

Pros

- Full access to university social and academic life
- Requires greater focus on study
- Greater access to resources and supervision

Cons

- Could be expensive
- Often involves separation of learning from employment or professional career
- Produce graduates with relatively limited work experience

Pros

- Offers greater flexibility for combining work with studying
- Enhances professional career - through work experience
- A valuable option if unable to study full time

Cons

- Takes twice as long to complete
- Could be challenging combining work with studying
- Obtaining studentships/funding may be difficult
- Limited interaction with university's social/academic life

Pros

- Ideal for students unable to live near or travel to university
- Suitable if study/research materials are based at remote locations
- Possibility for a reduced tuition fees

Cons

- Can be very isolating
- Requires communication links with home university
- Options not always available
- Limited interaction with university's social/academic life

Figure 1.2 PhD study modes: full-time – part-time – distance learning

Purpose of a PhD and why do a PhD?

A pertinent question for any aspiring candidate is, Why do a PhD? While doing a PhD may be a matter of personal choice or preference for some people, obtaining a PhD degree is essential for those seeking employment in academia.

In many countries, the completion of a PhD is a key requirement for a university position such as a lecturer or researcher. Those who teach at universities or work in academic, educational or research institutions are usually expected to have a PhD degree as a basic requirement. Therefore, completing a post-graduate course leading up to a PhD may offer you a great deal of opportunities for professional career advancement in academia.

Besides this, doing a PhD through research is considered to be a privilege, and it comes with a sense of joy and feelings of exploration, excitement, challenge, involvement and passion (Phillips and Pugh, 2015).

Given that there are many types of PhDs, a key decision you need to make is, What type of PhD is appropriate for my needs? While a traditional PhD may be desirable as they are relatively well known, a professional or practice-based doctorate may well be what you need depending on your career ambition.

What does it mean to do a PhD?

Doing a PhD means different things to different people. Generally, doing a PhD offers an opportunity to make a significant contribution to the advancement of knowledge in a specific area in a chosen field of study. As a matter of necessity, a PhD should be an original piece of work. Your contribution to knowledge needs to be original, innovative and demonstrable as to how your work advances research or understanding of the issue you are investigating. The value of the contribution that your research makes to knowledge is judged through peer review in a viva voce examination. By the end of your PhD, not only are you going to be an expert in your field of investigation, but other experts in the area of your study will also be able to assess and certify that your contribution is significant enough to be awarded a doctorate degree.

Doing a PhD can be a terrifying experience that requires a great deal of courage and perseverance. The journey through a PhD is often exhausting and draining not only in terms of resources but also emotionally. It is a piece of work through which you may need to confront or face a personal feeling or sense of insecurity, self-doubt and intellectual inadequacies. Overcoming these, and many other obstacles and setbacks that you may face along the way, could be exceedingly rewarding. Hence, a great deal of bravery and self-belief is required to get you through your PhD journey.

Doing a PhD involves working independently. As an independent researcher, doing a PhD can be very lonely. This sense of loneliness could be exacerbated if you don't have support networks around you. If you are undertaking your PhD away from your home country or your usual place of residence, it is also possible to feel alone and homesick. While studying in different social, cultural and political settings does have its advantages, it may also pose some challenges to some international students and other PhD students studying away from home.

PhD is a massive project that needs to be undertaken with a great sense of understanding as to what will be required. As complex and daunting as the task of doing a PhD may seem, it is necessary to take each step at a time and work systematically through different stages in order to get to the end point. Therefore, there is a need to plan and to be strategic in your approach to doing a PhD. A systematic approach is more likely to get you to the destination, rather than a haphazard and unstructured approach. Procrastination is said to be the 'thief of time'. Timely action is required if you are to succeed in your PhD ambition. You need to know about the key milestones you need to achieve and how to get through them. (See Figure 1.3 for key stages in a PhD journey).

Doing a PhD involves a great deal of personal investment. Even with the network of support around you in form of your director of study, supervisors, academic mentor and other institutional support structures such as the library, PGR office and the like, success in a PhD depends largely on your personal investment into your study. Doing a PhD requires that you challenge yourself to a level that will enable you to grow intellectually and emotionally to succeed in your research.

To succeed in a PhD, it is often necessary to be able to network and be part of a research community locally within your institution and nationally or globally within the field of your enquiry. You need to be able to work with peers in your field in a collaborative way to benefit you and your study. Your PhD research offers you the opportunity to contribute to academic discussions organised through, conferences, seminars, workshops and so on that relate to your study.

Before commencing your PhD research, it is now a general requirement in many institutions to seek ethical approval for your study. This is to ensure that your PhD follows ethical standards and you comply with various regulations relating to conducting research. Ethical issues and laws regarding PhD research and personal data are discussed in Chapter 7.

Despite the challenges involved in doing a PhD, it can be one of the most rewarding pieces of academic work you will ever have to do in your career or lifetime. When successfully completed, a PhD stands as a symbol of personal success. It offers you an opportunity to produce something special and worthwhile and that means something to you and to the academic community working in your area of study.

Key *stages in a PhD journey*

Doing a PhD involves a series of actions and processes that need to be undertaken. The degree of success in completing the tasks involved at each stage of a PhD goes a long in shaping the outcome of your study. There are 15 key steps in a PhD journey (Figure 1.3). These are the following:

- Deciding on doing or not doing a PhD
- Reviewing existing literature to identify knowledge gaps
- Setting your own research questions and main focus of investigation
- Deciding which university or research institution best suits your PhD research
- Preparing your research proposal and application
- Going through enrolment and settling in your university/research institution
- Refining and focusing your PhD research questions
- Completing your MPhil or transferring onto full PhD
- Conducting your research/experiments and collecting your data
- Synthesising and analysing your data
- Drafting your PhD thesis
- Submitting an original PhD thesis or dissertation
- Getting ready for your viva voce examination
- Defending your thesis in a viva voce examination
- Post-viva clean-up and final submission

These key stages or phases in doing a PhD are discussed in greater details throughout this book. Each institution may set specific guidelines and

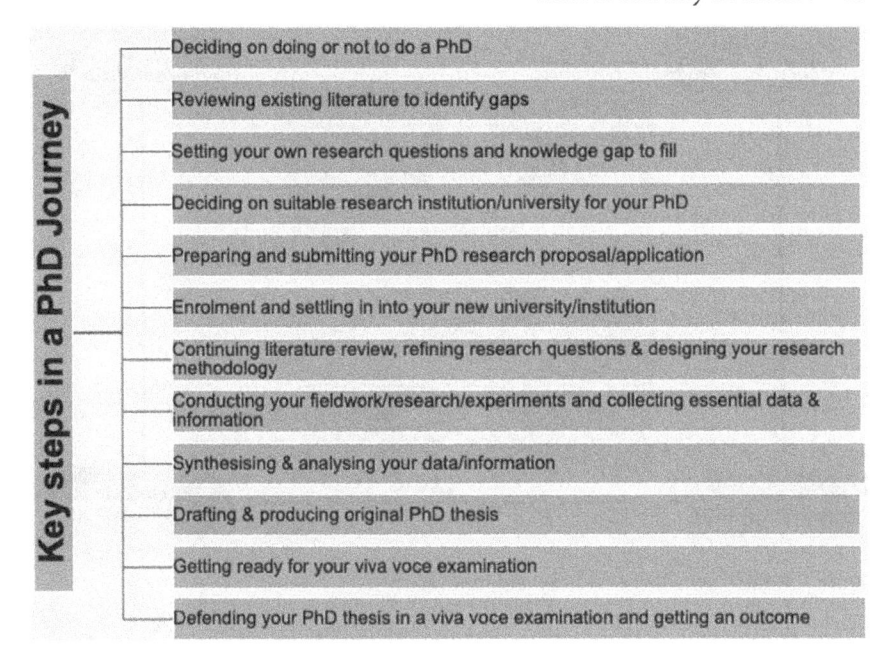

Figure 1.3 Key steps in a PhD journey

timelines as you move through each of these phases or stages. It is crucial that you are familiar with the requirements of your institution for each of these phases.

It is important to stress that having decided to do a PhD, it is essential to establish the gap in the knowledge that you want to fill with your research. This will involve setting out your own research goals or questions and identifying the main focus of your investigation. Essential issues that you need to consider in choosing the university or institution to undertake your research are discussed in Chapter 2 together with guides on how to write an effective PhD proposal. Supervisory support that you may expect to receive from your chosen institution of study is explored in Chapter 3. Ethical considerations in PGR are discussed in Chapter 7 while Chapter 8 covers essential tools and training you need to get through the key milestones in your study.

To do a PhD you need to be prepared to go through a dynamic process of searching, learning, growing and changing and searching again not only in relation to yourself but also with regards to your PhD research and/or professional development. Doing a PhD is an enterprise in knowledge creation and exchange that comes through personal and professional development and training. In this enterprise, you learn about, search for or change and grow

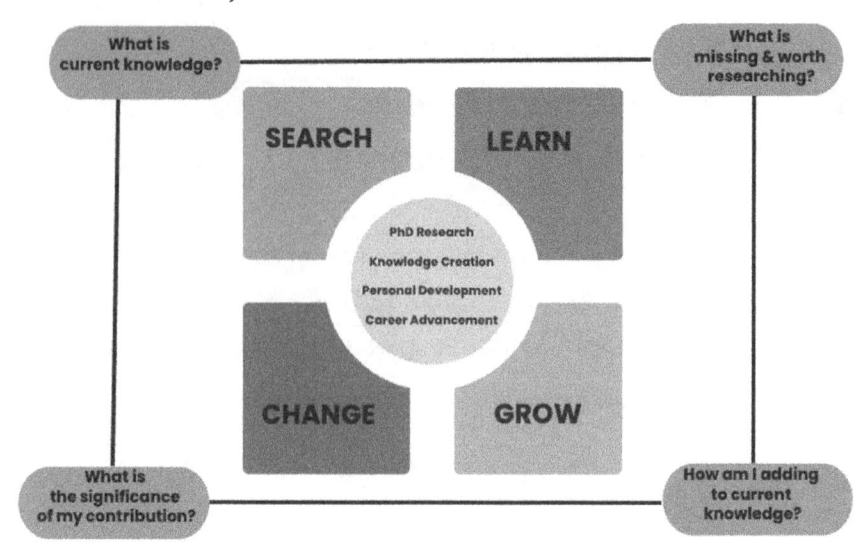

Figure 1.4 PhD, knowledge creation and innovation

ideas through a continuous circle of knowledge creation and innovation in your specific area of study (Figure 1.4).

PhD is a project that will test your sense of self-belief and endurance. It will challenge your intellectual ability and your organisational skills to the limit. It will change you and your understanding and perception of learning through which you will grow as a person and as a researcher. In the course of your PhD, you will understand what is current knowledge, idea and theories in your area of research or profession. You will be able to identify knowledge gaps through an extensive search for literature. You will learn about how to articulate the specific contribution that you are making to existing knowledge, thereby growing the knowledge exchange base relating to your topic. Also, your PhD will offer the opportunity for you to explain the significance of your research and how that will change or is likely to change current thinking or understanding of the issue you are researching into. The overall benefit of your research to the research community and your profession will become apparent.

Preparing for your own PhD journey

It is worth stating that you need to be clear from the onset and at the early planning stages of your PhD journey what exactly you want to get out of your PhD. Once you decide you are doing a PhD, start preparing for it now. Amongst the questions that you should be asking yourself at the early stage are the following:

- Do I need or want to do a PhD?
- Have I understood what it takes to do a PhD?
- Have I sought and obtained advice from someone who has done a PhD or has experience as to what is involved?
- Can I make the personal, financial and emotional commitments to undertake this 'big project' over the required period?
- Have I got a contingency plan in place in case things don't go according to plan doing a PhD?

The degree to which you prepare for your PhD will dictate your success in wading through the various stages of your PhD journey. Good planning and preparation in the early stages are critical for success in doing a PhD.

Why many who started never complete a PhD

In 2014, 25,020 PhDs were awarded in the UK across all subjects. The top ten countries with PhD awards in 2014 were the US, Germany, the UK, India, Japan, France, South Korea, Spain, Italy and Australia (Table 1.1). These countries also have the highest number of students currently doing research degrees leading to PhDs.

The rapid growth in the number of people enrolled in PGR in the last decade suggests that possession of a PhD degree is no longer perceived or considered as the prerogatives of those seeking a career in academia. Most people now seek to do a PhD for a variety of reasons.

However, the PhD completion figures in Table 1.1 hide the fact that a large number of students who start a PhD never complete their programme. Non-completion rates vary hugely across disciplines and countries around the world. Globally, about a quarter of students who start a PhD never complete it.

Table 1.1 Top 10 PhDs awarding countries in 2014

Country	PhDs Awarded
US	67,449
Germany	28,147
UK	25,020
India	24,300
Japan	16,039
France	13,729
South Korea	12.931
Spain	10,889
Italy	10,675
Australia	8,400

Source: World Economic Forum 2021 - https://www.weforum.org/agenda/2017/02/countries-with-most-doctoral-graduates/

In the UK, there has been a steady rise in the number of PhD completions over the last decade. However, about a fifth of students who started a PhD in some universities in England may still never complete it or get a degree (Jump, 2020). The attrition figures include non-completion by students who voluntarily withdraw themselves for reasons such as health, financial difficulty and changes in personal circumstances, among others; those who had their registration terminated by their universities due to a lack of engagement and poor standard of work; and students exceeding maximum registration without reaching the required milestones, among other reasons.

There are complex factors responsible for the attrition rates amongst PhD students globally. Some of these factors have been explored by academic scholars (see Spronken-Smith et al., 2018; Cuthbert and Molla, 2015; Golde, 2005; Humphrey et al. 2012; Kyvik and Olsen, 2014; Seagram et al., 1998). Generally, PhD students drop out of PGR study without a degree for the following reasons:

- Poor or a general lack of preparation
- Unrealistic expectations as to what it takes and costs to do a PhD
- Poor choice of PhD research topic or project leading to a dead-end
- Inappropriate research design and weak methodology
- Poor judgement in choosing institution/supervisor for PhD research study
- Personal issues relating to health, loneliness, depression/mental health
- Loss of motivation and the like
- Financial hardship and a lack of sufficient means to support and sustain the PhD study
- Poor or a lack of supervisory or mentoring support

To compound these myriads of inhibiting factors, the general lack of essential texts providing easy-to-follow advice and information for students before they start their course means many post-graduate students' dream of obtaining a PhD were never realised. While the market is full of textbooks focusing on students doing their undergraduate studies. There are relatively few textbooks and educational resources available to support PhD students. This book seeks to fill that gap, providing essential guides to anyone thinking of, starting or is in the process of doing a PhD. Ways to mitigate against some of the inhibiting factors to success in a PhD are discussed throughout the following chapters. Where necessary, references are made to PhDs awarded by non-UK universities/institutions in other parts of the world; however, it is important to note that the main focus of this book is UK-based PhDs. Nevertheless, readers may still find the information in this book relevant regardless of which PhD model they are operating under in any part of the world.

Keys to a successful PhD

The key to success in a PhD depends upon a number of complex and intervening factors that could be personal, institutional, locational/environmental and financial, amongst others. Essential skills you need to develop along the way to help your success are summarised in (Figure 1.5). These skills are also discussed in various sections in the subsequent chapters to provide you with the grounding and the knowledge you need to succeed in your PhD journey.

Generally, to succeed in your PhD, it is essential that you do the following:

- Maintain a healthy and good work–life balance to sustain your well-being throughout your PhD journey (see Chapter 8).
- Have a good relationship with your director of studies or supervisors and make the most of their supervisory support (see Chapter 3).
- You have a good grasp of what your PhD research is about and what you want to achieve in terms of goals and how to get there (see Chapter 2).
- Pay attention to details (see Chapter 8).
- Understand all the milestones required along the way on your PhD journey and set yourself specific, measurable and attainable goals or targets to achieve those targets in a timely fashion (see Chapter 8).
- Develop your organisational skills to save yourself time by getting the right things done at the right time (see Chapter 8).
- Read! Read!! Read!! and Write! Write!! Write!!! Read everything relating to your PhD topic and write things down as you go along – this will help towards your literature review and drafting your thesis (see Chapter 5, 6 and 11).
- Learn to present your research ideas in academic group meetings such as conferences, seminars, workshops and the like as that may help you in your viva and in publishing your research at a later stage, if you so wish (see Chapter 12 and 13).
- Network with others and make good use of other support you may get for your PhD (see Chapter 4).
- Have resilience. Don't give up when things go wrong. Keep going and keep driving your research forward in spite of any odds or obstacles that you may face (see Chapter 8).
- Comply with ethics and regulations regarding your PhD research and the way you collect, store and manage personal data (see Chapter 7 and 9).

Key messages

- A PhD can be done in a wide range of disciplines and professions through a variety of routes and mode of study – part- or full-time.
- Doing a PhD is not necessarily for everyone. If you must or want to do one, then do it well by understanding what it entails and what it means for you.

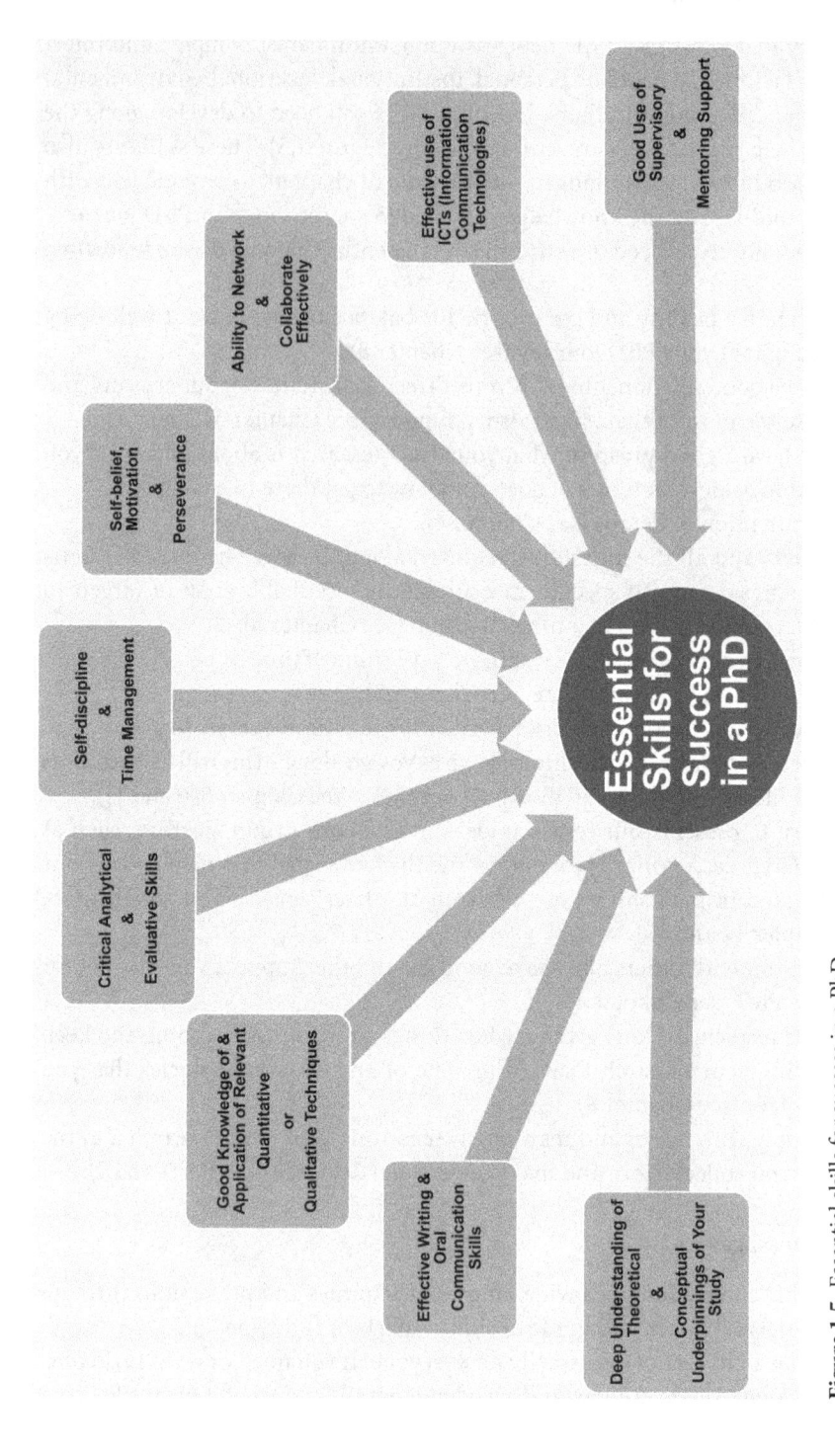

Figure 1.5 Essential skills for success in a PhD

- To do a PhD, you need to prepare yourself and plan effectively for the journey before you start.
- In the course of your PhD journey, you will learn, grow and change as a person and intellectually and experientially.
- Although there might be some element of good luck involved to succeed in a PhD, a great deal will depend on your own actions – your hard work, dedication, perseverance and strategic approach.
- As an independent researcher, you are responsible for your own work. However, networking and developing collaborative links with other researchers in your field will help your success.
- While doing a PhD could be very daunting, challenging, frustrating and sometimes lonely, you can still enjoy the overall experience and take pride in the fact that every milestone completed is a step towards your goal.

Further reading

Bogle, D. (2017). *100 Years of the PhD in the UK* [Online]. Available at: www.vitae. ac.uk/news/vitae-blog/100-years-ofthe-phd-by-prof-david-bogle

Churchill, H., and Sanders, T. (2007). *Getting Your PhD: A Practical Insider's Guide.* London: SAGE.

Clark, W. (2006). *Academic Charisma and the Origins of the Research University.* Chicago: University of Chicago Press.

Cuthbert, D., and Molla, T. (2015). PhD crisis discourse: A critical approach to the framing of the problem and some Australian 'solutions'. *Higher Education*, 69(1), pp. 33–53.

Dunleavy, P. (2003). *Authoring a PhD: How to Plan, Draft, Write, and Finish a Doctoral Thesis or Dissertation.* Basingstoke, UK: Palgrave Macmillan.

FindAPhD. (2020). *Types of PhD* [Online]. Available at: www.findaphd.com/advice/phd-types/

Finn, J. A. (2005). *Getting a PhD: An Action Plan to Help Manage Your Research, Your Supervisor and Your Project.* London: Routledge.

Golde, C. M. (2005). The role of the department and discipline in doctoral student attrition: Lessons from four departments. *The Journal of Higher Education*, 76(6), pp. 669–700.

Hall, S. (2019). *The History of the Doctoral Degree* [Online]. Available at: https://www.theclassroom.com/history-phd-degree-5257288.html.

Higginbotham, D. (2018). 4 routes to getting doctorate. *Prospects* [Online]. Available at: www.prospects.ac.uk. Accessed on 18th June 2020.

History of the Doctoral Degree [Online]. Available at: www.theclassroom.com/history-phd-degree-5257288.html

Humphrey, R., Marshall, N., and Leonardo, L. (2012). The impact of research training and research codes of practice on submission of doctoral degrees: An exploratory cohort study. *Higher Education Quarterly*, 66(1), pp. 47–64.

Hutcheson, P. A. (2007, Winter). Academic charisma and the origins of the research university (review). *The Review of Higher Education*, 30(2), pp. 206–207.

Jump, P. (2020). PhD completion rates, 2013. *Times Higher Education*. World University Ranking [Online]. Available at: www.timeshighereducation.com/news/phd-completion-rates-2013/2006040.article. Accessed on 20th June 2020.

Kyvik, S., and Olsen, T. B. (2014). Increasing completion rates in Norwegian doctoral training: Multiple causes for efficiency improvements. *Studies in Higher Education*, 39(9), pp. 1668–1682.

Lee, N. (2009). *Achieving Your Professional Doctorate*. Maidenhead, UK: Open University Press.

Noble, K. A. (1994). *Changing Doctoral Degrees: An International Perspective*. SRHE and Open University Press Imprint, Society for Research into Higher Education Series, the University of Michigan, USA.

OECD (2019). Education at a Glance 2019. *Organisation for Economic Co-operation and Development* [Online]. Available at: https://www.oecd-ilibrary.org/education/education-at-a-glance-2019_f8d7880d-en. Accessed on 27th February 2021.

OECD (2020). Education at a Glance 2020. *Organisation for Economic Co-operation and Development* [Online]. Available at: https://www.oecd-ilibrary.org/education/education-at-a-glance-2020_69096873-en Accessed on 27th February 2021.

Peabody, R. (2014). *The Unruly PhD: Doubts, Detours, Departures, and Other Success Stories*, 1st ed. Basingstoke, UK: Palgrave Macmillan.

Phillips, E. M., and Pugh, D. S. (2015). *EBOOK: How to Get a PhD: A Handbook for Students and Their Supervisors*, 6th ed. McGraw-Hill, UK: Maidenhead Berkshire. Available at: VitalSource Bookshelf.

Potter, S. (2006). *Doing Postgraduate Research*, 2nd ed. London: The Open University in association with SAGE Publications.

Rugg, G., and Petre, M. (2020). *The Unwritten Rules of PhD Research*, 3rd ed. McGraw-Hill, UK and London: Open University Press. Available at: VitalSource Bookshelf.

Seagram, B. C., Gould, J., and Pyke, S. W. (1998). An investigation of gender and other variables on time to completion of doctoral degrees. *Research in Higher Education*, 39(3), pp. 319–335.

Spronken-Smith, R., Cameron, C., and Quigg, R. (2018). Factors contributing to high PhD completion rates: A case study in a research-intensive university in New Zealand. *Assessment & Evaluation in Higher Education*, 43(1), pp. 94–109. https://doi.org/10.1080/02602938.2017.1298717

Taylor, L. (2018). *Twenty Things I Wish I'd Known when I Started My PhD* [Online]. Available at: www.nature.com/articles/d41586-018-07332-x. Accessed on 11th April 2020.

Times Higher Education. (2020). PhD completion rates, 2013. *The Times Higher Education*. World University Ranking [Online]. Available at: www.timeshigher education.com/news/phd-completion-rates-2013/2006040.article. Accessed on 20th June 2020.

World Economic Forum. (2019). Which countries have the most doctoral graduates? Education at a Glance. *World Economic Forum*. Available at: www.weforum.org. Accessed on 20th June 2020.

CHAPTER 2

The PhD application process

Introduction

This chapter discusses the essential steps involved in making a PhD application. It highlights key features of PhD research programmes in UK universities and the key issues to consider in choosing a university for your doctoral study. The chapter also provides essential guidelines on how to write your PhD proposal and how to apply for PhD studentships. A general process of admissions and criteria for selecting applicants for admission into doctoral studies is discussed together with what to expect during your enrolment and induction, key stages and milestones in a PhD journey are discussed with reference to academic and administrative processes and procedures involved in a PhD.

By the end of the chapter, you will have a better understanding of

- overview of doctoral research studies in UK universities,
- general admissions requirements for PhD research study in UK universities,
- key issues to consider in choosing a university for your doctoral study,
- how to write an effective PhD proposal and apply for admissions and studentships,
- what to expect during your enrolment and induction onto your doctoral programme and
- key stages or milestones in a PhD journey from start to finish.

UK universities and doctoral studies – an overview

In the 2018–19 academic year in the UK, there were 130 higher education (HE) institutions, including public and private universities, with a license to run and award PhD degrees. In the same year, there were 2.38 million students studying in UK HE institutions, and about a quarter of this (0.59 million) were post-graduate students (HESA, 2020). In addition to the growing number of home students, UK higher institutions attract a large number of students from the EU and non-EU countries. There were 1.9 million students from the EU and 0.34 million non-EU students in UK institutions in the 2018–19 academic year (HESA, 2020).

The Research Excellence Framework (REF) of 2014 rated 76% of the research conducted and submitted in the UK as 'world leading' or internationally excellent, and UK academic research productivity was judged to be 3.6 times higher than the world average (REF, 2014). Most of the research was linked to the work of doctoral students and their supervisors. Set up by the Department for Education, the Office for Students (OfS) acts as the official government regulator and competition authority for the HE sector in England. With some variations, most UK universities require that you have at least a first- or upper-second-class honours degree before you can be enrolled in an MPhil/PhD programme. Others will not accept anything less than a master's degree before you start a doctoral programme. Although degrees from a UK university are preferred for admissions to a PhD programme, equivalent qualifications from non-UK institutions are also usually accepted.

Enquiring about PhD opportunities and choosing where to do your PhD

Once you have made the decision to do a PhD, it is worth making an initial enquiry about PhD opportunities in your area of interest from two or three universities and then decide which one is best for you. For each potential university, you may wish to consider their research environment, supervisory capacity and other resources available to support PhD students. The research environment relates to the structures, strategies and general infrastructures available to support research such as training facilities, research equipment and facilities, laboratories, study space, opportunity for teaching experience and so on. Opportunities for studentships may also be a factor to consider in your choice of university and how the university fares in the league tables such as the Postgraduate Research Experience Survey (PRES).

Universities in the UK vary widely in terms of their PhD programmes, research environment, criteria for admissions, documents required for submission when applying for admission and the duration and procedures for processing PhD applications. There is no one-size-fits-all advice that can be given here other than to say that you may want to find out a bit more about the specific requirements of the university you are planning to apply to. Given the diversity of factors you need to consider in choosing the right university for you, it is essential to look at a range of information sources and then choose wisely on the basis of what is most important to you.

Main sources of information for UK universities

(a) International recruitment agents and representatives

Some UK universities have recruitment agents and representatives in different parts of the world who coordinate admissions onto their PGR programmes. If you are an international applicant, you may well want to contact the university representatives in your country. In some cases, this could be the only option you have to process your PhD admissions to a UK university. These agents often serve as the bridge between applicants from specific countries and the UK universities they represent. These agents can support you with the necessary information about the university and what it is like to study in the UK. They may also offer support regarding your application process and student visa application. While many agents may offer support free of charge, others may charge a fee for their services. It is, therefore, important you check their fees before you use any third-party agents for your application.

(b) Published PGR prospectus and university websites

Universities in the UK have information available online on their websites. The information details their admissions requirements, fees, enrolment procedures, induction and other essential information for prospective PhD students. Published websites may also offer specific information on research areas the university is seeking applications for PhD admissions and the potential or named supervisors who are able to take on new students.

(c) Government institutions' and independent organisations' reports

There are a number of governmental and non-governmental organisations (NGOs) and institutions that provide valuable information on UK universities and the services they provide to students and their stakeholders. Some of these organisations or institutions perform statutory regulatory functions, while others provide public information on universities and the HE sector in the UK.

Examples are the Quality Assurance Agency (QAA) and the Universities UK.

The QAA is an independent organisation set up to safeguard standards and improve the quality of UK HE wherever it is delivered around the world (Quality Assurance Agency, 2020). The agency is responsible for ensuring that students working towards a UK qualification get the HE they are entitled to expect and that the standards are as high as they should be. Amongst other things, the QAA provides guidelines on issues relating to standards and quality in all universities and colleges in the UK. Information on the function and role of QAA in the UK HE sector is available at www.qaa.ac.uk.

Universities UK is the representative organisation for all UK universities. It was founded in 1918 as an umbrella organisation for UK universities. The organisation serves as the representative and voice of all 137 universities and colleges of HE in the four nations of the UK: England, Scotland, Wales and Northern Ireland. Information on the function and role of Universities UK is available at www.universitiesuk.ac.uk/.

(d) UK Universities league tables – PRES

Every year UK universities are independently assessed in terms of the quality of services they provide with regard to key factors such as entry standards, student satisfaction, research quality, graduate prospects and degree completion, amongst others. This results in the publication of a highly completive annual league table with listings of university rankings. While a university ranking in the league table may not always provide the most appropriate reflection on the suitability of the university for you, it can offer a general insight into what to expect if you decide to choose the university for your PhD.

Factors to consider when choosing where to go for your PhD study may also include, amongst others, the university ranking in relation to your specific subject, the general cost of living at the university town, the university's overall PGR ranking, the proportion of university's students who are classed as international students, the rate of post-graduate degree completion and the like.

The UK University league table varies, depending on the indicators used and the priority of the publishers. The most popular league tables are published by *The Guardian*, *The Times* and The Complete University Guide. *The Times* and *Sunday Times Good University Guide* is generally regarded as good and trusted quality indicator of UK universities. The web link to the 2020 complete guide to the UK University league table is www.thecompleteuniversityguide. co.uk/league-tables/rankings?tabletype=full-table.

(e) PRES

Apart from the league table, post-graduate students of UK universities are surveyed annually to collect information on the experiences of their post-graduate studies. Run by the Higher Education Academy, the PRES is conducted at all publicly funded universities across the country. The survey provides insight into and valuable information on students' perceptions of their post-graduate studies across the UK universities and HE sector.

The PRES survey covers areas such as the following:

- The general standard of supervision provided by universities as perceived by PGR students
- Opportunities for developing PGR students research skills
- General research culture within the university
- Students general feelings of progression in their studies
- Development of PGR students' understanding of their responsibilities and those of their supervisors and others within the university connected with their study
- Development of students' skills in research, creativity, innovation and application of research methodologies
- Professional development of PGR students with regards to their ability to manage projects, communicate information to diverse audiences and manage contacts and professional networks
- Provision of advice or opportunities for personal training in relation to personal development, transferable skills and research skills
- Provision of general development opportunities, such as placements, internships, attendance of academic conferences and publications in academic journals or books
- Opportunities to get trained and undertake paid teaching work as a graduate teaching assistant or graduate demonstrator
- Overall satisfaction with research experience/environment and general feeling of confidence in completing students' own research at the university

While the PRES may not provide the full picture, it offers a good indication of the research environment and facilities available at each university in the UK. The PRES report is particularly important because it is based purely on PGR students' own experience at their universities. Therefore, you may want to consider the PRES ratings of the university before you choose where to do your PhD. The web link to Higher Education Academy and the PRES is www.advance-he.ac.uk/reports-publications-and-resources/postgraduate-research-experience-survey-pres.

(f) University Open Days – PGR

Universities in the UK regularly run Open Days for prospective candidates. Open to the general public, Open Days provide opportunities for prospective candidates and the public to visit university campuses to speak face-to-face with faculty or admissions team regarding opportunities for doctoral studies. It is also a good way to find out, firsthand, about physical facilities available to support PhD students at the university. While you may need to book in advance for such visits, attending an Open Day can also provide an opportunity for you to meet with your potential supervisor. Such an initial contact or meeting with your potential supervisor may be especially beneficial to you if you have to do an interview to secure an admission.

Most post-graduate admissions to PhD programmes in UK universities are very competitive, especially if you are not self-funded and you may want to apply for studentships to support your study. So making a good impression at the early stage on an Open Day and showing that you are really keen, passionate and interested in doing your PhD with the university may give you an advantage over others who did not make such an initial effort. Such early contact with your potential university could also provide an opportunity for you to know what is good and what is not so great about the university and whether, on balance, the university is the right one for you.

What you need to know about the university before you sign up for your PhD

If you do make early contact with your potential university, either through an Open Day visit, direct communication or through an agent, some of the key questions you may wish to ask regarding the PhD opportunities at the university include the following:

- Is there a supervisor or director of study to supervise my research?
- Is my supervisor a full-time academic staff who will be available to me when I need him or her or a part-time associate staff?
- Is the potential supervisor likely to remain both in post and on campus for the duration of my PhD research?
- Is my potential supervisor recognised as an expert in the field of my research or enquiry?
- What is the research environment and PhD students' community like in the university?
- Are there other experienced post-doctoral students in the department, faculty or university who are working in the same or similar area of my research that I could bounce ideas off?
- What is expected of me as a PhD student in terms of a research agreement or contract that I may be required to sign, and what is the university providing me?
- What physical resources, (e.g. own office, own/hot desk facilities, own PC, access to telephone, etc.) are available to support my research?
- Is there any opportunity for me to get a university-funded PGR studentship, such as research assistantship, teaching assistantship, fees-only bursary and so on?

- When are the possible times or periods of the year for enrolment?
- Does the university have any support system or plans for people from Black, Asian and Minority Ethnic (BAME) groups, female doctoral students, disabled students, international students?

Writing your PhD research proposal

Whichever university you choose, a written research proposal will most certainly be required for admissions onto a doctoral study. A PhD proposal is an outline of a proposed research project that contains detailed information on the main questions the study is designed to answer and the ways or methods you adopt to carry out the study in order to answer the questions. Your proposal should not only define the aim and objective of your study but also underline the significance and originality of your study in terms of how your research will either challenge or contribute to the advancement of existing knowledge.

It is essential, therefore, that you present a clear, credible, feasible proposal and research plan if you were to have any chance of getting onto a PhD programme in a UK university. It is advisable to make your proposal interesting, original and novel with regards to your topic of investigation and the contribution you are seeking to make to existing knowledge. Your proposal should also demonstrate a deep understanding and knowledge of literature relating to your study (see Chapter 5). The more you read about existing studies, the more you will be able to identify knowledge 'gaps' that need filling. The ability to identifying the right knowledge 'gap' to be filled is critical in writing a good research proposal. Your proposal needs to clearly evidence that the research is

- of a standard worthy of a PhD,
- novel and original and
- forms an academically worthwhile project to embark on.

Key features of a PhD proposal

A PhD research proposal that stands any chance of success, as shown in Figure 2.1, should have all the following key features.

(a) An appropriate title

An appropriate title is one that reflects the essence of your PhD research and generates interest in your proposal. Your title and subtitle, if required, should be concise, clear and unambiguous as to what your PhD is about. From your title, readers should have a clear understanding of what your study is about

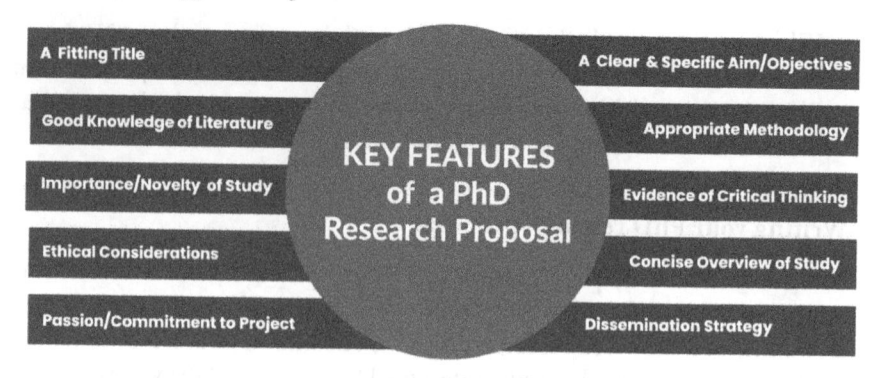

Figure 2.1 Key features of a PhD research proposal

and a sense of what to expect with regards to your study and where it sits in the structure of existing knowledge and research.

(b) Specific aims/objectives and poses the right question to be answered

A clearly defined question that lends itself to scientific, analytical or empirical study is essential. Your research question needs to relate to the central research objectives. Also, the study aims and objectives should be clearly stated in your proposal. The general purpose of research is to advance human understanding and knowledge.

The original contribution to human understanding or knowledge in your chosen field must be evident. Therefore, in your proposal, you need to

- ask the right question,
- highlight your specific focus on the issue you are investigating and
- provide an explanation for why you are investigating the issue(s) identified.

It is useful to provide background information to the project to give your study some context. This could be a social, political or historical event that necessitated the study. Alternatively, it may be new evidence that came to light on a particular issue that needs further analysis or investigation.

(c) Knowledge and understanding of existing literature

The level of your knowledge and understanding of literature in your area of study will be used to assess your proposal. So undertaking an extensive review of existing literature and using that to inform your proposal are critical to your success in gaining admission onto a PhD programme. It is advisable, therefore, that you show familiarity with key literature and make copious references to credible sources and to ensure that your proposal not only identifies 'knowledge gap' that you want to fill but also demonstrates a deep knowledge of academic literature relating to the general and specific areas of your research. A good proposal will show that you have detailed and extensive knowledge of the subject matter and that you possess the necessary skills and competency to undertake the proposed study.

(d) An appropriate methodological approach to study

The methodological approach you want to take to answer your research question should be clearly shown. Also, justifications for using a particular approach needs to be provided. Your methodology should be scientifically sound and should indicate a clear study plan and logical research design. There should be evidence of your understanding of key concepts and theories relating to your study that you will engage with in your study (see Chapter 6). The basis for using a particular methodological approach, cases studies and analytical techniques also needs to be clearly stated and how these will support the central argument of your study. An overview of how you will undertake data collection and the analysis of your data needs to be provided in your proposal together with the significance of the analysis to answering your central research question. Information on the general logistics of data collection such as the distribution of questionnaires, the location and length of interviews and so on, together with your sampling strategy and the required sample size for your study, needs to be provided. Also, the limitations of your research methodology need to be recognised and acknowledged.

(e) Highlights the importance and the novelty of the study

The importance and significance of your study and its novelty should be clearly highlighted. The possible value added to knowledge resulting from your study needs to be clearly stated. This could make a potential supervisor or university to take special interest in your study. It could also help you in securing financial support or funding for your research. The more original your research proposal, the more interest it will generate in potential supervisors and universities. So let your proposal communicate the importance of your research to the reader.

(f) Demonstrates critical thinking

An indication of your ability to think critically should be made clear. Essential critical thinking skills such as clarity of thoughts, rationality and an ability to engage in reflective and independent thoughts are important traits that are required of a PhD candidate. So your proposal should give an indication that you possess some of these attributes and that you are able to make logical connections between ideas.

(g) Considers ethical issues relating to study

Any ethical issues relating to your study should be evident. This involves ensuring that valid and informed consent will be sought and obtained before any human participants are involved in your research. It also requires ensuring that no potential and willing participants are unduly prevented or discriminated against in the study by taking reasonable steps to identify and remove barriers to participation. Your proposal should demonstrate a knowledge of and intention of complying with all data protection laws with regards to the protection of the confidentiality of information about research participants and their identities (see Chapter 7).

(h) Shows interest and passion for the study

In addition to making a strong and persuasive argument about the academic merit of your study, the proposal should also convey your passion and interest in the topic. The advice is to write a proposal that shows that you are really interested in the topic, given that you will be spending 3 to 4 years of your life working on this project if you are a full-time student and even longer if you are doing your PhD on a part-time basis. Make sure that you have the passion for your topic or subject of investigation and that you feel it is really what you want to do. This passion will drive you through the next 3 to 4 years and beyond.

(i) Indicates feasibility of work schedule and timeline

The feasibility, achievability and realism of your research must be highlighted in terms of the research aim and objectives. Note that a good PhD topic may not be doable or realistic within the time scale available to you and that a feasible topic may not necessarily be novel or interesting. Your proposal should give an indication of the work schedule and the time scale for each stage of your proposed study. A typical PhD study in the UK takes about 3 to 4 years for a full-time student and 6 to 7 years for a part-time student. The scope of your study needs to be stated in your proposal to show that you will be able to complete your PhD within the time period stipulated for your study mode. Including a carefully generated Gantt chart in your proposal may help show your work schedule and indicate that you have a realistic plan for completion.

(j) Offers comprehensive but concise overview of your study

All the requirements of the PhD proposal must all be detailed within the word limits specified by the university to which you are applying. Most universities will ask you to write a 3,000-or-so-word proposal as part of your application.

(k) Provides information on research dissemination strategy

Your proposal should provide some indications of your research dissemination strategy. This could be in terms of papers you may wish to write, research conferences you may want to attend or seminars you may wish to present to share the results of your research.

Applying formally for PhD admissions and studentships

Admissions onto PhD programme in most UK universities can be made through an online application. It is essential to follow any specific guidance given by the university or its agents for submitting applications and to give yourself enough time to meet any submission deadlines that may be specified for the enrolment cycle you are aiming for. Many universities have up to 3 or more enrolment cycles that will allow you to join or start your doctoral study at different times of the year, usually September, January and June. Applying for funding or studentships can be very competitive. It is therefore important that you have a secured source of funding for your tuition fees and living expenses for the whole period of your PhD before you start.

Certificates, transcripts, academic references and other documents

In addition to a good research proposal, many UK universities may require that you provide evidence of your qualifications in the form of copies of your certificates and transcripts. Other documents that are usually requested to be provided include academic references and proofs of identity which could be a copy of your passport, national identity card or residency permit. Some non-UK/EU/EEA citizens are also required to provide Academic Technology Approval Scheme (ATAS) certificate.

Under this scheme, all international students who require a visa to study in the UK and are subject to UK immigration control are required to have an ATAS certificate if they want to do a doctoral study, especially in certain sensitive subjects relating to national security. Examples are topics relating to STEM (Science, Technology, Engineering and Mathematics) subjects, whereby scientific knowledge gained through study could be used for military or terrorist purposes. For information on ATAS guidelines, see the UK government's web link at www.gov.uk/guidance/academic-technology-approval-scheme.

PhD studentships and scholarships opportunities

There are a number of sources of funding for post-graduate study offered by charities, foundations and trusts that you may wish to explore. Some of these grants are available to UK students only and are subject-specific. Others provide grant awards to any student regardless of subject or nationality.

For information on funding opportunities and grants see the following web links:

Postgraduate studentships www.postgraduatestudentships.co.uk/

Alternative guide to postgraduate funding gateway www.postgraduate-funding.com/gateway

UK Research and Innovation (UKRI) funding opportunities www.ukri.org/funding/funding-opportunities/

Awaiting the outcome of your PhD application

Once your application for PhD admission is submitted with your proposal, the next step is to wait for the university to process it and then give you an outcome. While some universities have a quick turnaround of about 3 weeks in processing their PGR applications, others may take a couple of months or longer. This time of waiting for an outcome could best be used for reading more literature relevant to your proposed research, especially the new literature published after you have submitted your proposal. New ideas or information gained may become useful in refining your proposal, if necessary.

PhD application review process

PhD application review and admissions decision-making processes vary from one university to another. Generally, all PhD applications received are most likely to go through a formal internal review process. This, depending on the university and the programme, is most likely to be undertaken by the admissions department or a panel of people with relevant knowledge and expertise in the area of your proposed study. The review panel may include faculty administrators, potential supervisors or project director, representatives of the post-graduate school or department your study will be based on.

Whichever form the application review panel takes, your PhD application will be considered in relation to

- the overall academic merit of your application as provided in your proposal;
- your academic qualifications and the degree to which you meet the university's requirements and any other subject-specific requirements relating to your research;

- verification of the institution you claimed to have obtained your qualifications and copies of certificates or professional registration you may have submitted;
- the suitability of your proposed study and whether it fits into the existing university/department research framework or strategy;
- the availability of subject experts and supervisory capacity to support your study;
- the available resources/facilities in the university/department, such as specialised equipment, computer software, hot desk/computing facilities, telephone and the like to support your study;
- evidence of your general research aptitude and ability to carry out a PhD research;
- the quality and sufficiency of your existing publications, if applying for PhD by publication; and
- an assessment of your competency in English at the appropriate level in terms of listening, reading, writing and speaking.

Pre-admission interviews

Many universities conduct oral interviews for their prospective PhD students as part of their admission process. Conducted either through face-to-face or via telephone or using any communication media such as Zoom, Microsoft Teams or Google Meet, amongst others, your performance at the interview can be critical to your success for admission. You need to be prepared and able to speak about your proposed research in a convincing way and explain why you are considering applying to do your PhD at a particular university or department within it.

Conditional/unconditional offer of PhD admissions

After careful consideration of your application, the university may decide to accept or reject your application or ask for more information. If your application is rejected, it does not necessarily mean the end of the road for you with regards to your PhD ambition. You may decide to try again at a later date at the same university with an improved application, or you can apply to other institutions that may look at your current application/proposal more favourably. Most universities will give you written feedback on the reasons why your application did not succeed. Figure 2.2 shows common reasons why PhD applications may be unsuccessful.

If your application is successful, a formal offer of admission will be made to you, usually in a written letter that will set out the conditions of the offer. While an offer of PhD admissions and studentships could be unconditional,

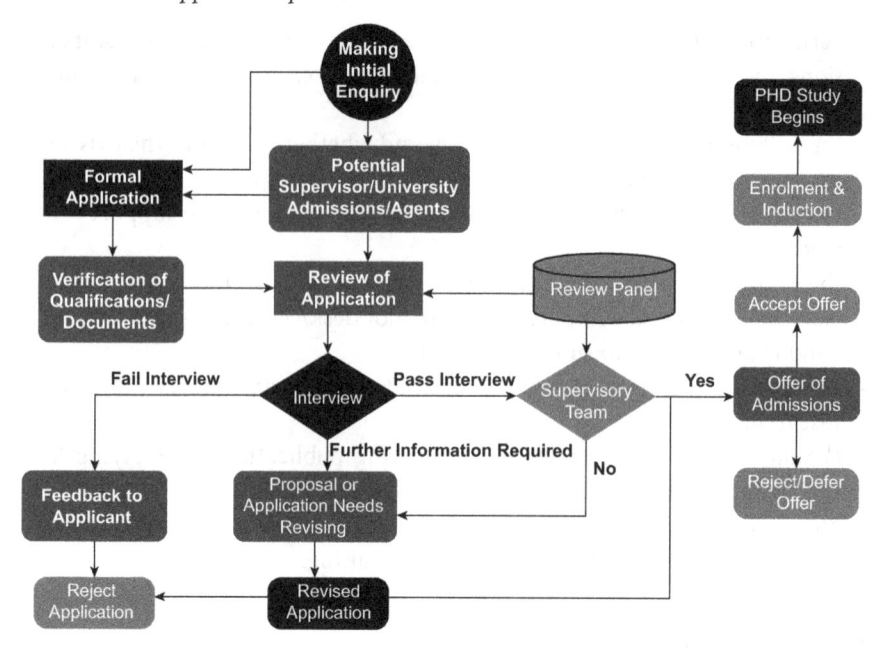

Figure 2.2 PhD applications review process

it is common for many universities in the UK to make an offer conditional on meeting a specified criterion. So if there are any other criteria you need to meet before you can be enrolled in a PhD programme, your university will expressly state that in its conditional offer of admission to you. For example, your admissions may be conditional on providing the university with evidence of your qualifications or certificates or showing that you have the required level of comprehension or communication in English. It may also involve providing evidence of your legal rights to study and live in the UK as verified through your student visas, citizenship or residency status.

Proficiency in English and English-language tests

All non-UK citizens may also be required to provide evidence of proficiency in the English language. This evidence and other required documents are usually checked and verified during enrolment.

If you are a non-native English speaker, your university may require that you meet the International English Language Testing System (IELTS) requirements before you can be enrolled in its PhD programme. Set up in 1989 and managed by the British Council, IDP: IELTS Australia and Cambridge Assessment English, the IELTS is an international standardised test of English-language proficiency. It is designed for those whose mother tongue or native language is not English. As a standard test of English, IELTS is now widely used to assess non-native English speakers applying to study in universities in the UK, Canada, Australia and many other English-speaking countries. The IELTS can be taken online. Valid for a period of 2 years, IELTS scores range from 0 to 9. Most UK universities require IELTS score of 7 or above for admission onto their PhD programme.

Other English-language proficiency tests accepted by some universities include the Test of English as a Foreign Language (TOEFL), the Pearson Test of English (PTE) (Academic), the Cambridge Advanced Certificate (CAE) and the Cambridge Certificate of Proficiency in English (CCPE).

Accepting or deferring a PhD admission offer

Once an offer of admission has been formally made to you, you are set to embark on your PhD journey. If you are still not sure whether doing a PhD is for you or you feel it is not the right time to embark on this journey, you may consider deferring your admissions to a later date to give yourself a bit more time to think and decide if doing a PhD is really what you want to do. Many universities in the UK will allow up to a 6-month period of deferment without going through a fresh PhD application process again. Any deferment of admissions longer than 6 months may require that you submit a fresh application and go through the admissions process again.

Accepting a formal offer of admissions sets you off firmly on the road to doing your PhD. That journey, as scary as it may feel for some, could be the most exciting and rewarding experience of your life. So get ready to face the opportunities and challenges that lie ahead.

International students and Student Immigration Routes visa application

If you are an international student that requires a student visa to study in the UK, you need to obtain the necessary visa by applying in good time before the commencement of your doctoral programme. In September 2020, new routes for international students to apply for visas were introduced by the UK government (Gov.UK, 2021). These replaced the old Tier 4 visa application system. There are two types of student visas – (a) Student Route Visas and (b) Short-term Study Visas. If granted, your Student Route Visa will cover the entire duration of your PhD programme of study, and will allow your legal entry into the UK a month prior to your enrolment date and 4 months after the completion of your PhD. Short-term study visas are valid for only 6 months and are usually issued for short-term courses. If you are a non-EU overseas student, you may want to check with the university or its admissions agents/representatives if you require a student visa to study in the UK. If you are a student from the EU, Switzerland, Norway, Iceland or Liechtenstein, and you or your close family member were residents in the UK before 1st January 2021, you may want to apply for the free EU Settlement Scheme to avoid any need for student visa application. Students from Ireland do not require visas to study in the UK and are not required to apply for the EU Settlement Scheme. For general guidance and information on regulations governing students visa, see the UK Visa and Immigration (UKVI) office website at https://www.gov.uk/student-visa.

Getting ready for enrolment and induction

Many universities have special enrolment and induction activities for their new PhD students. Enrolment is a formal process of registration which marks the official start of your engagement with the university and the beginning of your PGR research study. Your university may put up a number of activities during your induction to familiarise you with the university environment. It could also be a time when you are introduced to your supervisors, other PhD students, faculty staff and other administrative staff whom you will be working with during your studentship tenure at the university. The enrolment/induction period is also a good time to learn about facilities and resources for research that are available to you and the general research environment you will be working in. Information on any available skills training, development opportunities and specialists' facilities appropriate for your research may be provided to you during your induction.

Understanding key stages in a PhD journey

It is always useful, at an early stage, to have an idea of key stages in a PhD journey and what would be expected of you in terms of milestones. This can help you make an informed decision on planning for your doctoral study. Although universities vary in terms of their requirements and what they expect from their doctoral students at different stages of their PhD programme, it is possible to identify common milestones as illustrated in Figure 2.3.

Stage 1 – Making initial enquiries about universities

Your PhD journey starts the moment you decide you are going to do a doctoral study. This decision needs to be followed up with a formal expression of interest in form of applications to the university you choose to do your study with. The usual contact point is the post-graduate school or admissions department. Some universities have recruitment agents through which you

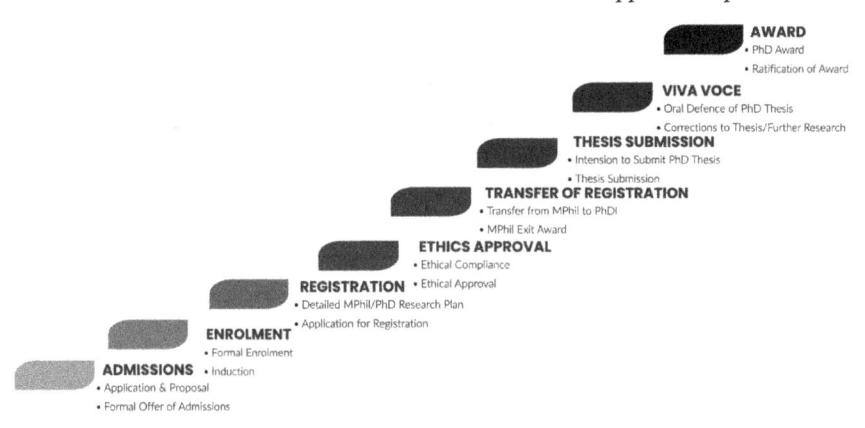

Figure 2.3 Key stages and milestones in a PhD journey

can make an enquiry about their PhD programme. Alternatively, you can get most information you need from the relevant university's website.

Stage 2 – Submitting a proposal and an application for admissions

The next stage is going through the admissions process by submitting a research proposal. This process may take between 1 to 4 months to complete depending on the university and the programme of study. It is advisable to give yourself enough time, as this process may take longer depending on whether you are a UK home student or an international student whose qualifications and documentation may need to be verified before any offer of acceptance is made.

Stage 3 – Undertaking enrolment/induction

Once you've accepted your offer of admission and it is all confirmed by either the graduate school, or post-graduate school or doctoral college (names can vary), the next stage is enrolment and induction. This is when you are formally accepted and welcomed into the PhD programme of the university. Depending on your programme and the university, the enrolment and/or induction is usually conducted through a face-to-face meeting during a campus visit, or it could be done through online registration. If not done before, you may be required to sign a learning agreement contract during your enrolment/induction. This is the stage at which you may receive a formal confirmation of the plan of your research study in terms of its duration, the time you are expected to meet key milestones such as the application for registration, transfer from MPhil to PhD, submission of thesis and amended thesis and so on.

Stage 4 – Submitting your application for registration

About 3 months after your enrolment, if you are a full-time student, some universities may require you to submit an application for registration for your PhD. This is a formal process by which universities consider and make a decision about whether your proposed research work is good enough and satisfies the academic requirements of a PhD award. This is an important milestone involving the submission of a detailed research plan for your PhD. A detailed and critical evaluation of your research plan or proposal will be undertaken at this stage. The main purpose of this is for the university to assess the feasibility of your research study. Your submission may go through the university's research review panel or committee for approval before you are allowed to continue your PhD research. The main objective here is for the university to be satisfied with the following:

a   Your proposed research and the work that you said you are going to do have the potential to satisfy the academic requirements of the university for a doctoral award.

b   The aims and objectives of your research are clear and reflect the proposed research work.

c   You have a realistic plan of work, and the plan is achievable within the target submission timeline of your PhD programme.

d   You clearly set out the rationale and the scope of your research in terms of what you want to achieve and how you want to achieve it.

e   The university has available the necessary resources and supervisory capacity to support your research.

f   You have considered all aspects of your research with regards to research governance, ethics, intellectual property rights (IPR), health and safety issues and other risk management issues.

Stage 5 – Applying for and receiving ethical approval for your research

Either after or in conjunction with stage 4, you may be required to submit a report detailing any ethical issues relating to your research and how you are going to address those issues. The main purpose here is to ensure that your PhD research is ethically compliant with the university's research ethics policy. It is essential you familiarise yourself with and understand the university ethical policy on research. Your ethical approval application will most likely go to the university's research ethics committee or review panel. Your university will most certainly require that you obtain ethical approval for your PhD research before you start your data collection, interviews or a field study.

Stage 6 – Transferring of registration from MPhil into a full PhD

For students enrolled in an MPhil/PhD programme, the expectation is that you will need to pass or have done an equivalent of level 7 before you are allowed to proceed to a full PhD. About 15 months after your enrolment (full-time students), your university may ask you to submit a report and undertake a mini viva voce examination with an assessor. The assessor, who could be internal or external to your university, is usually a researcher with expertise in your area of study. This could be one of the most important milestones in your PhD journey as your ability to continue is conditional on your success at this critical stage. Most universities in the UK tend to offer admissions for MPhil/PhD at the first instance. Your ability to transfer or continue your study to a full PhD programme is predicated on your success in satisfying the university and the assessor(s) that you meet the required standard of work to proceed to level 8 (independent and original research that will lead to a doctoral award). Various terms are used by different universities to refer to this process of transfer such as 'Transfer of Registration', 'Confirmation of Registration' or 'Confirmation of Route'. Whichever nomenclature is used, if the standard of your research work, in the first 15 months or so, is deemed to fall short of the standard expected for a PhD, your university may de-enrol you or ask you to write up your work for a lower exit award of an MPhil. In some cases, in order to achieve a transfer of registration to a full PhD, you may be required to pass or demonstrate competence or sufficient knowledge in research methods or specific aspects of the subject of your thesis. This could involve enrolling in and passing a credit-rated module.

Stage 7 – Giving notice of intention to submit and submission of your thesis

This is an advanced stage of your PhD journey in which you have done most of your research and you are approaching the end of writing your thesis. It is a stage during which your university may require that you give a formal notice of your intention to submit your PhD thesis. This is usually about 3 months before the actual submission is due. Such notice is usually required to enable the university to commence arrangements for your viva voce examination. This is an internal administrative process undertaken mostly by the PGR office or graduate school and involves your supervisor and the internal and external examiners. Your university may request that you submit 2 to 4 soft-bound copies of your thesis and an electronic copy.

Stage 8 – Doing your viva voce examination

This is a stage at which you have finally submitted your thesis and the thesis will have been read by the internal and external examiners and others who are experts in the field. The viva is a formal oral defence of your thesis detailing the research you have been doing since you started your PhD. The main purpose of your viva is to establish that you are the true author of your thesis. Through your viva, your thesis and matters relating to it will be examined and your research findings and conclusions will be subjected to scrutiny and rigorous testing and validation before an expert in the area (see Chapter 12).

Stage 9 – Receiving an outcome of your PhD

This is a nerve-racking stage in which you are made to wait in anticipation of what the outcome of your viva is going to be. This is the last stage of your PhD journey in which the outcome of your viva voce examination will be orally communicated to you. It can be an emotionally charged stage, and it is not unusual for people to see people cry either for joy or sadness depending on the outcome of the viva. It is a watershed moment with a crucial and profound significance when you are told that you have either

1 passed with no further work required apart from perhaps correction of minor typographical errors or
2 required to make minor revisions but not requiring resubmission and re-examination of the thesis or
3 required to make major revisions requiring resubmission and re-examination of the thesis.

It is not uncommon to pass a viva but with some minor or major amendments required to the thesis before an award can be confirmed. Such amendments or corrections can take up to 12 months for the thesis to be resubmitted, without any need for another viva, or in some cases, a second viva may be required.

If after your viva examination, your thesis is judged to have failed (see Chapter 12), some universities will give you the opportunity to resubmit and go through the viva voce examination process again. This may take up to a year before you can resubmit depending on the amount of work that you need to do to make good of the failed thesis. Other universities may decide to terminate your PhD with a lower award of MPhil or no award.

Underlying the key stages and milestones described earlier are complex administrative/academic structures and processes within the university system. They ensure that academic quality and standards are maintained for doctoral studies. In addition to your supervisors and your faculty academic staff, various departments/units of the university may be involved in your doctoral studies (Figure 2.4).

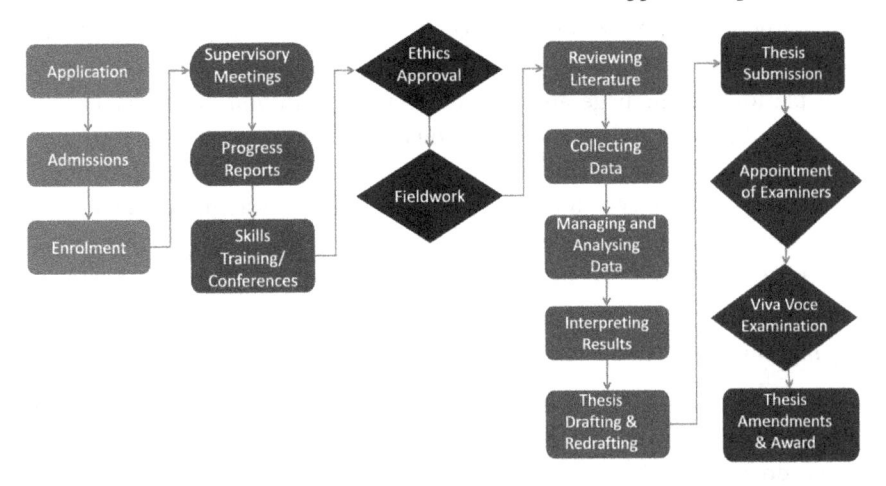

Figure 2.4 Administrative/academic processes and structures underpinning PhD research study

Maximum registration and termination of a PhD programme

Many UK universities run time-limited PhD programmes. This means your doctoral study will have an expiry date. Typically, full-time students are required to complete their PhD programme within 3 to 4 years. For part-time students, this may range from 5 to 7 years. Each university has its own regulations and guidelines regarding the maximum registration period permitted for their PhD students. Generally, the maximum registration is the total time permitted for the completion of a PhD programme. This is usually set at the expected or target date of thesis submission plus 1 year of corrections for full-time students or expected date of thesis submission plus 2 years of corrections for part-time students.

Alternative route to a PhD programme – research master's (MRes/ResM)

Some UK universities offer research master's programmes (MRes or ResM) that allow successful students to transfer onto a PhD programme. MRes programmes usually run for 18 months full-time or 3 years if done on a part-time basis. Eligible MRes students could transfer to a PhD programme. However, these students still need to complete the requirements or mini viva examination relating to the transfer of registration process before they are accepted to a full PhD programme.

PhD and student information management systems

Universities in the UK use different information technology platforms to manage and process their students' information and progression. The most commonly used PhD information systems are PhD Manager and GradBook. You may be required to use your university's preferred information management platform to manage and record meetings with your supervisors and submit applications and evidence that you have met key milestones. Your university will be able to provide you with training on the use of its PhD management systems. Once you have gained access to the system, the university/supervisors will be able to monitor your progression and engagement with your research study.

Key messages

- Reading and reviewing existing literature will help you find an interesting and feasible topic or area of study that you are passionate about to do for your doctoral study.
- To gain admissions into a PhD programme, you need to write a convincing research proposal that clearly sets out your research aims and objectives, and your research questions need to be clearly stated.
- UK universities vary widely in their admissions procedure and requirements for doctoral studies as well as in the research environment and support for PhD students. You need to choose your university wisely based on what is important to you.
- PhD research is underpinned by complex university administrative structures and processes that ensure quality and maintain standards from the application stage right through to the confirmation of an award stage. Understanding your university's processes can help your doctoral study's experience.
- Studying in the UK can be very expensive, especially for international students. Make sure you have sufficient funds and financial means to support your study and your living expenses for the duration of your study.
- Some non-EU PhD applicants may need to obtain a student visa before they can study in the UK. Others also require authorisation (ATAS certificates) if their PhD research relates to sensitive national security areas. Check your visa status and what you need to travel to, live and study in the UK.
- Understanding key milestones and making effective plans to meet them will help you with your PhD journey.

Further reading

Bickerton, P. (2016). 10 things you need to know before starting a PhD degree. *Earlham Institute* [Online]. Available at: www.earlham.ac.uk/articles/10-things-you-need-know-starting-phd-degree. Accessed on 12th April 2020.

Complete University Guide. (2020). *University League Tables 2020*. Complete University Guide Limited, Bedford, England. https://www.thecompleteuniversityguide.co.uk/league-tables/rankings. Accessed on 19th May 2020.

Findaphd.com. (2020). *Writing a Good PhD Research Proposal* [Online]. Available at: www.findaphd.com/advice/finding/writing-phd-research-proposal.aspx. Accessed on 27th April 2020.

Gov.UK. (2021). *Study in the UK on a Study Visa* [Online]. Available at: https://www.gov.uk/student-visa. Accessed on 27th February 2021.

HESA. (2020). *Higher Education Statistics Agency* [Online]. Available at: www.universitiesuk.ac.uk/facts-and-stats/Pages/higher-education-data.aspx. Accessed on 18th June 2020.

Kramer, G., Bernstein, D., and Phares, V. (2019). Getting into graduate school in clinical psychology. In *Introduction to Clinical Psychology* (pp. 415–444). Cambridge: Cambridge University Press.

Postgraduate Studentships. (2020). *Where Ideas and Funding Meet* [Online]. Available at: www.postgraduatestudentships.co.uk/. Accessed on 14th June 2020.

Quality Assurance Agency (QAA). (2020). Available at: https://www.qaa.ac.uk/ Accessed on 7th June 2020.

REF. (2014). *Research Excellence Framework* [Online]. Available at: www.ref.ac.uk/2014/. Accessed on 18th June 2020.

SI-UK. (2020). *UK University Rankings 2020*. Available at: www.studyin-uk.com/uk-study-info/university-rankings/. Accessed on 19th May 2020.

Sturdivant, S., and Relles, N. (2016). Graduate Record Examination (GRE). In *Getting into Graduate School in the Sciences: A Step-by-Step Guide for Students* (pp. 22–37). Cambridge: Cambridge University Press.

Universities UK. (2020). Higher education in numbers. *Universities UK* [Online]. Available at: https://www.universitiesuk.ac.uk/facts-and-stats/Pages/higher-education-data.aspx. Accessed on 18th June 2020.

CHAPTER 3

Working with your supervisor/
director of study

Introduction

This chapter focuses on the relationship between you as a PhD student and your supervisor(s) or director(s) of study. It examines your responsibility as a PhD research student and highlights the role of your supervisors and directors of study in directing and supporting you through your PhD research work. The importance of developing a good working relationship between you and your supervisors are discussed and specific ways your supervisors can be of help to you and how you can make good use of their support are discussed.

By the end of the chapter, you will have a better understanding of

- the role of supervisors and directors of studies,
- what supervisors expect of their PhD students,
- how to work with supervisors to good effect,
- managing meetings with supervisors,
- reporting your progress to your supervisors and
- deciding when, or if, to change supervisors.

Role and purpose of a supervisor

Your university will most certainly provide some supervisory support for your research in terms of a named supervisor/director of study with expertise and knowledge in the area of your research. Your supervisors are most likely to be senior academic staff with a proven record and experience in supervising other PhD students and may have had a number of PhD completions in their career. Usually, but not always, a PhD student is allocated two supervisors. In some universities, a supervisory team could comprise three or more people, each having something to contribute to your supervision. One of your supervisors usually serves as the lead supervisor or the director of study (DoS). All your supervisors will, most likely, have undergone some training relating to their supervisory role. Many UK universities recognise the need to support their doctoral students by ensuring effective monitoring of their needs and requirements. Supervisors play a key role in this; hence, universities now provide, as standard, regular training for PhD-student supervisors to establish codes of practice with regards to the role and responsibilities of both supervisors and students (Phillips and Pugh, 2015).

Universities use different names for supervisors, such as mentor, DoS, first supervisor and so on. Whatever title or label is used, supervisors tend to be people with expertise and deep knowledge in your field of investigation. Hence, their role is to serve as 'critical friends' working with you to improve your work to the standard required. They are there to help and support you through your study. Understanding their role and making the most of what they have to offer are, therefore, central to your success. It is most likely, as some have suggested, that you will develop a close and strong personal and professional relationship with your supervisors (Petre and Rugg, 2010).

Your supervisors can help facilitate and support you by providing specific guidance and training for you and by introducing you to new contacts and networking opportunities where you meet other people who may be able to support you in your research. Supervisors also perform a central mentoring role. Many universities, in recognition of their role, run regular supervision training sessions for PhD supervisors to keep them up to speed with regards to regulatory and other academic and administrative processes relating to your study.

There is some element of luck and good fortune in getting the right supervisors for your PhD. A supervisor with a good record of completions or high academic status in the field of your research may not necessarily be the right person for you. Similarly, the right supervisor who may work well with you may not necessarily be a high-profile academic in the faculty or university. Whomever you chose or are allocated as your supervisors, they are there to perform key functions and play an important role in your PhD study (Figure 3.1).

Enabling access to and contacts with supervisors

Supervisors are expected to provide you with support in your doctoral study on a regular basis. They should be there and available when needed. Having access to your supervisor is critical to your success, and your supervisors are expected to enable access to and contact with them. Given that some academics may be busy or away from the university at conferences or on sabbatical leave from time to time, it is important that you know when and how frequently you can have face-to-face, one-to-one supervisory meetings with your supervisors. If face-to-face supervisory meetings cannot be arranged,

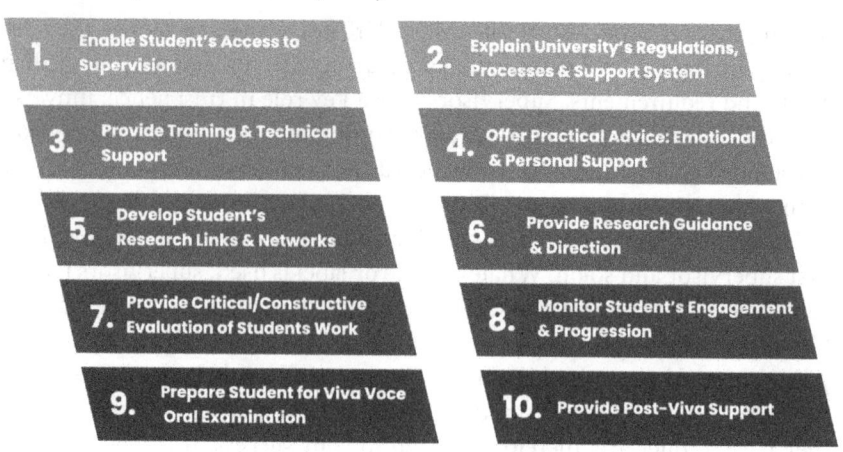

Figure 3.1 Role of PhD supervisors/directors of studies

your supervisor should provide an alternative means of access and communication to undertake their supervisory duties.

In some universities, there is an expectation that a PhD student should receive a minimum of six supervisions per annum, involving the whole supervisory team. Supervision could be done remotely over the telephone or using media such as Zoom, Teams or other communication platforms. Your university may require your supervisor to keep a record or log their meetings and contact with you as evidence that supervision has been provided to you. It is, therefore, important that you take notes of every meeting and contact you have with your supervisor in case you need to raise any issues regarding your supervision in the future. It is also useful and good practice to have a record of or summary of what was discussed or agreed with your supervisors at every meeting in relation to your study.

A useful tactic could be a brief email to your supervisor immediately after each meeting outlining what was discussed and agreed on. This effectively holds your supervisor to any agreement as much as you. While your supervisor should supervise you, you, on the other hand, should supervise your supervisor(s).

Mentoring you and directing your study

A key role of the supervisor(s) is to serve as your mentor or DoS. A supervisor can offer you a great deal of support in relation to the general direction of your study. They can help develop your ability to think critically and provide personalised training on key aspects of your study such as field study, survey design, data collection, analysis and interpretation.

Keeping regular contact with your supervisors will ensure that they know about and are involved in every stage of your work. Your supervisors should have oversight of your work and your achievements and development in the context of the stage you are at and the stage that you ought to be in your programme at any particular point in time. They should set clear milestones, timelines and expectations against which to monitor your progress to ensure that you are progressing satisfactorily.

Monitoring your engagement and progression

Another key role of the supervisor is to serve as progress monitors to ensure you are working at the right pace to meet your milestones. They can advise you on the timing for the various activities and stages of your research and help ensure you are working at the right pace to meet the required deadlines or milestones. Your supervisors should also be able to guide you in ensuring that your work meets the required standard. Where your work or progress is not of the required standard, they should be able to provide support and assistance to improve your performance. Most universities require PhD supervisors to provide evidence of their students' progress as completion rates are regarded as one of the key performance indicators that universities are judged by. The progress monitoring may involve completing an annual or quarterly report detailing the work you have done.

For home students, progress monitoring of your study may be a light touch and a simple exercise. However, if you are an international or non-EU student on a Tier 4 visa (now known as Student Visa), your progress monitoring exercise may have a more significant implication as any report of a lack of progress may affect your student visa. Under the regulatory framework, all Tier 4 PGR student visa holders doing their PhD in the UK universities are required to show quarterly progress with their study. Your university is required to submit a mandatory quarterly report on your progress to the UK authorities. It is, therefore, important that your supervisors know what you are doing regarding your study and that you are making steady progress without which you may lose your students visa. If your university believes and reports to the UK authorities that you are not engaging or making satisfactory progress, your PhD programme may be terminated and you may be asked to leave the UK.

Helping you with advice on how to conduct your research, writing and structuring your thesis

Your supervisors should be able to provide you with guidance and advise on how you conduct your research, the appropriate methodology to adopt and how to write and structure your thesis. They will be able to help you with advice on appropriate theoretical or methodological approaches to ensure a solid foundation for your study. They may also offer advice on literature sources and analytical techniques to assist you with your research. As experts in their fields, and as experienced researchers themselves, your supervisors are there to provide academic leadership and an encouraging and supportive environment for you to succeed in your research.

Providing you with a critical but constructive evaluation of your research

Your supervisors may offer to read and check through draft chapters relating to your literature review, methodology, analysis, results and the like to ensure that your findings and conclusions are consistent with your data. As the bedrock of your academic support, your supervisors should be able to provide an honest and critical evaluation of your work in order to help improve the standards of your written or creative work. They should serve as 'critical friends', working alongside you to achieve the best outcome for you.

Introducing you to and helping you to develop your research links and networks

Giving their wealth of experience and expertise in the area of your research, your supervisors may be able to introduce you to external contacts, publications, professional bodies, and useful sources in your field of study. They may also involve you in the activities of any research groups, workshops and conferences that may be beneficial to you in your own study.

Reading through and providing feedback on your written/creative work

Your supervisors may require you to submit your written or creative draft work in form of chapters, analysis, findings and the like so that they can give you feedback and constructive criticism that could help you improve your work. It is particularly important that your supervisors have oversight of your thesis and to ensure that it meets the standard expected before you submit for a viva voce examination and assessment.

Preparing you for your final viva voce examination

As directors of your study, your supervisors have an important role to play in preparing you for your viva. They should be actively engaged and involved in any decisions as to when you are ready and willing to be put forward for a viva voce examination. Through their experience of supervising other students, they should know when your work is up to the required standard to be examined and how best to prepare you for the critical viva voce examination. Usually, about 4 to 6 months before you submit your thesis, your university may require you to give your intention-to-submit notice. Through your supervisors, the university will need to organise and arrange your viva voce examination. Your supervisors have an important role to play here as they may need to liaise with you, the examiners, the PGR student office, chair of the viva voce examination and any other relevant people that may need to be involved in your viva voce examination. Your supervisors can also help with your preparation for the viva voce examination by doing a mock viva for you or giving you essential tips. In Chapter 13, further details on how your supervisors can help you prepare for your viva are discussed.

Offering you post–viva examination support

In addition to supporting you in preparing for your viva, your supervisors may also play a critical role in any post-viva support you may need. Viva voce examination can be very stressful and, depending on the outcome, can be emotionally and psychologically draining. Having your supervisors by your side at a critical moment when you receive the result of your viva can be very beneficial.

Working with an external supervisor

It is possible, in some cases, to have a supervisor or a second supervisor that is external to your university. This could be an academic or researcher with expertise or special knowledge on aspects of your study but working or based in other universities or institutions. Where such arrangements are in place, most universities will ensure that your external supervisor is formally appointed or set up as an associate lecturer with access to your academic records. Your external supervisor should normally be an established (full-time or fractional) member of the academic staff of another university with a specific schedule of work or tasks to undertake in relation to your supervision.

What your supervisors expect from you

In return for their support and advice for helping with your study, there are certain expectations as to how you should engage with your supervisors to make the relationship work. Some of the essential things that most supervisors expect from their PhD students are summarised in Figure 3.2.

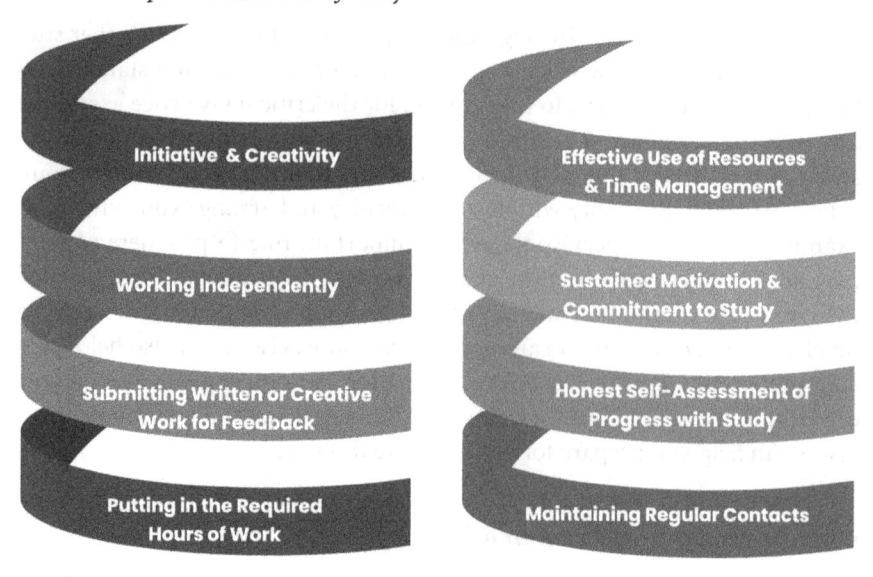

Figure 3.2 What supervisors expect from their PhD students

Working independently

You are required to take full control of your own research and to use your supervisors to provide support and assistance with your project only when needed or required. It is your PhD, after all, and it's your responsibility to ensure that you do the work and meet all the required milestones to achieve success. You should see your supervisor as a source of support and not the driver of your study. While your supervisors may be able to advise on stages or timings for various activities relating to your work and help with advice on things like chapter structures, work plans and general direction of your study, it is essential you take the lead and initiative and put in the efforts to work towards your own success. It is your responsibility to work independently and effectively and to take actions that will ensure your thesis is submitted within the stipulated or required period.

Read the regulations, understand your milestones and have some independent thoughts and insights into how you are going to drive your own progress (see Chapter 8). Seek help if you are struggling and have to, but you must be able to work independently and creatively.

Production and submission of written or creative work

Your supervisors will expect you, on a regular basis, to produce and submit written works, chapter drafts and the like that they can read and make comments on. Be responsive and creative. Doing a PhD is about creativity and developing new knowledge and ideas. The more creative you are, the more you are able to show or demonstrate your contribution to knowledge. You create and your supervisors evaluate. Your supervisors are there to support you in the creative process. Their reviews and feedback on your work and comments can help you improve your work and think of new ideas. Their feedback can also help you think critically and objectively about your work and how it is likely to be received in the academic community. While some supervisors prefer a chapter-by-chapter review, others may want you to submit several chapters or a whole draft of your thesis for them to comment on or critique. You and your supervisor can agree on what style of feedback works well for both of you.

Putting in the required hours of work onto your PhD research

If you are a full-time PhD student, you may be expected to devote no less than 37 hours per week to your doctoral studies. For a part-time student, at least 18.5 hours per week of work on your PhD may be required. Although many full-time PhD students do take up paid work in areas not related to their study, the number of hours international students on a student visa (Tier 4) can work is strictly controlled. If you are a non-EU international student on a Tier 4 general student visa, it is important that you check the number of hours you are allowed to work without breaching the conditions attached to your student visa. Part of the conditions for your student visa may require your university to provide evidence of your engagement with your doctoral study. Your university may, therefore, require your supervisors to monitor your commitments to your study in terms of your engagement and write reports on your progress on a quarterly or an annual basis.

Using resources and managing your time and resources effectively

Your ability to manage your time effectively and productively will contribute to your chances of success in your PhD. There is a long list of tasks to be completed at every stage of your PhD. Understanding what is required of you and getting on in earnest with the tasks within the time and resources available to you will enhance your chances of completing your PhD in good time. Procrastination, as the saying goes, is the thief of time. Getting the right task done and completed at the right time means you will be on top of your work schedule and able to meet your research work plan and the required milestones. Your supervisors will expect you to be respectful of their own time too. So they will expect that you don't turn up late for meetings. Also, not showing up at a supervisory meeting, without sending an apology or cancelling the meeting before the day or time of meeting will be considered unacceptable and disrespectful. You will be expected to participate in the academic and research life of the department by engaging in training activities, seminars, workshops and interacting with other PhD students, especially if you are a full-time student. You will be expected to spend your time wisely and manage your own work schedule.

Showing and maintaining motivation and commitment to your study

If you, as a PhD student, don't show much interest or motivation and evidence of commitment to your own study, it will be difficult for your supervisors or anyone else to help you. The more you demonstrate a sustained passion for your research, the greater your chances of getting the best out of your supervisors to support you. By showing that you are working hard and that you are committed to your own study, your supervisors are most likely to be motivated in helping and supporting you to achieve your goal.

You can show your commitment through your engagement in research activities or training opportunities provided, as an example. If you are less enthused about your own work, you can't honestly expect your supervisors to invest their time and be passionate about offering you support. Be punctual and turn up at supervisory meetings as arranged. Manage your time and use time and resources allocated to you wisely.

Most supervisors have a sense of responsibility towards their PhD students and will make the effort to help them if they struggle. Having invested a great deal of their time in your supervision, they will expect you to have a sense of dedication and be enthusiastic about your own study. They will expect you to have some degree of perseverance and not to give up easily when you are faced with challenges. It is in your interest as well as your supervisors' that you persevere through your study when faced with challenges along the way on your PhD journey.

Being honest and transparent in your assessment of your own progress

You should be absolutely honest with yourself and your supervisors with regards to your progress. The annual progress report, which your university may require you to submit is a good opportunity to be honest about the progress you've made and the challenges or obstacles you've faced during the year. Through your progress review, you can draw the attention of your supervisors and the department to areas where you need help. If you are struggling for any reason, it is strongly advisable that you let your supervisors know as soon as possible so that they can help you or point you to where you can get some help. Their experiences in supervising other students may be beneficial to you in times of crisis or when things don't go according to plan. If they can't help you, they may know someone who can. For detailed information on getting support for your PhD, see Chapter 4.

Maintaining regular contacts and communication

As a PhD student, you are expected to maintain regular contact with your supervisors through meetings, emails, telephones and so on and to be responsive to their advice and offer of support for your study. It is advisable to keep a record of supervisory meetings you have with your supervisors and that you follow up on any lead they may provide with regards to your research. You will also be required to engage with any training opportunities they provide that relate to any specific or generic aspects of your research. This could be in the form of specialised courses, training, workshops, conferences and the like which will keep your supervisors informed of your research activities. Giving your supervisors feedback on conferences or workshops you have attended can help them gain insight into your progress and engagement.

Some supervisors want meetings with their PhD to be formal, with key points for discussion or an agenda drawn up before the meeting. Others prefer an informal meeting on a regular or semi-regular basis over lunch or coffee. Whichever your supervisors prefer, try to make the most of the time with them. Be reasonable in your expectations and your demands on your supervisors' time as many supervisors often have a very tight work schedule, fitting everything else in, in addition to supervising your PhD.

Publishing with your supervisors

Having some publications under your name, while still doing your PhD, can be extremely beneficial not only for your viva but also for your career after your PhD. If you have the inclination and opportunity, publishing with your supervisors is a great and easy way to get into producing academic contents that are published in high-ranking journals and periodicals. This could prove useful, especially if you want to pursue a career in academia after your PhD. However, the drive to publish with your supervisor, no matter his or her academic standing or status should not detract you from the focus of completing your own PhD. Your main focus as a PhD student is successfully completing your PhD. Your future and your career may depend on that, rather than on being a co-author with your supervisors.

Many universities actively encourage their PhD students to publish papers, sometimes with their supervisors. Academics take on the role of supervisor for various reasons. One of these is connected with their passion or love for the topic or subject of investigation. Supervising PhD students, and producing joint publications with them, offers them the means to advance their own career. While publishing with their supervisors is a great way of training and developing PhD students' skills in academic writing, this can sometimes create a conflict of interest if not managed effectively. Some PhD students may feel pressured to publish with their supervisors, thinking that success in their PhD may be predicated on or affected if they don't comply. While the academic agenda of most universities is to promote scholarships through publications, it is not obligatory for you to publish articles or papers relating to your study with your supervisors. It is unethical and immoral for supervisors to subject their PhD students to unreasonable pressure to publish their PhD work with them or force them to do so against their wish.

It must be remembered that a PhD is judged entirely by what is presented in the thesis itself regardless of how many or how few, if indeed any, papers a PhD student has published. Prioritise doing the PhD thesis itself over trying to achieve publication.

Developing a good relationship between you and your supervisors could help you make the right decision regarding any suggestion or idea of a joint publication, but always remember that you own your PhD research work and have the ultimate rights to decide how and with whom it is published. Understanding your rights, as a PhD student, within the general framework of intellectual property and copyright law will help you manage or resist any pressure from your supervisors to publish your own work with them as joint authors. For further guidance on intellectual property and your PhD, see Chapter 7.

Core principles underpinning PhD student–supervisor relationships

There are five inter-related principles underpinning an effective, supportive and responsible PhD student–supervisor relationship (Figure 3.3).

Trust

A good student–supervisor relationship requires mutual trust between the supervisor and the supervisee. PhD student should be able to trust their supervisors to give them good advice and guidance when needed. Students should also be able to trust the professional judgement of their supervisors and understand that supervisors are there to work with them and not against them. The supervisors should also feel that the advice they give to their PhD students is valued and appreciated. It is essential for both PhD students and their supervisors to build trust between and amongst themselves and to

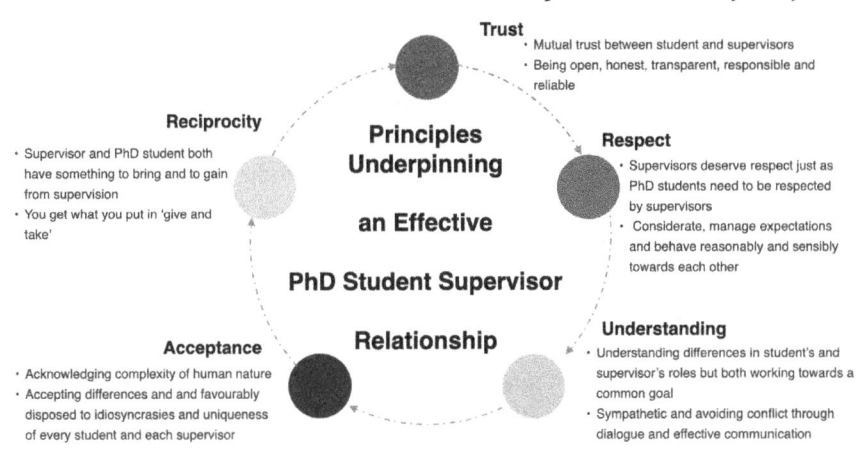

Figure 3.3 Principles underpinning PhD student–supervisor relationship

know that each one will work and meet their end of the bargain to achieve the goal – the student's PhD award. It has been suggested that trusted relationships are built, generally, through interactions that have gone well (Giang, 2020). Therefore, the more productive and resourceful supervisory meetings that supervisors and their PhD students have, the more trust they will build between them.

Respect

Mutual respect between PhD students and their supervisors is central to a good and effective professional working relationship. Supervising a PhD student is a trusted and highly respected role. It is a role that requires that supervisors respect their students and for students to be respectful and behave sensibly towards their supervisors. Supervisors need to understand that although a PhD student is enrolled to study under their tutelage and guardianship, they should not be treated as children or school pupils who need to be told what to do and what not to do. PhD students are adults, and supervisors should relate to them as such. Many PhD students have had successful careers before opting to do a PhD. Treating them as adults and with respect as colleagues will most certainly bring the best out of them. Similarly, PhD students should respect and value their supervisors, whose support and guidance they need in order to achieve their goal of getting a PhD.

Understanding

It is essential that both PhD student and supervisors understand each other's role and responsibilities in the relationship. PhD students should know that supervisors are not there to massage their egos, nor are they there to make PhD students' lives hell by making things difficult for them. There are times when supervisors may need to be critical, firm and honest in their advice, comments and feedback on PhD students work. Tough love may need to be applied as a goad to drive students forward in their studies. Supervisors' comments and feedback are normally directed at the work submitted for review and are not and never should be directed at the student as a person. However, impassioned they may be about supervising or supporting a PhD student, supervisors should understand that they are not dictators. PhD students have the rights not to follow their supervisors' advice. It may not be wise to do so; PhD students may choose to ignore or disregard advice or guidance received from their supervisors. After all, supervisors are there as a support and not to dish out orders that must be obeyed.

Once a supervisor and a PhD student, understand that they have each other's best interests at heart, then creating a conducive environment for imparting knowledge and learning becomes a possibility (Wenger, 2020).

Acceptance

For an effective student–supervisor relationship, both supervisors and PhD students should accept each other for whom they are. Knowing that supervisors are humans just as their PhD students and there is no such thing as a perfect human. A perfect supervisor does not exist; neither does a perfect PhD student. Also, there should be an acceptance on the part of supervisors and students that everyone is unique. No two students are the same, and no two supervisors are the same either. Every individual is different and unique and has some degrees of imperfection. Supervisors and their PhD students have feelings and are subject to all kinds of emotions. Humans respond differently to pressures and can sometimes have hidden personal issues that may affect views and judgements and how they respond to events, situations or other people. Getting to know your supervisor or your student well will help you accept them for what they are and work with them to bring the best out of them.

Reciprocity

The principle of reciprocity suggests the idea of give-and-take. For an effective student–supervisor relationship, there should be a mutual drive to give and to receive. For PhD students to receive good support and advice from their supervisors, they need to play their part by showing their commitments to their work, putting in the required hours of work and generally making the effort. For students to develop confidence in their own work and in their supervision, supervisors need to give good advice, support and guidance. PhD students can't do it alone. They need their supervisors to succeed, and the success of their PhD students often reflect well on the professional career of supervisors. PhD students can benefit from good advice from supervisors, which can lead to greater productivity and creativity of students, which, in turn, makes supervision easier and more rewarding for supervisors.

What to do with your supervisors' advice and guidance

You don't always have to agree with your supervisor or take their advice. Sometimes supervisors may advise you to take a particular methodological approach to your study that you consider not to be the right one. They may ask you to structure your analysis differently, or they may be pushing you in a direction you don't want to go or pushing you too far into a particular analytical approach that you consider unsuitable for your study. Such differences in opinions or disagreements on academic matters between PhD students and their supervisors are not uncommon. In fact, this is considered a normal process of developing your academic independence. Rather than taking it as something negative, such differences in opinions could be seen as a healthy way of advancing your knowledge and nurturing you as a young researcher.

However, you need to have the confidence and the courtesy to discuss your position with your supervisors and offer them a solid basis or foundation to back up your position. Willfully disregarding. your supervisors' advice, without giving any reason or explanation is never a good idea and may be perceived as discourteous or rude and some supervisors can take this very personal.

If you really don't want to go in the direction that your supervisors are pushing you and you don't feel that is what you want to do, you need to provide a strong and convincing argument backed with literature or facts to convince them that that is not the right way for you. Most supervisors will reason with you, support you in your decision and respect the fact that it is your PhD and that you have to do the right thing for you regardless of their supervision. If your supervisors are adamant and unyielding and still insist that you do what they tell you to do, the advice is that you may begin to reassess whether they are the right supervisors for you as this may cause you some difficulties in the long run (Lantsoght, 2018).

Whatever they feel about how you use their advice, knowing that your supervisors are not always right is a good way of developing an independent mind and taking control of your own PhD research. After all, this is your project, your own research and your PhD, so it is imperative that you own it and drive it to success (see Chapter 8). However, if you do take a different view to your supervisors' advice, make sure that you have a strong basis for doing so and that your approach is justified and backed up by evidence. It may be useful in this case to seek the views of a third party who is respected in the field.

You should also understand that your supervisors may have had a great deal of experience and their advice is worth listening to even if you don't take all the advice on board or apply it to your own study. Trusting your own thought process is also equally important and do not just follow everything your supervisors tell you to do. At the same time, you should avoid coming across as an arrogant PhD student who thinks they know better than their supervisors. It is important to bear in mind that whatever decisions you make about your PhD study, independent of your supervisors, it is your responsibility, and you should ensure it is the right one for you and your methodological approach to your study is systematic, rooted in good theory, backed up with data or evidence and is scientifically provable or verifiable.

Managing conflicts with your supervisor

Developing a good and effective working relationship with your supervisors is critical to your success. At the best of time, doing a PhD can be challenging on its own. If, on top of that, you find that you don't have a good relationship with your supervisors, this can be troubling and may have a profound effect on you and your study. It has been suggested that some of the problems PhD students have with their supervisors are avoidable and preventable as they relate more to misunderstanding and miscommunication rather than anything more sinister (Petre and Rugg, 2010).

As no two supervisors and no two students are the same, the type of conflict that may arise between you and your supervisors will depend on a number of factors such as your personality and those of your supervisors, their supervision style, the stage you are at in your PhD study, the type of relationship you've built up or set up with them and the degree of their involvement in your study, amongst many other factors.

Some supervisors can be very overbearing and sometimes overreach their role. In an attempt to push their students to succeed, some can become too pushy and overtly insensitive in driving their supervisees. Other common areas of conflict with supervisors relate to their supervision style which, rather than helping their students, could have a negative impact on their students. Effective dialogue and communication between you and your supervisor can sometimes resolve some of these problems. The earlier you let your supervisors know about your feelings and areas of conflict, the easier it is to have a resolution before the problem gets bigger. If you feel a particular style of supervision is not helping you or is beginning to have a detrimental or negative impact on you, it is advisable to speak to your supervisors or someone within the department or faculty with the necessary authority to intervene and help resolve the situation. Sometimes, the issue may relate to just one of your supervisors, in which case the other supervisors may be able to help resolve the issue.

In some cases, PhD students may be the cause of conflict with their supervisors. It could well be that some PhD students don't pull their weight and take responsibilities for their own studies, leaving their supervisors frustrated and unresponsive. Some students and supervisors simply don't work well together because of differences in personalities, temperaments, work ethics, rhythms of life and differences in expectations, amongst many other factors. Other common reasons why PhD student–supervisor relationships sometimes break down include personality clash, a lack of understanding of the role and responsibilities of supervisors, unrealistic expectations from the student and/or supervisors, inadequate or incompetent supervision, general feelings of a lack of support, poor or unhelpful feedback from supervisors and so on (Figure 3.4). In most cases, some of these disagreements or issues between PhD students and their supervisors are temporary problems that get resolved amicably without any lasting adverse effects on the students work.

The longer the strained relationship between you and your supervisors goes on, the harder your PhD journey may get. This could be extremely frustrating, especially if there is no more communication, contacts or synergy between you and your supervisors. Inasmuch as supervisors are critical in supporting you and working with you to achieve your doctoral study's objective, you don't necessarily have to stay with or stick to your supervisors at all costs. Nevertheless, the decision to change your supervisors should not be

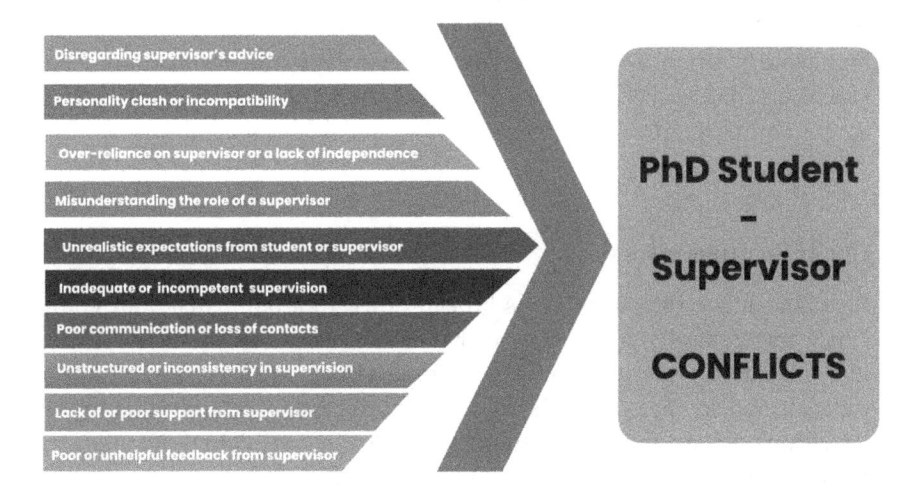

Figure 3.4 Main causes of PhD student–supervisor conflicts

taken lightly and should only be considered when all other options to repair the damaged relationships have been exhausted.

What makes a good PhD supervisor?

A good supervisor should be able to manage their PhD students and have the wisdom and experience to treat them with respect as individuals and as a part of a team or cohort while still providing academic leadership and direction. A great deal of initiative is required from a supervisor to know how best to help and support the individual student achieve success.

This may require an ability to know each students' needs and then develop a supervision approach that best meets those needs. A one-size-fits-all approach to supervision may not be suitable for all students. Hence, it is essential that the optimum combination of approaches is developed, as a supervisor, to support different PhD students (Lee, 2019).

A good supervisor should take and show interest in their students' research and study and offer them valuable research-based practical advice at critical moments. It is important for supervisors to get the necessary training that will enable them to function in this role and support their PhD students effectively. A supervisor new to the role should, as a matter of necessity, be mentored by more experienced supervisors. It is good practice for supervisors to regularly evaluate their own strengths and weaknesses and work towards improving their supervisory practice.

A good supervisor should not only provide personal and academic support to his or her individual student but also create an environment where students can work together and support each other while still working on their individual projects. There are greater efficiencies to be gained in supervising more than one PhD student as healthy interactions between the students can help avoid isolation, loneliness and other issues some students may face. Your role as a PhD supervisor is critical to the success of your students as your advice and pastoral care is key to their personal development (Walker and Thomson, 2010).

Changing supervisors

If, however, the relationship has broken down to a point that your confidence and trust in your supervisors have been completely eroded, it is time to think carefully about changing your supervisors. The need for a change of supervisors becomes particularly obvious and urgent if the conflict relates to serious issues such as bullying, racism, anti-Semitism, harassment, theft of your creative work, criminal or illegal activities and other serious misdemeanours.

Any of these may inevitably lead to a complete and irretrievably breakdown of trust between you and your supervisors. Experiencing any of these major issues or situation can be very traumatic and can leave you feeling very alone and demoralised. It is highly recommended, therefore, that you talk to other people you trust about what you are going through. This can be done in confidence and possibly with people outside the circle of your supervisors.

It is always a good idea to take notes or keep a record of your experiences and document all the issues that cause conflict between you and your supervisors. By doing so, you can help yourself articulate very well and other people understand the situation better and how best to help you sort out the problem. There may be other academic colleagues of your supervisors that may be in a position to take over as your new supervisor. However, you need to be extremely careful as to how you manage the change from the current supervisor to the new one without getting trapped in the internal politics of the department or faculty.

Most universities will have a standard process and stated conditions under which a PhD student can request a change of supervisor. It is important that you seek advice as to how to go about changing your supervisors and how that change may affect or impact your study. If the situation becomes too serious that you don't feel the department or faculty can resolve your supervisory issue satisfactorily, you may want to seek help beyond the department/faculty (see Chapter 8 on getting other support for your PhD).

Standing up to and calling out rogue supervisors

Most supervisors are honourable, decent and professional people who take pride in helping and supporting their students in their goal. Unfortunately, the world of academia is not all inhabited by well-meaning, good and ethical people. Supervisors work within the general context of what some people may consider as racially unequal and an unjust educational system. Institutional racism is believed to be rife in the very structure and systems of UK university institutions where supervisors work (Chouldhry, 2019; Seresin, 2019). So changing a supervisor if you encounter issues of racism may be one thing; changing the culture where racism exists is another thing entirely.

It is possible that you may come across rogue supervisors who may use their position of trust and authority to play out their racist or sexist behaviour towards you. Some PhD students are now getting empowered and confident to stand up against such attitudes and call out supervisors or institutions they believe exhibit or perpetuate racist, sexist, anti-Semitic, homophobic, transphobic and misogynistic behaviour. In the wake of #MeToo, #BlackLivesMatter and other social-change movements, there is growing evidence that society is becoming intolerant to these kinds of attitudes and behaviours in the public sphere and within the university system. In particular, the Black Lives Matter movement, formed in 2016 and became popular in 2020 following the death of George Floyd by white police in the Minneapolis, Minnesota, US, on 25 May 2020, has highlighted the racial injustice and structural racism in many aspects of our social, economic, political and educational institutions. Hence, some PhD students are now taking a stand and calling out racism, sexism and the like that are embedded in the structure of their academic institutions. In some universities, students are taking the lead to call for a general decolonisation of the university academic curriculum. Some universities have responded by setting up initiatives such as 'Staff–Student Decolonisation Working Group', 'Decolonised PhD Reading Group' and other similar initiatives (Seresin, 2019).

While, for fear of any possible repercussion, you may not necessarily want to take such direct actions if and every time you experience racist, sexist, misogynistic or anti-Semitic behaviour towards you from your supervisors or your university, you also do not need to put up with it. There are a number of avenues you can use for support if you have issues with any of these as a PhD student (see Chapter 4). It is important to stress that these attitudes may also come from PhD students and directed at their supervisors. Your university may already have their regulations about this and may take a very tough disciplinary action against you if you are a PhD student exhibiting racist, sexist, anti-Semitic and misogynistic attitudes towards your supervisors or any other students. In some cases, this may lead to the termination of your study at the university.

So it is critical that you refrain from any kinds of reprehensible behaviour that could ruin or jeopardise your chances of getting a PhD.

Key messages

- Your supervisors can play a critical role and support you through your PhD journey, but you also need to take charge of your own study.
- Having and maintaining a good working relationship with your supervisor is crucial to your success.
- Although your supervisor is there to support you through your PhD, you are still responsible for the outcomes of your doctoral studies.
- Whatever the pressure, you should not feel obliged to publish your PhD work with your supervisors as joint authors if you don't wish to do so.
- You can always change your supervisors if things don't go well, but such a change should be thought through carefully and should only be initiated when all options to resolve issues have been exhausted.

Further reading

Chouldhry, I. (2019). I've seen firsthand that academic spaces have a problem with racial slurs – No wonder PhD students are quitting. *Independent*, 8th July

2019 [Online]. Available at: www.independent.co.uk/voices/academic-racism-university-cambridge-n-word-priyamvada-gopal-a8993016.html. Accessed on 6th July 2020.

Giang, V. (2020). The 4 most important relationships you need at work. *Business Insider* [Online]. Available at: www.businessinsider.com/the-4-most-important-relationships-you-need-at-work-2013-3?r=US&IR=T. Accessed on 5th July 2020.

Langs, R. (1994). *Doing Supervision and Being Supervised*. London: Routledge.

Lantsoght, E. O. L. (2018). *The A-Z of the PhD Trajectory. A Practical Guide for a Successful Journey*. Springer Texts in Education. Springer International Publishing AG. Springer, 20180525. Vital Book file.

Lee, A. (2019). *Successful Research Supervision: Advising Students Doing Research*, 2nd ed. Abingdon, Oxon, UK: Routledge.

Petre, M., and Rugg, G. (2010). *The Unwritten Rules of PhD Research*, 2nd ed. Berkshire, UK: Open University Press. Available at: vbk://0335240267

Pugh, E. P. (2015). *How to Get a PhD: A Handbook for Students and their Supervisors*, 6th ed. London: McGraw-Hill. Available at: VitalSource Bookshelf.

Seresin, I. (2019). Withdrawal statement. *Medium.com* [Online]. Available at: https://medium.com/@indianaseresin/withdrawal-statement-56f7411b48b1. Accessed on 6th July 2020.

Snieder, R., and Larner, K. (2009b). The adviser and thesis committee. In *The Art of Being a Scientist: A Guide for Graduate Students and their Mentors* (pp. 53–64). Cambridge: Cambridge University Press.

Walker, M., and Thomson, P. (2010). *The Routledge Doctoral Supervisor's Companion: Supporting Effective Research in Education and the Social Sciences*. London: Routledge.

Wenger, J. (2020). *Seven Principles to Strengthen Relationships at Work* [Online]. Available at: https://medium.com/@johnqshift/seven-principles-to-strengthen-relationships-at-work-f861b0cbab06. Accessed on 5th July 2020.

CHAPTER 4

Finding support for your PhD

Introduction

In the course of your PhD, you will most certainly need some support. This could be in the form of academic, financial, personal/emotional, material or other practical support to get you through your study. This chapter provides essential information on where you can draw support for your PhD research study. It covers both financial and practical support and advisory services that may be available internally within your university and other support that may be available to you externally outside the university system. The chapter also covers issues of self-help, self-support and general issues of looking after your social, psychological and physical well-being. The chapter outlines the importance of drawing support from various sources such as health or medical centres, student well-being departments, faith and pastoral services, student employment agencies, student unions and international student support centres, amongst others, if and when needed.

By the end of the chapter, you will have a better understanding of

- the support commonly available at UK universities to PhD research students,
- key departments/units or centres within your university that provide help and support to PhD students,
- sources of external support available to PhD students within the UK community,
- specific support for women PhD students, students with disabilities and students from BAME groups and
- support available from within and outside the university in times of emergencies such as the COVID-19 pandemic and a health crisis experience.

PhDs and the need for support

Doing a PhD is never an easy undertaking, and you should never assume things will always go well or according to plan. The complex academic and administrative processes, the rigour of conducting research, fieldwork and data collection plus endless hours of reading and reviewing literature, together with the anxiety of getting the right results and the fear of failure, money worries, the politics around working with your peers, your supervisors, and the like, all suggest there is so much going on when you do a PhD. For some people, all these things could go well seamlessly without any major difficulty, but that is very rare. For most people, doing a PhD can be tough, and the pressure may soon take its toll on you as you progress through your doctoral studies journey. There may be moments of self-doubts, apprehension, physical and mental exhaustion and outright frustration. At such moments in time, you may need some support. Understanding how and when to ask and make good use of people around you and the support network available to you may be crucial to your success.

Your support network could comprise your directors of studies or supervisors, research assistants, fellow PhD students, friends and families, charities, sports or social group and other government and independent agencies that offer financial or advisory support to students, amongst other groups (Figure 4.1). These people, organisations or institutions can offer you valuable advice or give you a unique perspective on how you can deal with any issue that you may be facing. The more people and organisations you know that

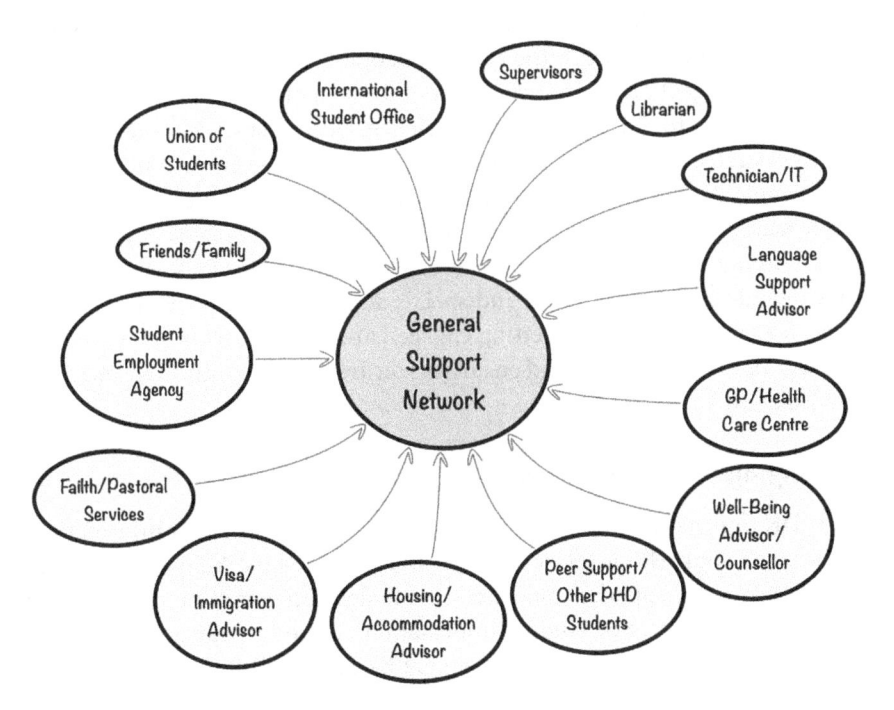

Figure 4.1 General support network for PhD students

could help you out, the better. By talking to different people, you can get different ideas that you can try out and apply to your own situation.

As an independent research project, doing a PhD can be a lonely and isolating experience. The hours and hours of time spent alone on your study can mean that you have less time to spend on other things and with other people. The more you lock yourself away from everything else in trying to catch up and make headway with your study, the less sociable you may become. Just when you need to connect with other people, you may find yourself spending less and less time with people who may be an important source of support and help to you. The general advice, therefore, is to be aware of this and to not isolate yourself or create an artificial barrier for people who may want to help and support you while doing your PhD.

Working flat out and very long hours on your study may also be counterproductive. You need to keep the right balance between doing your PhD and having a life and doing other essential things that contribute to your general well-being. You need to have some downtime when you temporarily stop working on your PhD in order to refresh and recharge your batteries. Taking time to socialise with other people and do something that you really enjoy is highly recommended. PhD students' to-do list may never be finished, so you just need to prioritise what is important and urgent at every moment of your PhD journey and still have a bit of time for yourself.

Each person is different in their needs, but generally speaking, it is also advisable not to just stay in the circle of people in your department, faculty, campus or subject area but to venture out to meet other people in other subjects or campus to share ideas and experience. Don't just stick to the people in your research centre or group. You really should try to venture out and meet new people. Go to events for post-graduate students and meet people from other faculties or campuses of your university or from outside your university. In many universities, regular events are organised for PGR students that may include sporting, cultural and socials activities – find time to take part in such events. Getting out, getting engaged and taking part in such events is one way of meeting people and ensuring you are socially connected and don't feel isolated.

Finding support from within your university

Most UK universities have a range of funding support and other information, advice and counselling services for their PhD students. Your first point of call for advice or support could well be the dedicated and often centralised student advice centre or student information centre in your university. The central students' information centre may be named differently in different universities.

University studentships and PGR Assistants (PGRAs)

Essentially, studentships are a form of scholarships or bursary awarded by Universities to some students to fund their PhD programme. This may include funding to support your tuition fees and other living expenses. PGRAs are a form of studentship whereby PGR students are obliged to undertake an approved and supervised programme of personal research and also carry out extra research-related or teaching duties in return for their funding. While the award of PGRAs is not a contract of employment, it is a form of contractual engagement with your university. You will be required to undertake research/teaching activities usually on a full-time basis alongside your PhD. Your PhD research could be related to the other research-related duties associated with your PGRA bursaries. However, some universities will expect that your PGRA duties are separate from your own PhD research. A PGRA award usually covers a period of 3 to 4 years, but this could be longer or shorter depending on the extra research-related activities or teaching you may be required to undertake.

Student advice/information centre

The student advice centre or student information centre, whatever it is called, tends to provide essential support services to students and offer advice on a wide range of academic and non-academic matters. These may include support or advice on areas such as accommodation, disabilities, mental health, careers, study skills, information technology, research training and the like. These centres tend to be situated within the general or central administrative structure of the university, outside of departments or faculties, which mostly deal with academic matters. Student advice or information centres may also be based or embedded within the departmental or faculty administrative structure

Information on the support available to you may also be contained in a single or multiple doctoral studies handbooks provided to you during your enrolment or induction. Handbooks for PhD students may also have been provided to you by your university in print or via online and digital format. Whichever format it was made available to you, it is important you are familiar with your university research handbook and take notes of where to get help or support for different things. Having this information can become handy as you may need it at some point during your study. Make the most of the available sources of support at your university by keeping yourself up to date with regards to key contacts and support staff within your university. Note their email addresses or telephone numbers. You may need these as you travel and navigate your way through the university system. Knowing what to do, who to call on and where to get help in times of need is essential for your success and will save you a lot of headaches and stress. Engaging with and using the support system and opportunities on offer at your university can also give you peace of mind, encourage and strengthen you if and when things get a bit tough.

Union of students/students' union

In many universities, the students' union or union of students plays an important role in the academic and social well-being of students. These are organisations run by students and for students. The type and level of activities led or run by the union of students vary across universities in the UK. These, generally, include sports, recreation, clubs, cultural events, performing and visual arts, politics and activism and religious and special interest activities, amongst many others. Developing an interest and participating in the union of students' events and activities organised for PGR students is a good way of being socially connected and getting support for your PhD. Some universities have student ambassadors or student representatives who can provide one-to-one support on an informal peer support basis.

Technical and information technology (IT) support

Most universities also have dedicated IT support for their PhD students. This is handy when you have IT-related issues such as printing, telephoning, photocopying, procuring specialist software for your study and other computing facilities you may need. Technical and IT support may also include skills development and training in specific areas relating to your study or how to use specialised equipment or software. It could also relate to training on research design, statistical data analysis and data storage, amongst others.

Library support

Seeking and getting library support while doing your PhD could be very beneficial in terms of knowing and understanding what is available at your university and how to access and use your university's vast learning resources and databases. Most universities invest substantial resources in their library stock and resources and services available to their post-graduate students. In addition to the physical stock of books, journals and audiovisual materials, amongst others, your university will most probably have institutional license to use many online services such as Scopus, JSTOR, PsycINFO, ERIC, EconLit, IBSS, ASSIA and CINAHL databases, amongst others. Access to these online resources means you are able to access a vast number of resources and databases from all over the world, usually under an open access arrangement. JSTOR, for example, offers open access to more than 12 million academic books and journals and materials in about 75 disciplines. For detailed information on some of these databases and sources commonly used in the social sciences and how to access them, see Jegede et al. (2020). Your university/subject librarians may be able to help organise a group or one-to-one induction for you to show you how to access and use the resources available in your library.

Drawing support from your library staff can be extremely beneficial especially if you have queries relating to sourcing or access critical reading materials, reports, data, journals and general information relating to your PhD. Most universities provide general training or have an online or paper-based guide on how to use the services and resources available to PhD students through their library. Your supervisors may also be able to help you with arranging essential training to support you. You just need to ask and keep asking until you get the support you need that could help you in your study. In many universities, library services may also include inter-library loan facilities and support for acquiring essential transferable skills such as confidence-building skills, effective communication skills, presentation skills and analytical skills, amongst others.

Your university may also have institutional licence for videos, digital and multimedia resources that can help you with your PhD research. A good example is Angel Productions – an educational video production project by partner institutions including Birkbeck, the University of London and Royal Holloway that is designed to support and develop the skills of doctoral students and their supervisors (www.angelproductions.co.uk/index.html). You may also find its video resources, made available through its new Dr.App for IOS and Android devices, very useful (www.angelproductions.co.uk/drapp.htm).

Peer support from other PhD students

One source of support that you will find useful, in the course of your PhD is that which comes from your fellow PhD students. Sometimes underrated, peer support often provides the best way to get by in a PhD. Your fellow students currently doing or about to complete their PhD can offer advice that you may not be able to get elsewhere. Support and advice from fellow PhD students tend to be well informed and based on the real experiences of the students at your university. Also, there may be people in your department who are doing their post-doctoral research. Their recent experiences on doing their own PhD could well be valuable to you, especially in relation to issues such as how to deal with or manage your supervisors, how to collect your data or carry out a particular analysis or how to use particular equipment or software, amongst others. They may be able to warn you of what to watch out for and tell you about any unwritten rules or code of conduct regarding the research culture in your department. Through this source, you may be able to gain an insight as to what to do and what not to do in your department or faculty as a PhD student. This information can help you fit in well and blend nicely into the research culture of your department and avoid any embarrassment to yourself or any other persons in your department or research centre.

In some universities, post-graduate students set up support groups that provide advice and support for other students. Generally, these groups tend to operate informally either as meeting groups, social media network or discussion groups. While such student-led support groups are not intended to and should not replace official advice, they, nevertheless, can play an important role as an independent source of information about your university or your supervisors. Student support groups can be very flexible and can offer personal, moral or emotional support which may not be otherwise possible through the official university channels or other sources.

Support from outside your university

Outside of your university, there are support networks that you can tap into to help you through your PhD journey. Getting external support in addition to what you have in your university can help smooth your PhD journey and enrich your doctoral research experience.

Family and friends

The support from your family and friends could be extremely valuable while doing your PhD. The support you get from a spouse, partner, boyfriend or girlfriend could give you the courage and confidence you need to face everything that doing a PhD throws at you. The emotional and psychological support received from friends and family can be invaluable at critical stages of your PhD. This could make the difference between success or failure. For example, if you are doing a PhD and you have young children, the support of family and friends could be doubly important to you if they are able to help look after your children at critical moments. Juggling childcare responsibilities with studying full time for a PhD is never an easy task, especially in the UK where the costs of childcare and babysitting can be quite substantial.

Funding and financial support from charities, government and NGOs

There are many possible ways of funding your PhD (Figure 4.2). Many universities in the UK provide bursaries, scholarships or studentships that could

Figure 4.2 Funding your PhD

cover all or part of your PhD tuition fees and/or living expenses. However, the vast majority of funding support for PhD research comes from self-funding and government and NGO sponsorships, including charities and trusts.

The type and level of funding, the reasons for award and terms and conditions attached to bursaries, scholarships or studentships can vary from one institution or organisation to another (Figure 4.3). Funding support may also be conditional upon the nature of your PhD research project. Generally, studentships tend to be comprehensively funded, covering tuition fees, living expenses and other costs relating to a specific PhD project. Similarly, scholarships tend to be fully funded, covering tuition fees and/or living expenses but not usually restricted or attached to a particular project. Scholarships are awarded for different reasons, such as the recipient's financial need, academic merit, personal circumstances and the like. The UK Research Councils is the main and the biggest PhD studentship-awarding organisation. Bursaries tend to be awarded usually on the basis of recipients' financial need and often targeted at low-income or underrepresented groups (Scholarship Hub, 2020).

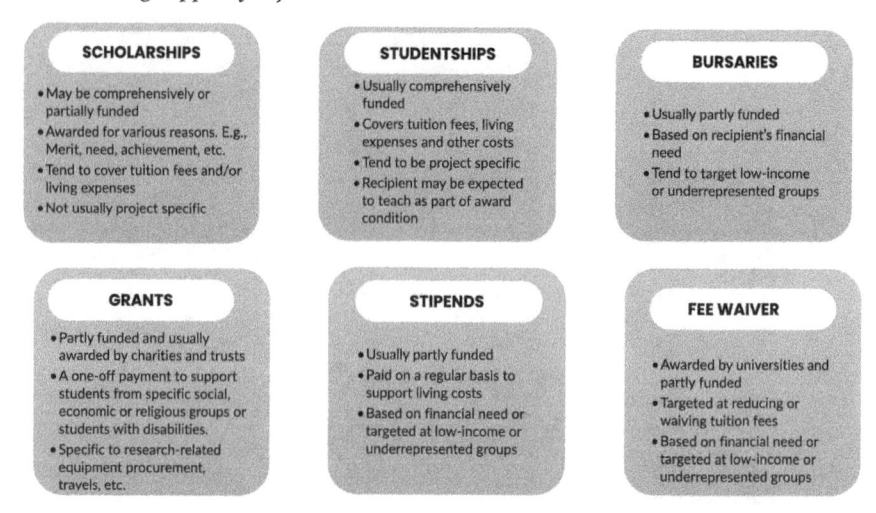

Figure 4.3 Types of financial/funding support available to PhD students

In terms of the level of funding and support, some universities or organisations offer PhD students small grants or stipends. Stipends tend to be paid on a regular basis to support students' living costs, while a grant is usually a one-off payment awarded to support PhD students research, equipment procurement or research travels. Some universities provide financial support to PhD students by reducing or waiving their tuition fees. The fee-waiver award could be based on students' financial situation or targeted at low-income or underrepresented groups. Some universities, however, use fee waivers as a marketing or promotional strategy to boost their recruitments. Whichever form they come, it is advisable you check your eligibility for any funding opportunities from your university or external organisations to support your PhD. Apart from bursaries, or offer of studentships, some universities provide short-term financial support for their students for different purposes. The financial support provided could be used for sustenance, living expenses, the procurement of essential materials relating to your study and so on. Some universities also have dedicated hardship funds for post-graduate students or development funds to support students with costs of living and other expenses relating to attending conferences, workshops or events.

Funding from government sources and Research Councils

The UK government provides a range of funding support for PhD students. Notable amongst these are the Research Councils' studentships or grants. These grants tend to cover tuition fees and living expenses and are awarded for various PhD projects in a wide range of subjects or disciplines (Higginbotham, 2019).

The Research Council, composed of seven different councils, funding awards are managed through the UK Research and Innovation (UKRI). The seven constituent councils, based on subject and areas of research, are the following:

- Arts and Humanities Research Council (AHRC) – www.ahrc.ukri.org
- Biotechnology and Biological Science Research Council (BBSRC) – www.bbsrc.ukri.org
- Engineering and Physical Sciences Research Council (EPSRC) – www.epsrc.ukri.org
- Economic and Social Research Council (ESRC) – www.esrc.ukri.org
- Medical Research Council (MRC) – www.mrc.ukri.org
- Natural Environment Research Council (NERC) – www.nerc.ukri.org
- Science and Technologies Facilities Council (STFC) – www.stfc.ukri.org

These seven councils together with Innovate UK and Research England came together under a general structure to form the UKRI – the biggest research-funding organisation in the UK with a budget of more than £7 billion. Although managed through the UKRI, funding applications and decisions on awards are made by and through individual universities. For detailed information on funding opportunities, eligibility criteria and how to apply, see www.ukri.org/funding/funding-opportunities/.

Financial support/funding from charities, professional bodies and independent organisations

General information on key charities and NGOs offering funding support for PhD students and how to apply for support could be obtained from the following sources:

Alternative Guide Online (AGO) – Offers a comprehensive online database of charities offering financial support and funding for Postgraduate Studies in the UK. www.postgraduate-funding.com/

Grants Register 2020 – A complete guide to postgraduate funding worldwide. Edited by Palgrave Macmillan. https://link.springer.com/referencework/10.1057%2F978-1-349-95943-3

Amongst the main charities, foundations and trusts that award studentships or grants for PhD studies are the following:

The Welcome Trust – an independent organisation that supports research mostly in the area of health and biomedical science https://wellcome.ac.uk/grant-funding

The Leverhulme Trust – an independent organisation that offers support and fund research in diverse areas such as the arts, humanities, sciences and social sciences www.leverhulme.ac.uk/schemes-at-a-glance

Rosetrees Trust – a private charity, that offers a range of funding opportunities for PhD students, mostly in support of medical research https://rose treestrust.co.uk/apply-for-funding/

British Federation of Women Graduates (BFWG) – a leading organisation of women with degrees or equivalent qualifications that offer grants, bursaries, exchange programme funding, living-costs grants, fee waivers and the like to women as part of an international strategy to improve the lives of women and girls. Current membership of BFWG includes membership of GWI (Graduate Women International) and UWE (University Women of Europe) and representation from the six leading women's groups in the UK. www.postgraduatefunding.com/provider-206

Nuffield Foundation – Although not designed for PhD support, the Nuffield Foundation Research, Development and Analysis Fund supports research in social policy relating, in particular, to education, welfare and justice. www. nuffieldfoundation.org/funding/research-development-and-analysis-fund

TURN2US – A national charity offering financial support to people in tough times. It also provides a list of other charities that offer financial support. www.turn2us.org.uk/

The Vegetarian Charity – Offers small grants of up to £500 to vegetarians and vegans in need and who are younger than 26. See: www.vegetarian charity.org.uk/apply-for-grant-may-may.html

Leathersellers' Company – an independent organisation that offers funding of up to £5,000 per year to support students from any part of the UK who are in real financial need. https://leathersellers.co.uk/grants-for-students/

UK PhD Loans – loans of up to £25,00 for students resident in England and Wales to undertake doctoral study. www.freedomfinance.co.uk.

While almost all funding opportunities, such as scholarships, studentships, stipends and the like, are non-repayable, PhD loans are repayable. Hence, it is essential you understand the terms and conditions of these loans before you decide to take out loans to finance your PhD.

The Prospects offers a good web link to other sources of funding as provided on its website – www.prospects.ac.uk/postgraduate-study/funding-postgraduate-study.

Support for disabled PhD students

If you are a disabled student, you don't necessarily have to disclose your disability while applying for a PhD or funding. Under UK law, it is illegal for university or any funding bodies to discriminate against applicants on the basis of their disability. Many universities have dedicated support system for disabled students. It is therefore essential that you know what support and resources are available to you as a result of your disability. You may also be entitled to free computer equipment, specially designed or adapted furniture, specialised software and visual or hearing aids, amongst others. Aside from the general funding sources available to all students, if you have a disability, mental health condition, learning difficulty, or long-term health condition and so on, you may be able to access additional financial support from sources such as the following:

Disabled Student's Allowance (DSA) – A UK government financial support to disabled students, covering expenses incurred as a result of disability or chronic illness. These could include the cost of getting the equipment you need to function effectively as a PhD student. It could also cover non-medical mobility support, travel expenses, personal assistance, British sign language interpreter, etc.

For information on criteria for eligibility and how to apply for DSA, see www.disabilityrightsuk.org/applying-disabled-students%E2%80%99-allowances-dsas

For detailed information on other support available to disabled students, see Disability Rights UK – www.disabilityrightsuk.org/funding-postgraduate-education-disabled-students.

Also, there are other resources available to support PhD students and researchers with disabilities and useful materials to help supervisors understand disability in the context of research and how best to support their disabled PhD students (see Vitae, 2020b) – www.vitae.ac.uk/doing-research/every-researcher-counts-equality-and-diversity-in-researcher-careers/resources-and-support-for-disabled-researchers.

Other funding sources and how to apply

There are other funding arrangements such as an employer-funded PhD, crowdfunding and religious organisation–sponsored support. Also, a direct approach to a relatively unknown organisation may also yield a positive outcome in terms of getting financial support for your study.

Whichever source of financial support you seek, ensure that you understand the eligibility criteria and put forward a strong and convincing application. There is usually strong competition for funding. So the stronger your application, the greater your chances. In order to apply, you may be required to submit a research proposal to show what you are aiming to do in your PhD study. Through this, the funding organisation may want to assess the relevance or uniqueness of your study and its impact on human, environmental, social, economic, cultural or political issues facing society. You may also be required to justify the level of funding you are seeking and explain how you will expend the funds or resources that will be allocated to you if successful. A robust and convincing personal statement detailing your situation and explanation of why you deserve to be awarded the students, grants, bursaries or scholarships are often necessary.

You also often need to get some backing or recommendations from reputable people to serve as your references. Your application should demonstrate that you meet all the requirements specified by the funding organisation. Some funding is restricted to applicants with UK residency status or UK/EU nationality. Other criteria for eligibility could be based on gender, ethnic group, religious affiliation or relevance of research to specific areas of enquiries, amongst many other factors. In any case, your qualification will most certainly be considered. Most funding organisations will expect that you have a good academic qualification, usually not less than a second-class upper division at the undergraduate level and/or a master's degree qualification or equivalent professional qualification.

Applications for studentships are usually made directly to the university you want to do your PhD study at. The process may involve filling out an application form, submitting your research proposal, references and other supporting documents and a cover letter. Application for scholarships, bursaries or grants may also be made directly to the awarding institution or charities. The outcome of your funding application for scholarships, studentships, or bursaries may be determined by a combination of factors such as

- your qualifications and how best you fit the eligibility criteria;
- the overall quality and strength of your application;
- the relevance of your study to the strategic research or business aim/goal of the awarding institution;
- the interdisciplinarity of your research and its application to social, economic, political or environmental policy;
- number of applications received in relation to the available funds;
- the novelty or uniqueness of your research project; and
- the strength of recommendation and support from your referees.

If your application passes the funder's initial review, you may be invited to an interview before you are given the final outcome.

Self-support and self-care

Whatever support you get from others while doing your PhD, supporting yourself and caring for your own well-being is of paramount importance to your success. You can self-support by doing five main things that could enhance your well-being and improve your productivity. These are sleep, eat, exercise, plan, ask, reflect and network (SEEPARN). Following the SEEPARN advice, as explained next, you can self-care and ensure that you live well, keep healthy and stay connected with people while doing your PhD (Figure 4.4).

S – Sleep

Resting well and having the right amount of sleep will help your concentration and keep you healthy. Most people try to catch up with work by sleeping less. However, it has been suggested that sleeping 1 hour less does not necessarily lead to greater productivity. Sleep deprivation may significantly reduce your productivity and affect your health and well-being (Rath, 2013). The longer you sleep and rested, the more you can get done. Everyone is different as to the minimum hours of sleep we require to function effectively. However, about 8 hours of sleep a day is recommended, and it is believed that getting fewer than 6 hours of sleep at night could lead to burnout, and losing 90 minutes of sleep can reduce your alertness during the day almost by one-third (Rath, 2013). It is not just about the number of hours you sleep but the quality of sleep that you have. If you sleep long hours without feeling rested, you may need to see your general physician. Sleep deprivation is generally believed to lead to high blood pressure and an increase in the risk of heart disease and stroke.

If you do suffer from a sleep disorder, such as insomnia, sleep apnea, narcolepsy, hypersomnia or any related condition and it's affecting your study, you need to seek help. For more information on sleep disorder, see the SleepFoundation.org website at www.sleepfoundation.org/sleep-disorders. A general lack of sleep can make you feel drowsy and sluggish, and this can significantly impact your study and daily activities (SleepFoundation.org, 2020).

E – Eat

There is a general saying that 'you are what you eat'. This is particularly relevant when doing your PhD. Eating well can help your general well-being. So cooking for yourself or knowing where to get the right food, if and when you need it, will help towards ensuring you eat, study and function well. Having a healthy diet can also contribute towards your general well-being. If you eat poorly and do not eat enough fruits, vegetables and other nutrients that your body needs to function well, you can become ill or be deprived of energy. It has been suggested that adding more fruit and vegetables to your diet can significantly boost your mood and emotional well-being (Mail Online, 2019). According to a National Health Service (NHS) report, a survey of UK

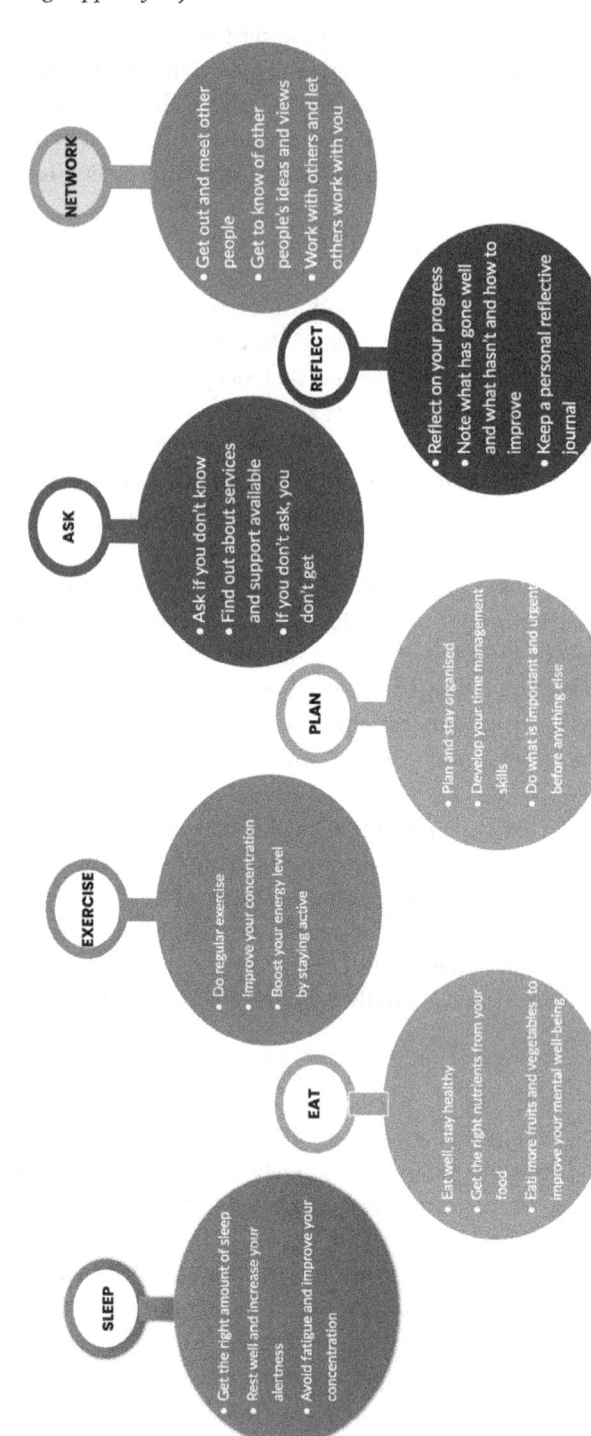

Figure 4.4 Living well, keeping healthy and staying connected while doing a PhD

families has shown the link between how much fruit and vegetables people ate on a typical day and their mental well-being. The study also suggests that people reported feeling happier, more purposeful and less anxious when they ate more fruit and vegetables (nhs.uk, 2020).

The UK government currently advises people to eat five portions of fruit and vegetables a day – www.nhs.uk/live-well/eat-well/why-5-a-day/.

A number of organisations in the UK provide support for people with eating disorders such as www.beateatingdisorders.org.uk/types/do-i-have-an-eating-disorder.

E – Exercise

Regular exercise is known to have a positive effect on health and well-being. Taking time to do some exercise could improve your concentration and productivity. So it's good to know about any sports facilities that may be available to use in your university. Find out about gyms near your university and how you can join or subscribe to the services they provide. Some sports clubs or gyms may offer discounts for students. Exercises such as aerobic, balance, flexibility, endurance and strength training all have their benefits. Going biking or walking may also be a good way to get regular exercise. There may be other sporting activities and hobbies, such as dancing, that you may be interested in that can keep you active and moving. Take time to find out what is available in your local area and what it costs to join or sign up.

Instead of working on your PhD all day without a break, having regular exercise interspersed with your study can help boost your energy and make you feel less lethargic and less tired. Sitting down for hours and hours and extended periods without moving is believed to be bad for your health and can lead to what has been described as 'sitting disease' (Rath, 2013). So it is advisable to stand, move around, stretch and walk rather than spending most of the day sitting down. It can also help you to concentrate more as you need a fresh mind to think clearly, get creative, write well and stay productive.

P – Plan

An effective planning strategy is essential in your PhD study as this will help you stay organised and work in a systematic way to meet your milestones. List what needs doing and when you need to do them by and plan how to get them done. Project time management is an essential skill you may need to learn while doing your PhD. If you are struggling with this get some training. By being able to identify specific tasks that you need to do and to schedule your time and allocate time to them, you will make your whole PhD journey more pleasurable. Also, you need to set realistic expectations with regards to your research. Don't over-promise yourself and then under-deliver.

Apart from using the manual paper daily/weekly/monthly/yearly planner, there are a number of apps that can help you plan your tasks, remind you of things, monitor your progress and keep you generally organised. Notable amongst these are

- **Calendars** – Google Calendar, iCal, Fantastical, Outlook Calendar, Apple calendar, Any.do and My Study Life;
- **Goal tracking** – Strides, Way of Life, Goals on Track, Habitica, Coach.me, ATracker and Toodledo; and
- **To-do lists/reminders** – nTask, Wunderlist, Microsoft to-Do, Todoist, Any.do, ToodleDo, Habitica and Remember the Milk.

An essential part of planning is learning to do the right task at the right time. This needs some skills in setting priorities for all the things you think you need to do while doing your PhD. Some things are very important, and others may be less so. Similarly, there are different levels of urgency relating to tasks. Some tasks may be very urgent while others can wait without any problem. The ability to differentiate among (a) what is important and urgent, (b) what is urgent but not important, (c) what is not urgent but important and (d) what is not urgent and not important neither is critical to effective planning and management of your time. The general advice to be effective is to do what is urgent and important, plan for those things that are not urgent but important, delegate things that are urgent but not important and eliminate things that are neither urgent nor important (Covey, 1989).

A – Ask

It is always a good idea to ask people if you don't know something. Get into the habit of asking questions and actively seeking help. Don't be too shy about asking for advice and keep asking questions that can help you through your PhD. There is no such thing as a 'stupid question'. If you don't know something, you don't know it. There is no point pretending that you know something when you don't. If you don't know, you can ask someone who does. So ask questions all of the time of all the people that may know better than you. They may be able to help find an answer to your question, no matter how stupid you think the question may sound. If you don't ask, you don't get.

Beyond your academic support, you may need to find out and ask about other services and support systems available to you in the course of your PhD. Examples of these are the following:

- Health/medical services
- Student well-being or counselling services
- Faith and pastoral services
- Student employment agencies
- Student unions or unions of students
- International student support services
- Language support services
- IT/technical support services

Finding out and knowing what is available to you can significantly reduce your levels of stress and anxiety. Your supervisors may be able to point you in the right direction of where to get help and support.

R – Reflect

Personal reflections on how your PhD research is going is a good way to monitor your own progress. Through your reflections on your research, you will know what is going well and what is not going well and how to fix it. Keeping a personal reflective journal, for example, could help develop your writing skills and enable you to identify areas of stress, stress triggers and ways to manage or avoid them.

N – Network

Finding time to meet and get together with other PhD students and other people in the community is highly recommended while doing your PhD. This may help you to be socially active and less isolated. Through this, you may be able to meet people or get to know about essential information that may help you with your personal or study-related issues. The saying that 'it's not what you know but who you know' is particularly important here. Whether through attending conferences or direct or indirect contact with relevant people in your field, you can build up a network of support that could be very beneficial to you in your PhD. Digital networking through media such as LinkedIn, Facebook, Twitter and the like can help you connect with other researchers, professionals, and organisations that can help you with your doctoral studies.

The support that you get from other people that you meet along the way or that you network with can be critical to your success while doing a PhD. Apart from knowing other people's views and gaining new ideas, there are several other reasons why communicating, connecting or collaborating with other people could be beneficial to you while doing your PhD. It can make you feel less isolated and lonely, and it can also make you achieve or do things quicker than you will otherwise have done if working all alone and by yourself. It has been suggested that your life will be a lot easier, as a PhD student, if you create a conducive environment in which other people can find it easy to work with you, especially those people outside your circle of friends whom you don't normally interact with (Gosling and Noordam, 2011).

Attending academic conferences is a great way to network, meet new people and share your research ideas with others. There are a large number of social science conferences hosted all around the world that encourage PhD students to present and share ideas about their research. If you are unable to attend international conferences, there are other national or local conferences and workshops that you may consider. These academic meetings provide a great forum for PhD students to present their research ideas, share experiences and connect with new people.

Dealing with self-doubt

There may be a stage during your PhD journey when you may begin to self-doubt. In times like that, it has been suggested that confidence in your abilities can become handy in getting you through a rough patch and helping you move forward (Vozza, 2020). Self-doubt sets in when we begin to think that we don't have what it takes or we are not good enough (Warrell, 2020). It's a general feeling of inadequacy or a feeling that you are lacking in certain skills or ability. If this thought is allowed to fester on for too long, you may begin to think you are not up to your PhD.

The advice is not to focus too much on what you are not good at or areas you are lagging behind but to believe in yourself that you can do it. Instead of letting self-doubt rob you of success in your PhD, it is advisable that you let it spur you to seek help and support as to how to get what you want and succeed in your goal (Warrell, 2020). In what has been described as 'second-year blues', you may begin to feel a sense of lethargy and a general lack of motivation when you get to the second year of your PhD study (Higginbotham, 2018b). This usually happens when the excitement and novelty of being a PhD student have worn off. That is precisely the time when you need to get support from all around you to get you through. You need to find the strength to carry on.

Reducing stress and looking after your mental health and well-being

Doing a PhD can be mentally and physically draining. It is, therefore, important to pay attention to your mental and health and well-being. You need to take practical steps towards your own well-being and self-care by overcoming stress and anxiety and staying healthy. This will not only help you in your study; it will also help you to stay focused and remain motivated.

Doing a PhD in a pandemic – COVID-19 and support in times of emergency

The coronavirus pandemic that started in December 2019 in Wuhan, Hubei, China, spread around the world and reached the UK in January 2020. This led to the UK government 'stay-at-home' order that banned all non-essential travel and contact with people outside one's home and the shutting down of schools, universities, businesses, sports venues and facilities, amenities and places of worship. In what has become known as the worst pandemic to hit the world, the unprecedented order for people to keep apart and maintain social distancing has caused severe disruptions to normal social, economic, political and cultural life. PhD students, like everyone else, have been affected by this pandemic, and the full ramifications of the impact of the pandemic on individuals, community and society at large are yet to be fully uncovered. However, the general feeling of anxiety created by COVID-19 has exacerbated health and well-being concern amongst the university community.

Therefore, many universities in the UK and indeed around the world, have come up with new and innovative ways of supporting their students during an enforced period of isolation and lockdown. While the full impact of the COVID-19 lockdown on PhD students' well-being is yet to unravel, a number of individuals, organisations, institutions and charities have been working hard to support PhD and other university students and staff through this difficult period.

Free online resources (time-limited)

During the first wave of coronavirus epidemic in early 2020, some of the leading publishing organisations offered support to students and their lecturers by offering free online access to their learning resources, databases and journals, albeit, for a limited period. For example, a number of US university presses made their content free on Project MUSE. These include the following:

- Johns Hopkins University Press – (all books and journals, through 31 May 2020)
- Ohio State University Press – (all books and journals, through 30 June 2020)
- University of Georgia Press – (all books, through 30 June 2020)
- University of Nebraska Press – (all books and journals, through 31 May 2020)

- University of North Carolina Press – (all books, through 30 June 2020)
- University Press of Colorado – (all books, through 30 June 2020)
- Temple University Press – (all books, through 30 June 2020)
- Utah State University Press – (all books, through 30 June 2020)
- Vanderbilt University Press – (selected books, through 31 May 2020)

Project MUSE is a non-profit collaboration between libraries and publishers encompassing an online database of peer-reviewed academic journals and electronic books. Project MUSE contains digital humanities and social science content from over 250 university presses and scholarly societies around the world (https://muse.jhu.edu/).

Similarly, Cambridge University Press made HE textbooks in HTML format free to access online during the coronavirus outbreak. More than 700 textbooks, published and available on Cambridge Core were made available. Free access was available until the end of May 2020 (www.cambridge.org/core/what-we-publish/books).

SAGE Publishing offered valuable resources and advice in the form of webinar questions and answers relating to how the research community is adapting to the changing world as a result of COVID-19. Some of the series offer methodological help and advice to students on conducting research in a lockdown.

With all libraries closed and physical access to research materials impossible, many universities also adapted their library services by setting up remote library services for students to access learning materials remotely. Other initiatives include making inter-library loans available in the form of electronically delivered journal articles, an extension of library loans periods, and the procurement of e-books covering a wide area of subjects and study/research skills.

Also, there are vast and freely available open-access materials on how to conduct research remotely, detailing how researchers are adapting to and innovating on conducting research remotely (QSR International, 2020; Lupton, 2020).

Although many of the free online resources are no longer available, as they were time-expired, the general support for remote working has continued. Most UK universities have developed their own system through which their PhD students are being supported to work remotely. Online supervisory meetings between PhD students and their supervisors are now commonplace. Apart from remote supervision, most universities have also moved the viva voce examination online. So instead of the traditional face-to-face meeting between PhD students and their examiners, viva voce examinations are now conducted remotely. This trend is likely to continue for the foreseeable future until academic life returns to normal when the COVID-19 heath pandemic comes to an end.

Also, in response to COVID-19, there has been a renewed effort to support students through this unprecedented and unsettling time by focusing on students' mental health and general well-being. Examples of these initiatives include the following:

The Wellbeing Thesis – This is an online resource for PGR students to support their well-being, learning and research. It covers, amongst other things, areas such as the goals, meaning and motivation behind PGR; PGR myths; taking time off; managing your supervisors; enhancing your creativity; how to support yourself when things go wrong; and planning your career post-PhD. https://thewellbeingthesis.org.uk/

Vita Blog – Mental Health and Wellbeing – Staying Sane while Working Remotely – A blog covering important tips and information on how to mentally prepare for time working in isolation www.vitae.ac.uk/news/vitae-blog/mental-health-and-wellbeing-staying-sane-when-working-remotely

Times Higher Education – Tips on Working from Home with Children – Essential information and tips on mixing home-working and childcare www.timeshighereducation.com/blog/tips-working-home-children

Times Higher Education – Studying Online: Tips and Experiences from a Student in Singapore – Information on how to make studying online work www.timeshighereducation.com/student/blogs/studying-online-tips-and-experiences-student-singapore

Student Minds – Coronavirus Resource Hub – A collaborative mental health programme to support students through unique circumstances such as those created by the coronavirus pandemic. Offers information and guide on how to survive in challenging times www.studentminds.org.uk/coronavirus.html

Support for PhD students from BAME groups

The Higher Education Funding Council's analysis has been reported to show that in 2016, BAME students are more likely than white students to decide to take a master's course but less likely to do a PhD (Fazackerley, 2019). The research also shows that while 2.4% of white students had started a PhD within five years of graduation, only 1.3% of BAME students did start a PhD within the same period suggesting that the academy is predominantly white as not many BAME students are doing PhDs compared to their white peer.

In light of the Black Lives Matter movement and campaign that advocates for non-violent civil disobedience in protest against police brutality and racially motivated violence against black people, there is a growing awareness of the need to support PhD students from BAME communities. UK universities are now pushing a diversity and inclusion agenda to promote race and social equality and widening participation. To assuage general concerns about racism in academia, some universities are now taking a tougher stance on racial and xenophobic harassment on campus, with initiatives such as the Report and Support programme, that allow students and staff to report racism and other forms of discrimination, harassment and bullying.

Other universities, such as Birkbeck University of London, are offering funding support to BAME students to undertake PhDs (www.bbk.ac.uk/news/birkbeck-offers-funded-phds-for-bame-candidates). To help you contextualise and understand issues such as institutionalised racism, harassment, discrimination and bullying in educational settings, see **Institutionalized Racism: A Syllabus – Catherine Halley – JSTOR DAILY https://daily.jstor.org/institutionalized-racism-a-syllabus/**. If you are a PhD student and you are experiencing direct or indirect race, sex or disability discriminations, you need to raise the issue with your university and get help. Under the Equality Act of 2010, you are legally protected against any form of racism, harassment, discrimination and bullying. Information on how to complain is available at www.gov.uk/discrimination-your-rights/what-you-can-do.

Knowing when to take a study break

If life events suggest that you need a break from your study, it is advisable you do so. Be kind to yourself and be honest with your feelings. Feeling nervous, confused, stressed, irritable and angry may be a sign that you need a break or help.

Taking a break from your PhD doesn't mean that you have failed. Whether it is for a short while or a long time, never consider taking a study break as a failure or sign of weakness. In fact, you can turn your study break into something positive and an opportunity to relaunch yourself with a renewed energy. So be kind to yourself and don't beat yourself up as a result of your decision to take a study break. It may be the best decision that you ever made.

Interruptions to your study may be short term or temporary. A short-term interruption means that when your situation improves, you may decide to go back to your PhD study at the point where you left, if your university allows you to do so. If you have made appreciable progress and you have run out of your funding and it is a real struggle for you to continue, you may wish to apply for an emergency funding or loan to enable you to continue. You may also apply for a fee waiver to your university. If you are at an advanced stage of your PhD and you have already completed your confirmation or transfer of registration, you can request to change your PhD registration to MPhil. If your university regulations allow this, it will enable you to write up the work you have done already for a lower award. Although this may not be an attractive proposition, it is still better than abandoning your PhD altogether without any reward or award for what you have done so far.

Even if you decide not to return to your PhD, the experience you have gained will remain with you, and that could offer you an opportunity to do something else that will be most beneficial to you. Many universities will let you suspend your PhD with the hope of resuming this later when your circumstances improve. Study break can range from a few months to a year. Many universities will not accept any student with a study break longer than 2 years to reconnect with their study. It is advisable that you check the regulations relating to study break in your university. It is perfectly OK to change your mind completely about doing a PhD and pursue a different career or move on to something else. There are other opportunities outside academia that are equally as rewarding.

Key messages

- Doing a PhD can be a lonely and stressful experience and making good use of the support system available to you can help make your PhD experience less stressful.
- Take care of yourself and avoid burning out or running yourself down by overworking yourself.
- Eat well and set yourself a regular time for exercise, physical activities and hobbies you enjoy. These can keep you fit and improve your well-being and creativity.
- Learn to prioritise and do things that are important and urgent first before moving down to things that are less important. Delegating duties that are urgent but not important may save you some time.
- If you need help, ask. It is better to be honest with yourself and your feelings if you are not coping and let other people help you.
- Usually there is a network of support system that you can tap into when needed, including your friends, colleagues, university support services and outside services.
- When things get too tough and you are run down and physically or emotionally unable to carry on with your PhD, an approved short study break can help you recharge your batteries before getting back to it.

Further reading

Agarwal, P. (2020). Tips on working from home with children. *Time Higher Education* [Online]. Available at: www.timeshighereducation.com/blog/tips-working-home-children. Accessed on 7th July 2020.

Barron, E. (2014). *The PhD Experience: An Insider's Guide*. Macmillan Education. London: Palgrave.

Bickerton, P. (2016). 10 things you need to know before starting a PhD degree. *Earlham Institute* [Online]. Available at: www.earlham.ac.uk/articles/10-things-you-need-know-starting-phd-degree. Accessed on 12th April 2020.

Castle, P., and Buckler, S. (2009). *How to Be a Successful Teacher: Strategies for Personal and Professional Development*. London: Sage Publications Ltd.

Castle, P., and Buckler, S. (2018). *Psychology for Teachers*, 2nd ed. London: Sage Publications Ltd.

Covey, S. R. (1989). *The 7 Habits of Highly Effective People: Powerful Lessons in Personal Change*. New York: Free Press.

Cox, R. (2020). Mental health and wellbeing – Staying sane when working remotely. *Vita Blog – Realising the Potential of Researchers* [Online]. Available at: www.vitae.ac.uk/news/vitae-blog/mental-health-and-wellbeing-staying-sane-when-working-remotely. Accessed on 7th July 2020.

Disability Rights UK. (2020). Funding postgraduate education for disabled students. *Disability Rights UK Factsheet F52* [Online]. Available at: www.disabilityrightsuk.org/funding-postgraduate-education-disabled-students. Accessed on 21st July 2020.

Fazackerley, A. (2019). 'Look at how white the academy is': Why BAME students aren't doing PhDs. *The Guardian.com*, Thursday 12th September 2019 [Online]. Available at: www.theguardian.com/education/2019/sep/12/look-at-how-white-the-academy-is-why-bame-students-arent-doing-phds?CMP=Share_iOSApp_Other. Accessed on 22nd July 2020.

Gallagher, P., and Gallagher, A. (2020). *The Portable PhD. Taking Your Psychology Career Beyond Academia*. Washington, DC: American Psychological Association.

Gosling, P., and Noordam, B. (2011). *Mastering Your PhD: Survival and Success in the Doctoral Years and Beyond*. London: Springer Heidelberg Dordrecht.

Gribben, M. (2012). *The Study Skills Toolkit for Students with Dyslexia*. London: Sage Publications Ltd.

Hawkins, K. (2017). *A Little Guide to Mindfulness*. London: Sage Publications Ltd.

Hawkins, K. (2017). *Mindful Teacher, Mindful School. Improving Wellbeing in Teaching & Learning*. London: Sage Publications Ltd.

Higginbotham, D. (2018). 5 challenges faced by PhD students. *Prospects* [Online]. Available at: www.prospects.ac.uk/postgraduate-study/phd-study/5-challenges-faced-by-phd-students

Higginbotham, D. (2019). Research council funding. *Prospects* [Online]. Available at: www.prospects.ac.uk/postgraduate-study/funding-postgraduate-study/research-council-funding. Accessed on 20th July 2020.

Holmes, E. (2019). *A Practical Guide to Teacher Wellbeing*. London: Sage Publications Ltd.

Jegede, F. Hargreaves, C. et al. (2020). *Writing Successful Undergraduate Dissertations in Social Sciences: A Student's Handbook*, 2nd ed. London: Routledge.

Krause, C. (2019). *Mindful by Design: A Practical Guide for Cultivating Aware, Advancing, and Authentic Learning Experiences*. New Delhi, India: Corwin Press, Sage Publications India Pvt. Ltd.

Lantsoght, E. O. L (2018). *The A-Z of the PhD Trajectory – A Practical Guide for a Successful Journey*. Basel, Switzerland: Springer International Publishing AG.

Lupton, D. (ed.). (2020). *Doing Fieldwork in a Pandemic* (crowd-sourced document) [Online]. Available at: https://docs.google.com/document/d/1clG jGABB2h2qbduTgfqribHmog9B6P0NvMgVuiHZCl8/edit. Accessed on 22nd July 2020.

Mail Online. (2019). Now you need to eat TEN-a-day! Adding more fruit and veg to your diet boosts your mood and emotional wellbeing as much as landing a new job, study finds. *Mail Online*, 5 February 2019 [Online]. Available at: www.dailymail.co.uk/health/article-6669419/Eating-fruit-veg-improves-mood.html

Malone, E. (2020). *Your Booksmart, School-savvy, Stress-Busting Primary Teacher Training Companion*. London: Sage Publications Ltd.

Minton, S. J. (2012). *Using Psychology in the Classroom*. London: Sage Publications Ltd.

National Health Service. (2020). Eating more fruit and veg 'improves mental wellbeing' [Online]. Available at: www.nhs.uk/news/food-and-diet/eating-more-fruit-and-veg-improves-mental-wellbeing/. Accessed on 21st July 2020.

Phillips, E. M., and Pugh, D. S. (2015). *EBOOK: How to Get a PhD: A Handbook for Students and Their Supervisors*, 6th ed. Maidenhead, Berkshire, UK: McGraw-Hill. Available at: VitalSource Bookshelf.

Pinterest. (2020). *Quick + Healthy Recipes for Busy Students*. Available at: www.pinterest.co.uk/sageeducation/quick-%2B-healthy-recipes-for-busy-students/. Accessed on 19th June 2020.

QSR International. (2020). *Remote Research Center: Discover How Researchers Are Innovating, Rethinking Research, and Teaching in a Remote World* [Online]. Available at: www.qsrinternational.com/nvivo-qualitative-data-analysis-software/resources/remote-research-center. Accessed on 8th June 2020.

Rath, T. (2013). *Eat – Move – Sleep: How Small Choices Lead to Big Changes*. Arlington, Virginia, United States: Missionday.

Sage Publishing. (2020). *Being a Mindful Teacher – Videos* [Online]. Available at: https://uk.sagepub.com/en-gb/eur/being-a-mindful-teacher. Accessed on 19th June 2020.

Sage Publishing. (2020). *Don't Forget Your Wellbeing* [Online]. Available at: https://uk.sagepub.com/en-gb/eur/dont-forget-your-wellbeing. Accessed on 19th June 2020.

Sage Publishing. (2020). *Do You Know Your Stress Triggers?* [Online]. Available at: https://uk.sagepub.com/en-gb/eur/do-you-know-your-stress-triggers. Accessed on 19th June 2020.

Sage Publishing. (2020). *How to Set Wise Goals for Yourself* [Online]. Available at: https://uk.sagepub.com/en-gb/eur/how-to-set-wise-goals-for-yourself. Accessed on 19th June 2020.

Sage Publishing. (2020). *Stress Busters* [Online]. Available at: https://uk.sagepub.com/en-gb/eur/stress-busters. Accessed on 19th June 2020.

Scholarship Hub. (2020). What is the difference between a scholarship, grant and bursary? *The Scholarship Bub* [Online]. Available at: www.thescholarshiphub.

org.uk/what-difference-between-scholarship-grant-and-bursary/. Accessed on 14th July 2020.

SleepFoundation.org. (2020). *Common Sleep Disorders* [Online]. Available at: https://www.sleepfoundation.org/. Accessed on 21st July 2020.

Student Minds. (2020). *Coronavirus Resource Hub* [Online]. Available at: www.studentminds.org.uk/coronavirus.html. Accessed on 7th July 2020.

Thompson, C., and Wolstencroft, P. (2018). *The Trainee Teacher's Handbook: A Companion for Initial Teacher Training*. London: Sage Publications Ltd.

Vitae. (2020). Resources and support for researchers with disabilities. *Vitae.ac.uk* [Online]. Available at: www.vitae.ac.uk/doing-research/every-researcher-counts-equality-and-diversity-in-researcher-careers/resources-and-support-for-disabled-researchers. Accessed on 21st July 2020.

Vozza, S. (2020). When you should listen to your self-doubt – and when you shouldn't. *Mindfulness at Work* [Online]. Available at: www.fastcompany.com/90516081/when-you-should-listen-to-your-self-doubt-and-when-you-shouldnt. Accessed on 7th July 2020.

Warrell, M. (2020). *You've Got This! The Life-changing Power of Trusting Yourself*, 1st ed. Milton, QLD, Australia: John Wiley & Sons.

The Wellbeing Thesis. (2020). A collaborative open access web-resource to support postgraduate research student mental well-being. *The Wellbeing Thesis*. The University of Derby, King's College London and Student Minds [Online]. Available at: https://thewellbeingthesis.org.uk/. Accessed on 7th July 2020.

Ye, A. (2020). Studying online: Tips and experiences from a student in Singapore. *Time Higher Education* [Online]. Available at: www.timeshighereducation.com/student/blogs/studying-online-tips-and-experiences-student-singapore. Accessed on 7th July 2020.

CHAPTER 5

Writing your literature review

Introduction

A literature review is an essential part of your PhD. This chapter covers essential information on how to search for appropriate literature and then write a comprehensive review of that literature. The chapter underlines the importance of conducting a comprehensive and detailed review of existing literature with the aim of finding 'knowledge gaps' that your research topic or question is designed to fill. Advice on places to search for publications – digital and non-digital, online or printed physical resources – are also contained within this chapter.

By the end of this chapter, you will have a better understanding of

- the importance of a literature review in PhD research,
- where and how to search for literature,
- effective strategies for reviewing existing literature and
- how to plan, draft and write your literature review chapter of your thesis.

The purpose of a literature review

A literature review is an extensive discussion and critical evaluation of published work that has already been done by researchers or scholars around your chosen field of study. It involves presenting and organising existing ideas and knowledge relating to your research in a systemic way so as to provide context for your PhD study. Through extensive reading of literature, you will be able to pull together key strands of work that underpin your own research. Your literature review will probably uncover a number of theoretical, methodological and practical issues relating to previous studies that are relevant to your research. Your review may also show how different approaches adopted by other scholars and researcher have helped shaped your research question. A good grasp of the relevant literature will enable you to frame your research question appropriately and position your study at the right place within the general discourse of your research area. A literature review also enables you to keep up to date with the development of ideas in your area of study and how those ideas have changed over time. An effective literature review will enable you to formulate and refine your research questions, provide you with a general context to discuss your own findings and demonstrate the depth and breadth of your understanding to your examiners and thesis readers.

By summarising and synthesising the works of other people and highlighting, critiquing or validating key ideas, concepts, theories, findings and other information relating to your topic, you will be able to articulate current debates and discussions within your field of study. Your literature review will provide the window through which readers can see the relevance of your work and the contribution you intend to make to the general discourse and advancement of knowledge in your field. Any new information your research brings to the table, in form of new ideas, new theories or concepts, a new approach, a new interpretation or a new analysis, amongst others, will be examined within the general context and in relation to existing literature and knowledge.

Searching for relevant literature

A key part of reviewing literature is to search for and access the literature in the first instance. You can't review what you haven't got. So your ability to search for or source the relevant literature is of critical importance. Literature covers a wide and diverse range of materials (Figure 5.1). You may, therefore, need to make a judgement as to what constitutes relevant literature in your PhD. Generally, literature includes published academic materials in any format and professional documents, conference proceedings and so on that provide information relating to your study.

Your search for literature may start from the first article or book you read about your PhD topic. Every journal article or book you read will most certainly contain a number of references or citations. These references and citations will open a trail for other sources and references. Those other references will point you to even more references and sources. So from a single journal you can begin to build a list of relevant literature, which can snowball into a long list of sources. The more materials you read, the longer the list of sources or references you will be able to compile. Your reference list can grow and snowball within a short time. It is therefore important that you sift through them, as not all the literature in your list of references will be relevant to your study. Only the references that are particularly relevant or critical to your study should form the basis for your review.

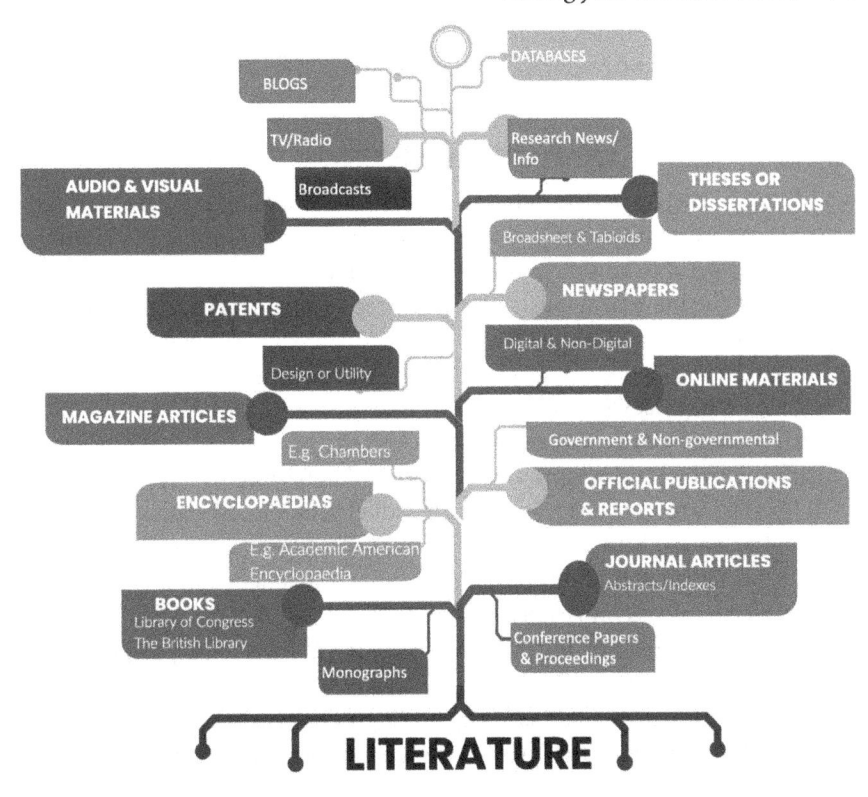

Figure 5.1 Diverse range of materials constituting literature

The essential tools for undertaking a literature search

In addition to searching manually, you may also look around for relevant literature using a range of electronic tools and database search engines. These are computer programmes or websites that enable you to find documents and materials by typing keywords. Some of the popular search engines include the following:

- Yahoo – https://consent.yahoo.com/
- Ask.com – https://uk.ask.com/
- Google – www.google.com/
- AOL – www.aol.co.uk/
- Baidu – www.baidu.com/
- Bing – www.bing.com/
- DuckDuckGo – https://duckduckgo.com/
- Lycos – www.lycos.com/
- WolframAlpha – www.wolframalpha.com/

- Yandex – https://yandex.com/
- Google Scholar – https://scholar.google.com/

The literature review and access to databases

In addition to the general search engines that are available publicly, as listed earlier, there are a number of databases that house a vast number of materials that may be useful to you in your literature review.

Amongst the popular databases for research in the social sciences include the following:

- Scopus – www.elsevier.com/
- PsycINFO – www.apa.org/pubs/databases/psycinfo/
- ERIC – www.ebsco.com/products/research-databases/eric
- CINAHL – https://health.ebsco.com/products/the-cinahl-database
- Web of Science – https://clarivate.libguides.com/woscc/citationreport
- The International Bibliography of the Social Sciences (IBSS) – https://proquest.libguides.com/IBSS
- Applied Social Science Index and Abstracts (ASSIA) – https://proquest.libguides.com/assia
- Sociological Abstracts: https://proquest.libguides.com/SocAbs
- ProQuest Dissertations and Theses – www.proquest.com/libraaries/academic/dissertataions-theses
- Kopernio – https://kopernio.com/
- PubMed – https://pubmed.ncbi.nlm.nih.gov/

While some of the databases listed earlier may be available free of charge, others may require some form of subscriptions. It is most likely that your university already subscribes to these databases, in which case you may already have free access. You can always check with your university librarian or supervisors which online databases you have free access to.

Selecting relevant literature

Whichever form of search method is used, it is essential to have a criterion for selecting relevant literature for your review. Ideally, you should read everything that is connected with your topic. Realistically within the time available to you and the ever-growing volume of materials being produced, the chances are that you probably will not be able to read every single literature connected to your study. This brings up the issue of knowing what to include and what to exclude. Making a decision as to which literature to include in your review and which literature to exclude or move into a 'read-later folder', time permitting, may seem simple. However, the complex nature of literature demands that you have a clear understanding of how to source and select literature. You may, therefore, need to define the inclusion and exclusion criteria for your literature search. Using specific keywords or string themes to filter literature during your search is a simple and commonly used strategy to select relevant literature.

For every literature or material you encounter, you may need to define and apply inclusion or exclusion criteria, based on your research and relevance to your review (Briner and Denyer, 2012). For most studies, the selection criteria are based on the degree of relevance of the literature, the quality of literature and the currency of publication. There are other criteria that you may also consider in selecting literature for your review such as diversity/inclusion criteria, location or geographical scope of literature, methodological approach used in studies, accessibility to publication, quality of publication, validity/reliability of contents, genre of literature and authors/publishers' academic standing and reputation, amongst others (Figure 5.2). Depending on your study, you may set multiple criteria for selecting materials for your literature review.

Engaging with and reviewing literature

Once you have decided on the relevant materials, the next stage is to start your review by perusing and reading through the materials. A literature review involves critical engagement with literature. Most universities would expect

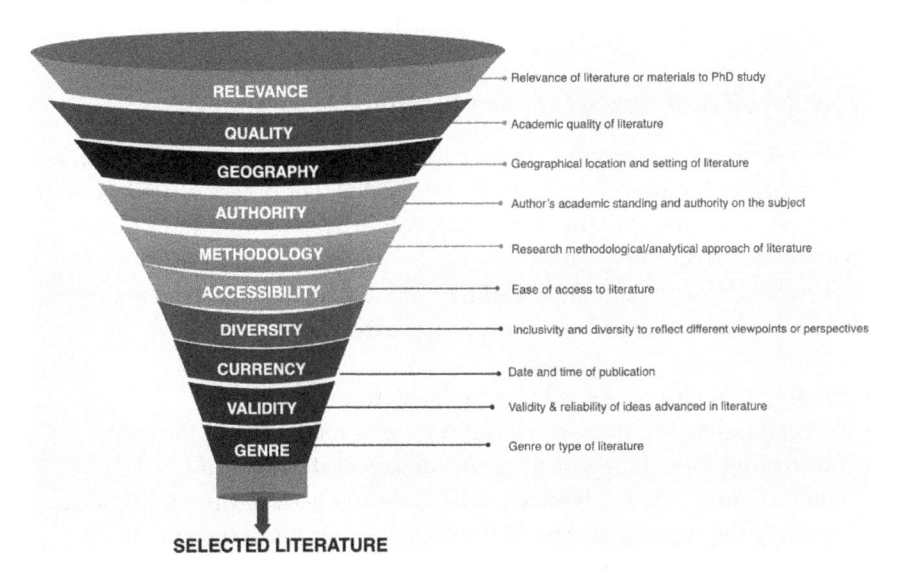

Figure 5.2 Criteria for selecting literature for review

you to undertake a critical and extensive review of existing literature relating to your research and present this about 3 to 4 months into your official enrolment, as part of your transfer or confirmation of registration for a PhD. A good literature review at this early stage could form the bedrock for a more comprehensive review that you will be required to provide when undertaking your final thesis. So it is important to get your literature review started in earnest and continue to refine and build it up as you progress through your PhD journey. The sooner you start writing your literature review the better for your supervisors to read through and offer you advice on improving it. Writing your literature review early can also help you detect any issue with your research design and fix this before you go too far into your PhD.

The simple advice is to read broadly. Read anything and everything that's closely related to your research, if you can and have the time. Sometimes, it helps also to read materials that are even unrelate to your PhD as these could help take your mind off your PhD when it gets really heavy and overwhelming. By reading extensively, you will develop a deep sense of knowledge and understanding of current knowledge in your area of research. You will know what has been done before by other researchers or scholars, how they were done and what needs to be done and the gap that your PhD research is designed to fill. Through an extensive and critical literature review, you may also find new inspiration, new techniques, new ideas and new ways of doing things that you hadn't thought of before that you could use or deploy in your own research. Your literature review and understanding of what has been done and how it was done will sharpen your theoretical/conceptual understanding and inform your methodological approach (see Chapter 6).

What does it really mean to review literature?

All literature reviews require reading the literature. For some literature, an exploratory or broad reading is all that is needed. For others, there is a need to be more engaging with the literature; hence, a deep reading and a thorough review may be required (Figure 5.3).

Generally, when you review the literature, the main things you are trying to do may include, but are not limited to, the following:

- Finding new ideas or knowledge in the literature
- Understanding key theories/concepts used or referred to in the study
- Identifying common themes within and across the literature
- Understanding the methodological approaches used in the study and recognising the appropriateness or limitations or merits of such methods
- Knowing the key assumptions underpinning the study and the basis for its analysis and conclusions

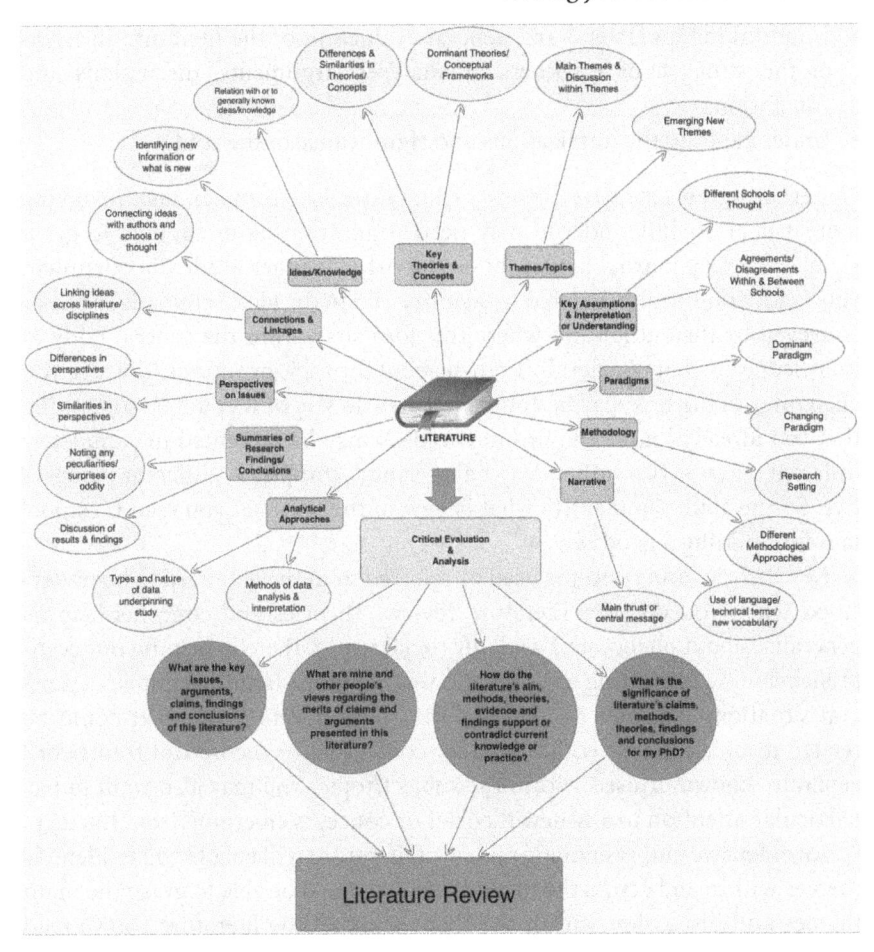

Figure 5.3 Essential issues in a review and engagement with literature

- Understanding of the narratives of the text and specific use of language, symbols and signs
- Recognising relevant paradigms that can be associated with the literature or any subtle or real change in the prevailing paradigms
- Comprehending the main thrusts or central argument of the literature and its conclusions and findings and identifying any flaws, inconsistency or illogicality
- Recognising the general/particular perspectives in which the literature is written, noting different schools of thought, ideological leaning and the like
- Grasping the analytical approaches used in the study and be mindful of the strength, shortcomings or limitations of such approaches
- Identifying any connections or linkages between ideas in the text and ideas in other literature

- Undertaking a personal and general evaluation of the literature in terms of the strength or weakness of analyses, arguments, discussions and conclusions
- Understanding the implications and significance of the study

Undertaking an extensive review of literature is a complex task involving a great deal of skill, and you may need some training or support to get it right. For every journal article, book, report and other academic document you read, you need to be able to identify the main idea being advanced or conveyed by the author and where this idea sits within the general body of knowledge or what is generally known about the topic or subject. The idea you encounter in the text may be completely new to you or it could be something that you already know. Old or known ideas may be presented in completely different ways or the author may be offering a completely different perspective. So the ability to identify what is new in the text that you read is important for building a good review.

Key theories and concepts used or referred to in the text need to be understood when you do your literature review. Theories and concepts help us generalise about phenomena and our social world, thereby helping our comprehension by presenting a systematic way of understanding complex events and situations (Chapter 6). Any theories or concepts in the text could be related to or compared with a broader contextual or theoretical framework generally known or used within the subject/topic. You may also want to pay particular attention to any new theories or concepts emerging from the text.

An extensive and systematic review of literature will enable you to identify themes within and across the literature. You should be able to grasp the main themes and discussion within the themes for all the literature you've read and be able to deduce if any new themes are emerging. To review literature effectively, you need to be able to understand the methodological approaches used in the study relating to the literature you've read and able to recognise or evaluate the appropriateness or limitations of such methods. Your ability to catch on to different research settings and different methodological approaches that could be used will help you in your review. Most studies are predicated on certain assumptions. Knowing the key assumptions underpinning the studies you read about and having the ability to ascertain the validity of those assumptions will enable you to critically review the text and help you make judgements on the reliability and/or accuracies of the studies' assertions and conclusions.

Reviewing the literature also requires an understanding of the narratives of the text and specific use of language, symbols and signs. You need to be able to understand the main thrusts of the text and its central message. You may need to pay particular attention to the use of language, technical terms or new vocabulary. Also, you need to take cognisance of the relevant paradigm that can be associated with the literature or any subtle or real change or shifts in the prevailing or dominant paradigm. Reviewing literature also requires a recognition of the general/particular perspectives in which the literature is written, noting differences in perspectives, context, schools of thought, ideological leaning and so on. Your ability to understand and grasp the analytical method or approach used in the study will help you in your review. You also need to be conversant with other approaches or methods in order to know whether a particular approach is appropriate for a particular study. Hence an understanding of the strengths, shortcomings or limitations of different approaches will help you understand different texts and undertake an informed review. An extensive literature review requires making links across literature and between authors. Therefore, being able to identify connections or linkages between ideas and authors of those ideas is crucial in a review. Ideas within particular schools of thought may need to be grouped together and the differences between and within schools highlighted.

Most important, you need to be able to undertake a personal and general evaluation of the literature in terms of the strength or weakness of their analysis, arguments, discussions and conclusions. Understanding the basis of the discussion in the text and being able to follow the logic of the author's conclusion – which you may agree or disagree with – are essential features of reviewing literature.

Your extensive review, together with your own personal assessment or evaluation of existing literature should be discussed in relation to your own study. When done effectively, all the bits and pieces of information you gathered from your review could form the basis for and bedrock of your literature review chapter of your thesis. Your review will need to be written up in a coherent and logical fashion with all the sources correctly and fully cited and referenced (see Writing Your Reference List or bibliography in Chapter 11). To do this effectively, you need to ask yourself three pertinent questions, that will help decide if you are ready to begin writing your literature review:

1   Have I read all the critical and essential literature relating to my research and understood the key ideas, narrative and themes, methodologies, theories and concepts, connections and linkages, among other elements, relating to the literature?
2   Is my PhD research informed by current knowledge in the field as evidenced in the literature and has a 'gap' in the literature been uncovered through my review?
3   Have I enough information and materials to start writing or drafting a literature review?

If your answer to any or all of these questions is yes, then you are in a good place to begin to pull all the information you gathered into writing or drafting your literature review chapter?

Notes and note-taking

One thing you will need to do over and over again in the course of your PhD is take notes. This is particularly important while doing your literature review. Whether it is about taking notes of important information or new discoveries relating to your study or putting together a draft chapter or conference papers, or writing a diary of your PhD journey and so on, you will need to write, write and keep writing notes again and again. As you browse or read through the relevant materials and literature you have selected from different sources, it is crucial that you take notes of titles of articles, journals, book chapters or books and their authors. Information on the publisher, place and year of publication, edition, volume and issue number also need to be noted as you will need all these to compile your references and citations. If your sources are from a website, you will need to also include the website address and the date you access the information.

As you begin to pore over or read through the literature, it is good practice to make a note of key points or summaries of the articles or books that you've read that are important to your study. You may also note down key theories or a particular method of analysis used in particular research that is similar to yours. You may also want to sum up different strands or arguments presented by different authors or schools of thoughts on a particular issue. Or, simply, you may want to outline how what you've read relates to your own research plan or thesis.

Whatever it is, writing things down, either manually using the traditional pen and paper or using digital means of word processing or using note-taking apps such as Evernote, OneNote, Apple Notes, Google Keep, Notion, Boostnote, Milanote, Simplenote or Standard Notes, amongst others, offer the opportunity to document, remember, recall and review your information when needed later. By writing up and using an effective system of documentation, you should be able to get more organised. Try to use a reliable system of storage for your written and creative work. Using cloud-based storage services such as OneDrive, iDrive, pCloud, Mega, iCloud, Box, NextCloud, SpiderOak or the like could save you a great deal of trouble and headache of losing your data if your computer suffers a fatal crash. It is advisable you start writing at the very early stage of your study as this may help you develop some writing skills and could be an effective way to reflect on your work and progress (Lantsoght, 2018).

Summarising and synthesising literature

As part of your literature review, you need to develop the skills of summarising and synthesising information. You also need to understand the logic and structure of arguments presented in the literature that you have read and how those arguments led to the conclusions arrived at by the authors. The more you are able to structure and logically present complex arguments, the better you will be at writing a critical review. Also, being able to identify conflicting and sometimes contradictory arguments in a text is very useful in a review.

Your skills and ability to judge the quality or value of the text being reviewed are central to a good review. So you need to consider the pros and cons of the texts, the merits and demerits of the arguments and the claims advanced in the text. You will also need to be able to relate and compare the text with other texts on the subject or topic and note any differences and similarities in assumptions, approaches and conclusions of the authors of these texts. A good review will also require an ability to synthesise the diversities in the methodologies employed and summarise evidence presented in the literature. As part of your own evaluation, you should be able to determine whether such evidence is strong, persuasive or adequate enough to support the conclusions arrived at. The conclusions of various texts on a topic, whether final or preliminary, need to be summarised in order to identify any common threads or contradictions. Overall, your ability to provide a comprehensive overview of the literature in relation to specific research questions and how the questions have been answered, analysed, interpreted and evaluated is important to writing a good review.

Arguably, the literature review is the most complex part of your thesis. Hence, you may need to write several drafts of your review to ensure it is logical, coherent and accurately reflect the literature being reviewed. That means you need to carefully plan for and have enough time to carry out and write a thorough review.

Writing up your literature review

Writing your literature review involves pulling together all the materials, ideas, concepts, theories, opinions, analysis, conclusions and so on you have gathered in the course of reading the literature and presenting them in an engaging, logical and coherent way.

Approaches to a literature review

There are several approaches to reviewing literature, each with its merits and demerits (Figure 5.4). The approach or method of literature review employed

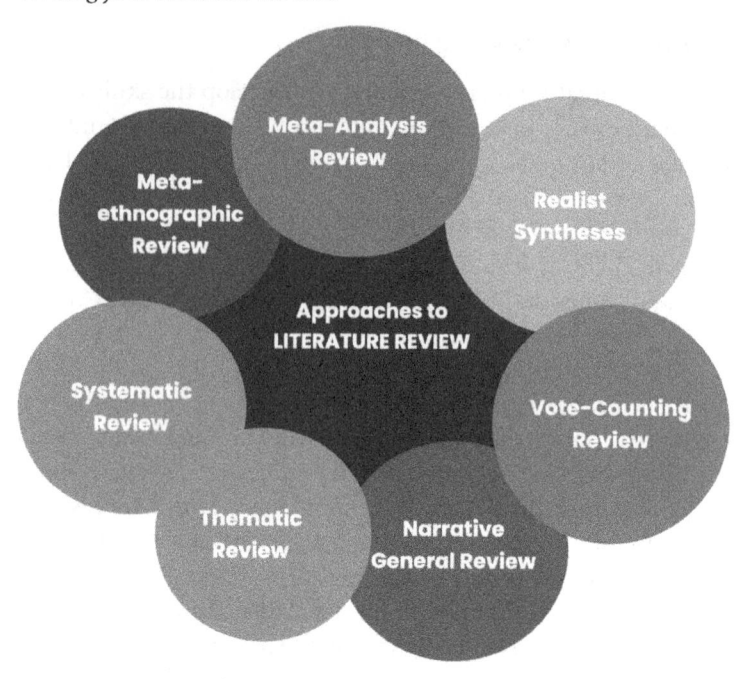

Figure 5.4 Approaches to reviewing literature

will depend on your research topic, the nature of the literature to be reviewed in terms of size and diversity and the purpose for which the review is being undertaken and the intended audience of the review report (Rickinson and May, 2009).

Depending on your study objective and types of literature, the essential information gathered through your review can be pulled together or synthesise in several ways. The approach you take to your review may also depend on your style of writing experience and your university guidelines on your thesis.

Narrative/general review – This form of review does not follow any particular approach or style in term of synthesis of literature. Rather, it is based on a generic overall synthesis of literature. Essential summaries of what has been written on a subject or topic are presented with regards to basic facts as contained in the literature. In essence, narrative review involves summarising what has been written on a subject or topic, identifying methodologies used on what samples or populations reporting the key findings (Davies, 2000; Pawson, 2002).

Systematic review – A systematic literature review is done using a structured process designed to find and analyse literature. This may involve a step-by-step approach based on the factors researchers consider essential in the review. Generally, a systematic review of literature involves a five-stage process of defining or formulating your research question, locating the relevant studies, selecting and evaluating the studies, analysing and synthesising the information in the studies and reporting and using the secondary research results (Denyer and Tranfield, 2009).

Thematic review – Thematic review of literature involves a review based on the categorisation of literature in order to explore common themes. From a thematic analysis or review of literature, you will be able to extract key themes from literature and identify essential elements relating to your study. A thematic review of literature covering multiple topics or themes is usually organised in chronological order of the development of knowledge or themes over time (Lawrence, 2011).

Meta-ethnographic review – This approach relates to the synthesis of literature based on interpretative comparison and inductive analysis. Widely used in health care studies, the meta-ethnographic review approach relates to determining how studies are related, translating different studies into one another, synthesising translations and presenting the summary or synthesis of arguments (Cahill et al., 2017). This literature review approach requires essential skills in interpreting qualitative syntheses and has been suggested to provide a much greater description of methods and higher-order interpretation of qualitative texts compared to other forms of literature review (Atkins et al., 2008).

Meta-analysis/review – Meta-analysis is a systematic review of the literature which involves mostly quantitative syntheses of the strengths, weaknesses, assumptions and biases of existing studies on a particular topic. The meta-analysis review approach requires a systematised and structured evaluation of existing research with a view of uncovering inconsistencies, contradictions that may call to question the validity of expert or popular opinion on a subject (Russo, 2007). Commonly used in health care studies, the meta-analysis provides the basis to assess whether the conclusions reached by existing studies are consistent with the evidence provided. A meta-analysis requires a systemic review of empirical evidence and the application of statistical methods to summarise or synthesise the evidence in order to establish the validity of the studies.

Vote-counting review – This is a form of meta-analysis review in which vote counting is used to register the number of positive studies against the number of negative studies with a view of determining if there are any significant differences or effect. Usually, the vote-counting procedure involves dividing studies into three main categories: (a) studies with significant positive results, (b) studies with significant negative results, and (c) studies with nonsignificant results (Bushman and Wang, 2009). Studies with significant positive results are generally highly rated and considered to have a positive effect while studies with significant negative results are often underrated. Due to the subjective nature of determining whether a study is 'positive' or 'negative', this type of review of empirical studies is less commonly used. The review approach takes no account of differences in the size of studies and weight of evidence provided in studies as it may only focus on studies' findings as positive or negative.

Realist synthesis – This is a form of research review that seeks to uncover causal structure in order to establish what works and under what conditions. Under specific settings or conditions, it explains how and why some programmes work and others fail. It is an approach widely used in evidence-based policy study of care management and delivery. Through an evidence-based mechanism, realist synthesis reviews literature on service interventions, especially in health care, by taking a long-term view of what works and what didn't work. As this approach takes cognisance of the weight of evidence in existing studies, it has been suggested that it is far more useful than the meta-analytic approach (Pawson, 2006).

It is worth noting that the approaches to doing a literature review, presented earlier, are not mutually exclusive. Some reviews may adopt multiple approaches and a meta-ethnographic review may be thematic or systematic. Whichever review methodology or approach you use in your study, it needs to fit into your research aims and objectives and should be appropriate for the literature being reviewed. Also, you should have a clear understanding as to what to include or exclude from your review and be consistent in your criteria for selecting literature. You also need to have a strong and convincing narrative to demonstrate your understanding of the development of ideas and knowledge in your field through your literature review.

Further guidance for drafting your review

Other essential guides in compiling, writing and presenting your literature review are provided in the following subsections.

Undertake an up-to-date review

While your review may cover old literature, especially if you want to show or highlight the historical development of an idea over time, it is critical that your literature review presents current information using up-to-date literature. As much as possible, recently published articles should be used in your reviews and to support your own arguments. Watch out for newly emerging themes in the literature and any recent changes in paradigm, methodological approach, definitions, appropriate use of language and the like. You may need to constantly add to or edit your literature review as new information emerges or new policies or practices are developed in relation to your study.

Structure your review

Your review should also be logically structured to develop a consistent flow and narrative so as to direct your thesis readers to the key points of your review and how the review relates to your own research. The structure should be clear, well defined and easy to understand with links between the sections and cross-referencing to show logical arguments. If using a systematic approach, your review should be presented and explained step by step to ensure you cover all relevant information.

Focus on the literature you read

Your literature review should encompass the literature you actually read, critiqued or evaluated rather than articles or literature that you intend to read but never get around reading or looking at them. Ensure that all works that you reference in your bibliography are cited in your text. Similarly, whatever work you cite in your text must be referenced in your bibliography.

Review literature, not the person

Your literature review could be a critique of existing knowledge or idea, pointing out the flaws, inaccuracies and inconsistencies in other people's work or argument, but it should never be directed at the persons who created the work you are reviewing unless this is critical to your argument or analysis. Acknowledge earlier works and recognise the strength of other people's work and not diminish them. At the same time, you can discuss or point out the limitations or flaws in such works.

Relate the literature review to your study and use the literature to justify the importance and relevance of your study

The main purpose of a literature review is to provide a context for your PhD research and to direct your thesis readers to what has been done, when it was done, by whom it was done, how and why it was done that way and so on and how your own study adds to, contradicts, disputes, negates or calls into question what has been done. Therefore, your literature review should endeavour to identify and justify the gaps and problems in the literature that your PhD research is intended or set up to address. These could be theoretical and or empirical gaps that the literature review has uncovered. In any case, you will need to validate, in your thesis, that the gaps or problems you have identified are significant, and previous study or research have not addressed them (see Chapter 12). Through that, the relevance and impact of your study could be demonstrated. To justify your PhD, therefore, you need to undertake a thorough and critical review, rather than just a descriptive or superficial review. Your review needs to highlight the issues or problems you are trying to solve and to demonstrate that the issue or problem needs addressing. The more tightly, you are able to tailor your literature review to your study, the easier it would be to justify your central research question, thereby providing a solid ground for your PhD. In essence, your literature review should help define or refine your research objective and dictate the scope of your study. Your literature review should be linked to your research objectives, research questions, framework and research instruments.

A thorough literature review can help you generate essential secondary data that can help set your research context and define your unique contribution to knowledge. After an extensive review of the literature, it is normal if you decide to change your original approach to your study, especially if you uncover new information that suggests a change of research plan or instruments is required. Such changes could involve a complete redesign of your research or a major or minor modification to your research aims and objectives and/or your methodology.

Be consistent in your review of literature

Be consistent in your review of literature. There are different ways of writing a review such as thematic or systematic approaches. Whichever approach you consider appropriate for your study, be consistent throughout your review. You need to write very clearly, succinctly and in a logical, structured fashion to make your review read fluently.

Highlight critical issues

Your literature review should be written in a way that unearths and exposes critical issues or ideas arising or emerging from the literature. These ideas or critical issues should then be presented to your readers without any ambiguity. In your review, you should highlight essential things such as

- the generally accepted explanations or understanding of the issue you are researching into,
- any comparisons with similar studies in the literature that you are making,

- differences in methods used by different researchers and
- the key issues that generate discussions, controversies and debate within the subject or topic.

A critical review of the methodological issues relating to doing research in your area of study may help in the design of your own research and data collection instruments. Similarly, your literature review could inform or provide the theoretical framework for your study (see Chapter 6). Overall, you need to undertake a meaningful and purposeful review that highlights the focus of your study and the substantive methodological or conceptual issues relating to your research.

Identify key theories, models or concepts

In your literature review, it is important to identify key theories, models and concepts that permeate literature that have been used to explain the problem or issue in relation to your research. By reviewing earlier works or reading pioneering publications which have been cited by subsequent studies, you will be able to uncover a number of theories, models or concepts that have emerged in relation to your study. Your readers should be able to see clearly from your literature review the key concepts on which your PhD is framed or based.

Review literature at an appropriate level

Your literature review should be pitched at an appropriate level. The standard of literature review you did for your undergraduate or master's programme may not be sufficient when it comes to your PhD. A much higher level of critical analysis is expected at the PhD level. You will be expected to have critically reviewed published peer-reviewed research papers. Undergraduate, pedagogically intended textbooks would definitely not be deemed sufficiently advanced to count in a literature review at the PhD level. So your review needs to be thorough, rigorous and critical. You need to demonstrate a comprehensive understanding of, if only to repeat for emphasis, the published peer-reviewed literature in your review.

Extend your review across disciplines

In social science research, as in any other academic disciplines, a literature review should be written to cut across disciplines. Your review should provide interdisciplinary perspectives to cover debates and discussions beyond the realms of your subject. A subject-specific and narrowly or too tightly focused review may be devoid of information on important related works being done in other subject areas. Your review should be extensive and broad enough to include a synthesis of studies and relevant information to your PhD research. Acknowledging the existence of relevant works in other disciplines can only help strengthen your thesis or reinforce your arguments. A multidisciplinary narrative of your literature review will be beneficial to your study.

Use literature review tools – *if required*

If required, you may use digital or academic tools to manage your review of the literature. Examples of literature management software include Mendeley, Zotero, NVivo, Wisdom and ReadCube. For a systematic literature review, you may also use software such as StArt (UFSCAR), Sistiller SR and Abstrackr. Other useful tools for meta-analysis are Open Meta-Analyst and OpenMEE. You may need some training on the use of these tools.

Use your review as a springboard to launch your publications

Apart from forming the bedrock of your PhD thesis, a well-written review could serve as a springboard to launch your academic publications (see Chapter 14). Your secondary research findings, through your literature review, could form the basis of a paper for a conference or for journal publication. This could significantly enhance the dissemination strategy of your research and help you during your viva voce examination (see Chapter 13).

Key messages

- A thorough and comprehensive review of peer-reviewed published literature is an important and critical part of your doctoral study.
- Apart from constituting the bedrock of your thesis, your review of literature should inform your research design, aims and methodology by highlighting gaps in the literature that your PhD is designed to fill.
- Sourcing, analysing, appraisal and synthesising literature in the social sciences is a skill that you need to develop as a PhD student, and you may need some training or support with this.
- There are several approaches or methods of reviewing literature. Whichever review methodology or approach you use in your PhD, you should be consistent with regards to the criteria for selecting literature for inclusion in your review.

- Your literature review needs to be manageable, meaningful, purposeful and relevant to your research aims and objectives
- You may need to write several drafts of your review to ensure it is logical, coherent and accurately reflect the literature being reviewed.

Further reading

Atkins, S., Lewin, S., Smith, H., et al. (2008). Conducting a metaethnography of qualitative literature: Lessons learnt. *BMC Medical Research Methodology*, 8, p. 21. https://doi.org/10.1186/1471-2288-8-21.

Aveyard, H. (2018). *Doing a Literature Review in Health and Social Care: A Practical Guide*, 4th ed. Maidenhead, Berkshire, UK: Open University Press.

Aveyard, H., Payne, S., and Preston, N. (2016). *A Post-Graduate's Guide to Doing a Literature Review in Health and Social Care*. Maidenhead, Berkshire, UK: Open University Press.

Briner, R. B., and Denyer, D. (2012). Systematic review and evidence synthesis as a practice and scholarship tool BT. In *The Oxford Handbook of Evidence-Based Management* (pp. 1–47). Oxford: Oxford University Press.

Bushman, B. J., and Wang, M. C. (2009). Vote-counting procedures in meta-analysis. In H. Cooper, L.v. Hedges, and J. C. Valentine (eds.), *The Handbook of Research Synthesis and Meta-analysis* (pp. 207–220). New York: Russell Sage Foundation.

Cahill, M., Robinson, K., et al. (2017). Qualitative synthesis: A guide to conducting a meta-ethnography. *British Journal of Occupational Therapy*, 81(3), pp. 129–137.

Davies, P. (2000). The relevance of systematic reviews to educational policy and practice. *Oxford Review of Education*, 26(3&4), pp. 365–378.

Denney, A. (2013). How to write a literature review. *Journal of Criminal Justice Education*, 24(2), pp. 218–234.

Denyer, D., and Tranfield, D. (2009). Producing a sys-tematic review. In D. Buchanan and A. Bryman (eds.), *The Sage Handbook of Organizational Research Methods* (pp. 671–689). London: Sage.

Lawrence, C. (2011). *Writing a Literature Review in the Social Sciences* [Online]. Available at: www.academia.edu/2911352/Writing_a_Literature_Review_in_the_Social_Sciences. Accessed on 31st July 2020.

Onwuegbuzie, A., and Frels, R. (2016). *Seven Steps to a Comprehensive Literature Review: A Multimodal & Cultural Approach*. London: SAGE.

Pawson, R. (2002). Evidence and policy and naming and shaming. *Policy Studies*, 23(3&4), pp. 211–230.

Pawson, R. (2006). *Evidence-based Policy a Realist Perspective*. London: SAGE.

Rickinson, M., and May, H. (2009). A comparative study of methodological approaches to reviewing literature. *The Higher Education Academy* [Online]. Available at: www.researchgate.net/profile/Mark_Rickinson/publication/

265008044_A_Comparative_Study_of_Methodological_Approaches_to_ Reviewing_Literature/links/56b31d6008aed7ba3fee2f8f/A-Comparative-Study-of-Methodological-Approaches-to-Reviewing-Literature.pdf. Accessed on 26th July 2020.

Russo, M. W. (2007). How to review a meta-analysis. *Gastroenterology & Hepatology. The Independent Peer-Reviewed Journal*, 3(8), pp. 637–642 [Online]. Available at: www.ncbi.nlm.nih.gov/pmc/articles/PMC3099299/. Accessed on 3rd August 2020.

CHAPTER 6

Understanding theoretical perspectives and developing your research methodology

Introduction

This chapter focuses on research philosophy and methodology. Using examples, it explains the philosophy underlying social science research, in general, and highlights some of the methodological decisions that you need to make with regards to your PhD research. It provides the basis for developing an appropriate theoretical and methodological framework for your PhD study.

By the end of the chapter, you will have a better understanding of

- research philosophy in general,
- ontology and epistemology,
- positivism and modern social sciences,
- social constructivism and interpretivism and
- research design and approaches in social sciences.

Types of research and ways of doing research

The process of choosing a research methodology involves developing your research question and then finding the means or tools to generate data or evidence for your answer. Depending on the subject matter PhD research can take several forms. PhD research could take the form of conceptual or empirical studies and or evaluations. Aimed at addressing specific research questions, PhD research may focus on literature reviews, impact evaluations, evidence assessments, systematic reviews, case studies, action research studies, process evaluations and socio-economic evaluations, amongst others, or a combination of these. Whichever form it takes, a PhD research involves the use of recognisable scientific methods to generate quantitative and/or qualitative data or information through a range of techniques (see Chapter 9). The techniques used in PhD research may include observations, surveys, interviews and focus groups, amongst others. Your choice of method should be consistent with a theoretical framework. An ability to develop an appropriate methodology for your study is one of the factors that your examiners will consider when assessing your thesis, hence designing a research methodology and analytical technique that is robust, credible and justifiable is critical to your success.

Deciding on your research methodology

Methodology is the foundation on which your research methods and whole thesis are based. It has been suggested that 'method' is what you do and that methodology is how and why you are doing it that way (Lawson, 2020). Methodology requires careful thought, deep reflection and justification of your choice of research methods. Your methodology should provide the philosophical and theoretical underpinning for your research and the methods you use in your study. Essentially, your methodology is the rationale (the science) underpinning your study and your choice of method in conducting the study. The methodology employed in your research will depend on your research topic, your study aims and your objectives, amongst many other factors. Your choice of methodology also depends on the values and assumptions that underpin your study. Your methodology should ensure that your research methods are reliable, valid, rigorous and appropriate for your specific study (Finn, 2005).

Choosing a methodology, therefore, requires an understanding of the goals or common reasons for doing research in the social sciences. Research in the social sciences is conducted generally with the aim of identifying and explaining general patterns and relationships; testing, refining or validating existing theory; making predictions on what is likely to happen; highlighting and interpreting the significance of a phenomenon; exploring diversity; advocating a new idea or giving a voice to a known idea; or developing or advancing new theories (Ragin, 1994). In order to achieve these goals, research in the social sciences tend to require specific actions or tasks and activities such as describing, explaining, evaluating, comparing, correlating, predicting, controlling and categorising, as highlighted in Figure 6.1.

Before deciding on specific tasks and the appropriate methodology to perform the tasks, you may need to consider a number of questions (Figure 6.2). First, you need to define or outline what exactly you want to achieve or do in your research and the best way to achieve it. You also need to know why what you want to do is important for your study and what are the possible different ways of doing what you want to do. Understanding different approaches to research in social science will enable you to choose the right methodology for your study. Then you need to have a clear understanding of the theoretical, conceptual or empirical bases for your preferred methodology and a sense of conviction as to why the methodology you've chosen is the right one for your

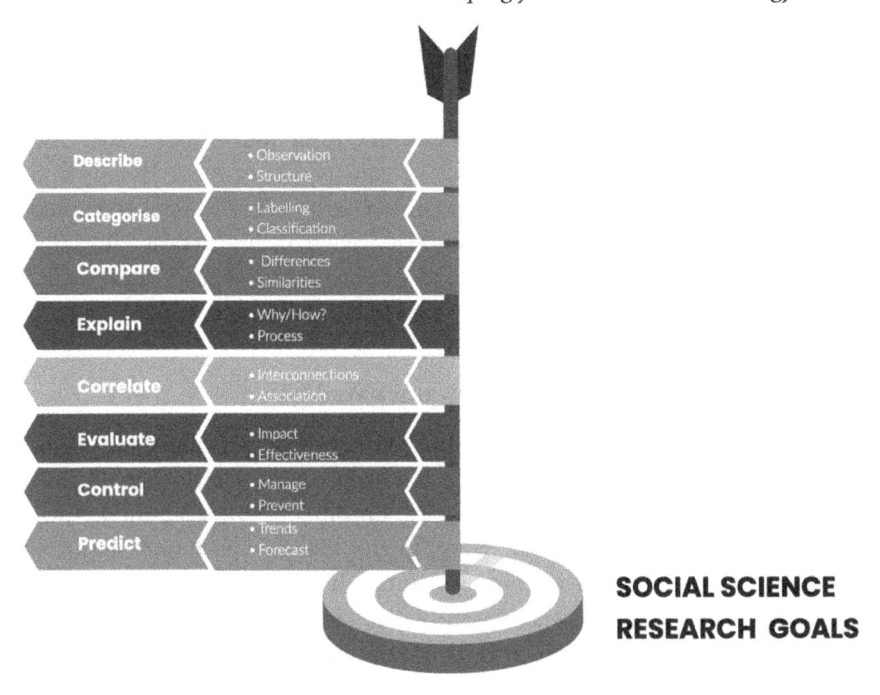

Figure 6.1 Social science research goals

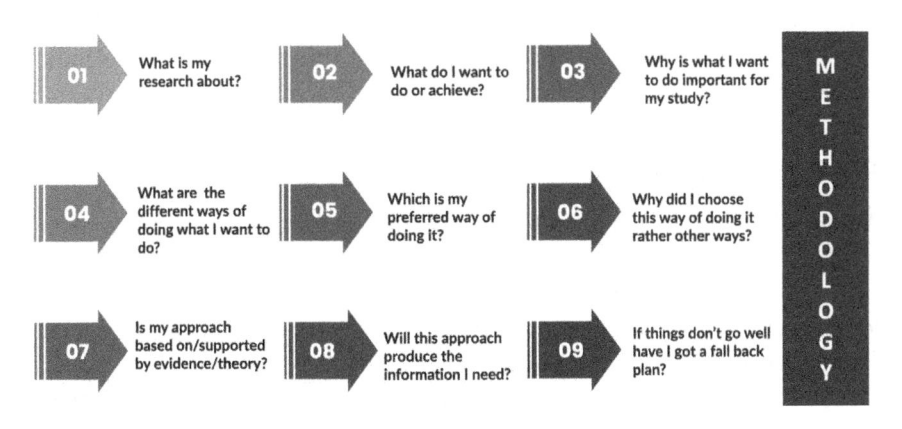

Figure 6.2 Key questions before deciding on your research methodology

study and you are able to defend this in a viva voce examination (see Chapter 12). In essence, the key issue is to ensure that whichever method you choose for your PhD research has to be appropriate for your study, and you need to be able to justify the choice of method and demonstrate that the chosen method answers your research question. Your research method should not be chosen simply because you like or prefer a particular method. While personal preference could be a factor in a choice of method, it should not be the main reason, as the method you like may not necessarily be appropriate for your study or suitable to answer your research question. Your thesis reader and your examiner should have confidence in your choice of methodology and the validity of your research design, if you are to have any chance of success with your PhD. Your contribution to knowledge will be more compelling and convincing if your research methodology is reliable, appropriate and justifiable for your study (Finn, 2005).

Understanding research philosophy and paradigms

Choosing a method for your PhD research requires an understanding of research philosophy and related theories and paradigms that underpin them. Philosophical theories are based on logical arguments. All scientific knowledge and ideas are based on good arguments that can be rationally justified (Dupré, 2007). The argument(s) presented in your thesis will be open to review, assessment and criticism. Scientific advancement is made through a continual process of review, reaction, revision and rejection of arguments and proposition. It is therefore essential that your research and the conclusions you arrived at have a strong theoretical and conceptual basis and can stand up to scrutiny. Regardless of whether your research focus is mainly theoretical and based largely on an extensive review of literature or is solving a problem, a policy evaluation or an intervention or impact study in an applied form, it needs to relate to a specific paradigm in terms of its analytical approach.

Research paradigms

A research paradigm is a set of ideas, common beliefs and shared agreements between scientists as to how to view, understand and solve a problem. It is, essentially, a worldview or an epistemological stance on which scientists seek to understand, analyse and address issues. Paradigms also offer a conceptual framework within which scientific theories are developed or constructed. Essentially, paradigms are sets of assumptions on which ideas and theories are predicated or formulated. Broadly, there are two main paradigms – positivism and interpretivism – each with its own sets of belief and ideas. Besides, humanism and structuralism also offer some perspectives as important paradigms.

The positivist approach favours an objective and realist approach to research based on quantitative statistical analysis to make a judgement on or proof of any causal relationships between social phenomena. Positivists work under the general assumption that society can and should be studied scientifically and empirically. Positivists seek 'the truth' through an objective and unbiased procedure that is devoid of a researcher's value judgement and subjective opinion. The positivist approach to conducting research, therefore, is based largely on empirical study involving formulating hypotheses that are subjected to validation or verification using objective data.

In contrast, the interpretivist paradigm suggests that there is nothing like 'the truth' as 'truth' is highly subjective and varies from one person to another. So depending on individuals' interactions and social context, different truths can be constructed. So the interpretivist paradigm or social constructionism suggests that individuals create their own reality based on their own definition or interpretation of truth and interactions with other people. While individuals may construct their own reality, social groups often agree or disagree on what is true and what is real (DeCarlo, 2018). Given that meanings are constructed socially and collectively, and there is no one single truth, the constructionist-interpretative paradigm tends to, therefore, rely on non-empirical data for problem-solving and mostly use descriptive methods (Figure 6.3).

Ontology

Underlying these two main approaches and traditions are the following ontological questions: What is real? How do we construct reality? Is reality subject to change? and If so, how do we know if reality is changing or has already changed? Answers to these questions and to the general question of the nature of reality are highly subjective and depend on individual viewpoint or stance within the general debate on reality and nature of knowledge. There are five main paradigms that inform or shape existing research traditions. These

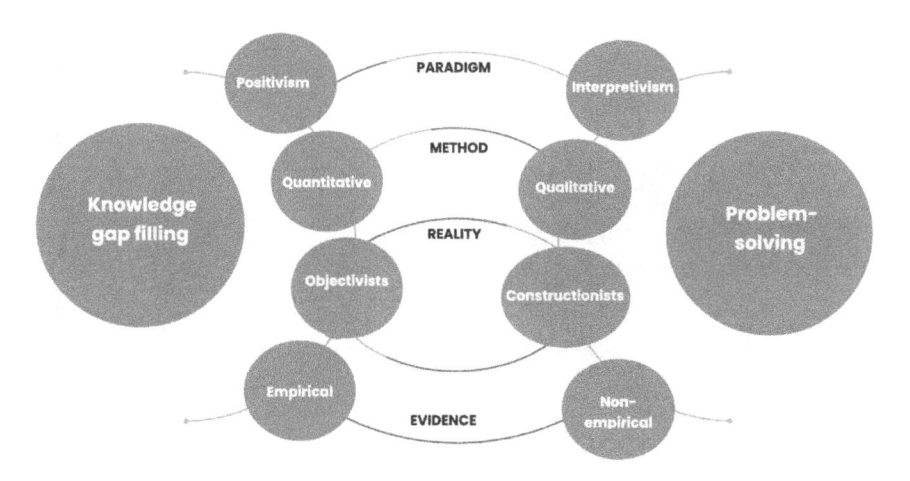

Figure 6.3 Paradigms and research methods

are positivism, constructivism, pragmatism, subjectivism and critical paradigms (Figure 6.4). Generally, **positivists** posit that there is a single reality or truth, which can be measured and known. Therefore, positivists or objective otologists are more likely to use quantitative methods to measure this reality. It is a tradition or paradigm that suggests that reality can be constructed, observed and measured objectively. They believe this can be done separately or independently of the researcher in a way that the observations or measurements will not change or affect reality.

Unlike positivists, **constructivists** believe that there is no single reality or truth. Therefore, according to this standpoint, reality needs to be constructed or interpreted. Qualitative methods of analysis are mostly used to construct those multiple realities. The approach suggests that researchers construct multiple realities which are affected by the participants or actors within the realities as well as by the researchers. Those who subscribe to this paradigm are generally known as **subjective constructivists**.

Pragmatism implies that reality is constantly being renegotiated, debated and interpreted. As a philosophical position, pragmatists suggest that an ideology or proposition is true if it works satisfactorily and that the meaning of a proposition is to be found in the practical consequences of accepting it. Hence, unpractical methods or ideas should be discarded or rejected. In any research, pragmatists would argue, the best method to use is the one that solves the problem or answers the question.

Subjectivists construe reality broadly from a subjective viewpoint, suggesting that reality is nothing but what we perceive to be real. Therefore, there is no external or objective truth; rather, it is a matter of opinion or perception.

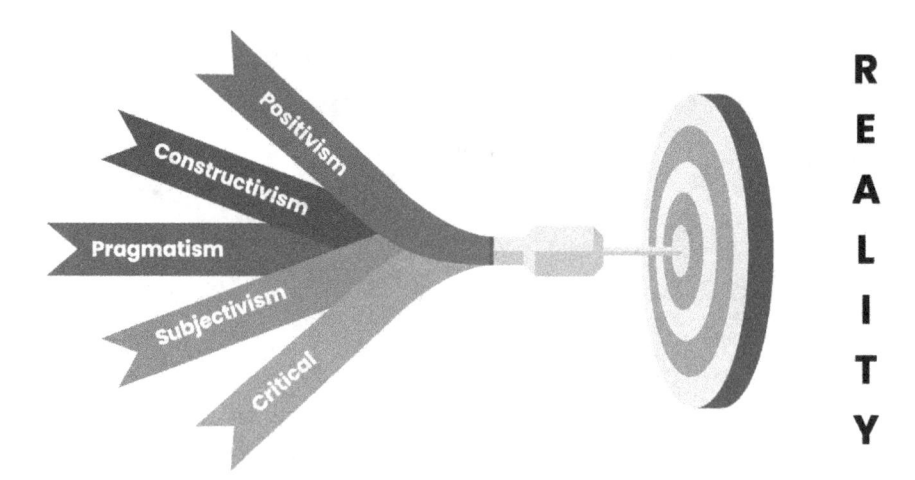

Figure 6.4 Notion of reality and social research paradigms

The **critical** paradigm school of thought believes that reality is socially constructed and is influenced or determined by socio-economic structures and power relations within society. It posits that there is an inherent inequality and imbalance within the social structure and that means social science can never be truly objective of all value-free. The focus is therefore on how to address and change the unequal power relations within society through effective social change.

It is essential to note that the paradigms discussed in this chapter are not mutually exclusive, as there are some research approaches that rely on mixed methods.

Epistemology

Epistemology is a theory of knowledge and how we acquire knowledge. It seeks to explain knowledge acquisition with respect to its methods, validity and scope. It also tries to make a distinction between what is considered a justified belief and what is an opinion. Essentially, it explains how we know something and how we attach meanings to the interaction between our idea and experiences. It is a study of the nature of knowledge, justification and the rationality of belief. As a branch of philosophy, epistemology seeks to provide a logical discourse and answer to questions such as What is knowledge? What does it mean to know something? How do we know what we know? and What is the justification or rationality for our claim to know something? It focuses on the nature of knowledge, conditions for acquiring knowledge, sources of knowledge and justified belief, structure of knowledge and claims and counter-claims to knowledge. What we believe may not necessarily be true; hence, there is a distinction between what we believe and what is proved to be true. While empiricists believe in the objective testing of hypothesis to establish reality or truth, constructivists prefer an interpretive approach, suggesting that reality can be constructed and interpreted in different ways.

From the foregoing, one can deduce that a paradigm provides the framework through which we approach knowledge. Paradigms are a way of framing what we know, what we can know, and how we can know it (DeCarlo, 2018). Different paradigms provide different ontological and epistemological perspectives. The traditional route of scientific investigation tends to follow empirical and quantitative methods that involve data collection, hypotheses formulation and statistical analysis. However, the decision as to which research paradigms you design your PhD to align with will depend on the nature of your research, your research questions and what you want to achieve in your study. It will also depend on the operating assumptions upon which you set up your study and how you think the world should or does work. It is not uncommon for some studies to reflect multiple paradigms and mixed methods as these research approaches and paradigms are not mutually exclusive of each other. The key issue is for you to justify why you have chosen a particular approach.

Understanding the role of theories in social science research

Theories are systematic explanations of the underlying phenomenon or behaviour (Bhattacherjee, 2012). Different theories or laws exist to explain different behaviour or phenomenon. Generally, social science laws and theories are established suppositions formulated to explain, predict and understand social phenomena. While laws relate to observed patterns in phenomena or behaviours that are yet to be scientifically challenged or disproved, theories imply suppositions backed with considerable evidence. Theories may not necessarily produce the same findings when applied, and that explains why some research is designed to test, confirm or modify existing theories.

Social science theories tend to provide generalised suppositions or knowledge about society and how our social world works. They tend to focus on socially constructed phenomena and how these phenomena relate to each other to create social systems (Shoemaker et al., 2004). One of the objectives of social science research is not just to formulate new theories that can be used to generalise or explain our social world but to test existing theories with a view of modifying or improving them.

Examples of theories in social sciences include the following:

Cognitive dissonance theory – a theory in psychology that seeks to explain how people react when their observations of an event are different from what they expected of that event (Bhattacherjee, 2012)
Deterrence theory – a social theory that explains why some people engage in improper or criminal activities or behaviours

Logic, reasoning and inductive–deductive research

Logical reasoning is central to the development and postulation of theories. Through critical observations, analysis and informed logical reasoning, your PhD research may help improve existing theories or lead to the postulation of new ideas or theories. Hence, it is essential you follow the scientific process of logic, evidence and validation to support your conclusions. It has been suggested that the two pillars on which scientific knowledge are based are logic and evidence (Bhattacherjee, 2012). Logic is manifested in theories and evidence is apparent through observation. Hence, both theory and observation are inter-related and constitute the basis for scientific reasoning. Theories give meanings to what is observed, and observation helps prove or validate or modify theories.

Research in social sciences can be conducted using an inductive or deductive approach. If your research is designed in a way as to deduce theoretical concepts and patterns from your data, then you are most likely using an inductive approach. Alternatively, if you are using new empirical data to validate test concepts and patterns known from existing theories, then you are most certainly using a deductive approach. Generally, inductive research tends to focus on theory-building or theory formulation whereas a deductive approach seeks to test, validate or falsify theories, usually with a view of improving or refining them.

Research design

Your PhD research can be aligned with any paradigms and can take various forms and based on specific theories. Most PhDs research in the social sciences is based on empirical work. That means sourcing, collecting, handling and analysing data, including those generated through your primary research and data that did not originate from your own fieldwork. Other PhDs may rely essentially on experiment or primary research, and yet others may be theoretically based, focusing on an extensive literature-based analysis, or it may be designed using a mixed-methods approach. There are many different approaches a study in the social sciences can take.

Evaluation research

This type of study, commonly used in social work, education, social policy and health care, is designed specifically to evaluate or assess the impact of an intervention. A range of methods may be used that require both descriptive data and data that identify outcomes.

Action research

Often used in education, health or social work settings, action research is based on action, critical analysis or evaluation study that is aimed at bringing about an improvement in a practice or service. As the term implies, action research is concerned with the action that results from the research process and the impact of conducting the research. This type of study is often initiated as a collaborative arrangement between the researcher and the organisation in which the research is being conducted. It places the researcher as an insider, rather than the traditional 'outsider' position. This allows the researcher and members of an organisation to work together to solve an organisational problem. Designed either as participatory action research involving sharing planning and data collection and negotiating the nature and significance of that data or as engaging in action from the research or as a means to exploring professional practice, action research can be based on quantitative or qualitative data or a mixture of both. It has been suggested that action research has four main cycles – planning, acting, observing and reflecting (Business Research Methodology, 2020). These are with regards to initiating change in an organisation, implementing the change and observing and reflecting on the process and consequences of change.

Case study research

Case study research places a great deal of emphasis on representing an accurate picture of the individual case and does not seek to propose generalisable results. Not commonly used as the main research design focus in a PhD, it can, however, provide essential information to support your study or test a hypothesis. As this type of study could provide supplementary data in PhD research, it can be used as part of a combined approach to data collection.

Ethnographic research

Ethnography is a mostly qualitative research design that is often aimed at exploring cultural phenomena. It is a systematic study of individual culture from the perspectives of members of that culture. Ethnographic research tends to see the world from the eyes of the participants. It is a type of study that is generally participatory in nature. Unlike any other form of study, ethnographic research is culturally sensitive. Ethnographic studies use a wide range of methods including observation, interviews, documentary analysis and analysis of visual and other media. An ethnographic study is mostly conducted in a participant's natural setting or environment. It mostly employs the interpretative analysis technique. Ethnographic approaches are used by researchers across a range of disciplines, including education, sociology and health.

Visual research

Visual research methods involve studies that are based essentially on the analysis of visual materials. Visual methods of conducting research are mostly used in sociology and anthropology. The research design is based on the idea that 'valid scientific insight in society can be acquired by observing, analysing, and theorizing its visual manifestations' (Pauwels, 2011). Through a range of methods such as discourse analysis, compositional interpretation, content analysis, semiology, audience studies, psychoanalysis, visual research methods are designed primarily to explore, contextualise and analyse visual materials. Visual research is essentially a way of interpreting and making meanings from images. This involves recognising visual images as embedded in the social world. These visual images have meanings or can be understood only when that embedding is taken into account (Rose, 2016).

Experimental research

Experimental research is a scientific approach to research in which the researcher manipulates variables. It often involves the control of one or more independent variables and applied to one or more dependent variables in order to measure the effect of the independent variables on the dependent variable. The effect of the independent variables on the dependent variables is usually observed and recorded over some time. Mostly used in the physical sciences, experimental and quasi-experimental research is also used in the social sciences, especially in psychology.

Policy research

Policy analysis research design tends to focus on evidence-based approaches to policy and review. It is a type of research that seeks to understand how and why governments initiate and push through certain policies and the effects of such policies (Browne et al., 2018). The growing connection between social lives, political objectives and policy formation at the local to national levels provides opportunities for researchers to undertake policy analysis research. Policy analysis has been greatly enhanced by the availability of a vast volume of secondary data and material published by government departments, institutions and organisations and the freedom of information law that enables legal access to materials and information held by government agencies. Three main approaches to policy analysis have been suggested. These are (a) the traditional approach that seeks to determine an optimal policy solution through an objective analyses of possible solutions, (b) the mainstream approach that examines the role of policy actors in policymaking and (c) the interpretive approach which examines the framing and representation of problems and how policies reflect the social construction of 'problems' (Browne et al., 2018).

Cross-/interdisciplinary and mixed-methods research

There is a growing tendency within the social sciences to adopt a cross-disciplinary or interdisciplinary approach to research. This has led to the increasing popularity of a mixed-methods research approach that embraces methodological adaptation and development from other disciplines. You may need to decide if your study is more suitable for an interdisciplinary mixed-methods approach. This is particularly important given that a single approach may be limiting in terms of answering your research question, in which case, using the mixed-methods approach could improve the reliability and validity of your study.

Whichever research approach you consider appropriate for your study, it needs to have a strong theoretical and empirical underpinning.

Key messages

- Your methodology is one of the pillars on which to build your thesis. As an essential part of your thesis, your methodology can make or break your dream of getting a PhD.
- Research methodology requires careful thought, deep reflection and justification of your choice of methods.
- Understanding theoretical perspectives will help you design an appropriate methodology for your PhD.
- Given that no single methodology is perfect, you need to understand the limitations of your methodology and highlight this is in your thesis.
- The validity, appropriateness and reliability of your research methodology and your ability to justify your choice of methodology may form an important theme of discussion during your viva voce examination.
- In order to successfully undertake PhD research, you need to have a good understanding of and well-developed skills in theoretical and methodological issues relating to your study.

Further reading

Badewi, A. (2014). YouTube video – Ontology, epistemology and methodology. *Research Methodology Course (Self-Study) – Session 2* [Online]. Available at: https://youtu.be/kf8wGvunyG8. Accessed on 4th August 2020.

Bhattacherjee, A. (2012). *Social Science Research: Principles, Methods, and Practices*, 2nd ed. Tampa, FL: University of South Florida.

Browne, J., Coffey, B., et al. (2018). A guide to policy analysis as a research method. *Health Promotion International*, 1–13.

Business Research Methodology (BRM). (2020). *Action Research* [Online]. Available at: https://research-methodology.net/research-methods/action-research/. Accessed on 7th August 2020.

Creswell, J. W., and Poth, C. N. (2018). *Qualitative Inquiry and Research Design: Choosing Among Five Approaches*, 4th ed. London: Sage.

Dawson, D. C. (2019). *Introduction to Research Methods*, 4th ed. London: Little, Brown Book Group.

DeCarlo, M. (2018). Paradigms, theories, and how they shape a researcher's approach. *Open Social Work Education* [Online]. Available at: https://scientific inquiryinsocialwork.pressbooks.com/chapter/6-2-paradigms-theories-and-how-they-shape-a-researchers-approach/. Accessed on 4th August 2020.

Dupré, B. (2007). *50 Philosophy Ideas You Really Need to Know*. London: Quercus Editions Ltd.

Finn, J. A. (2005). *Getting a PhD: An Action Plan to Help Manage Your Research, Your Supervisor and Your Project*. London: Routledge.

Gerring, J., and Christenson, D. (2017). *Applied Social Science Methodology: An Introductory Guide*. Cambridge: Cambridge University Press.

Gobo, G., and Marciniak, L. (2016). What is ethnography? In David Silverman (ed.), *Qualitative Research*. London: Sage.

Kellstedt, P., and Whitten, G. (2018). *The Fundamentals of Political Science Research*. Cambridge: Cambridge University Press.

Lamont, C. (2015). *Research Methods in International Relations*. London: Sage Publications Ltd.

Lawson, A. (2020). Musings on ways of doing research (and socks). *Musings on Methodology: Thoughts, Ideas and Opinions on Research Methods* [Online]. Available at: https://musingsonmethodology.com/tag/methodology/. Accessed on 4th August 2020.

Neuman, W. (2013). *Social Research Methods: Qualitative and Quantitative Approaches*. London: Pearson Education.

Patel, S. (2015). The research paradigm – Methodology, epistemology and ontology – Explained in simple language [Online]. *Dr Salma Patel: Research, Digital, UX and a PhD*. Available at: http://salmapatel.co.uk/academia/the-research-paradigm-methodology-epistemology-and-ontology-explained-in-simple-language/. Accessed on 4th August 2020.

Pauwel, L. (2011). An integrated conceptual framework for visual social research. In Eric Margolis and Luc Pauwels (eds.), *The Sage Handbook of Visual research Methods*. London: Sage.

Ragin, C. (1994). *Constructing Social Research: The Unity and Diversity of Method* (pp. 31–54). Pine Forge, Thousand Oaks: North-western University [Online]. Available at: http://faculty.uncfsu.edu/hlheem/09-f-420-social%20research. htm. Accessed on 10th August 2020.

Rose, G. (2016). *Visual Methodologies: An Introduction to Researching with Visual Materials*. 4th ed. London: Sage.

Shoemaker, P. J., Tankard, J. W., and Lasorsa, D. L. (2004). *How to Build Social Science Theories*. London: Sage Publications.

USC Libraries. (2020). Research guides. *University of Southern California* [Online]. Available at: https://libguides.usc.edu/writingguide/theoreticalframework. Accessed on 10th August 2020.

CHAPTER 7

Understanding ethical issues and laws regarding PhD research and personal data

Introduction

This chapter draws attention to essential ethical issues in conducting research. It examines ethical and legal issues relating to the collection, storage, and use of personal data that are used for social research. The chapter discusses the new EU's General Data Protection Regulations (GDPR) about processing personal data belonging to EU citizens. Issues of consent, anonymity, and non-disclosure of personal data in research are explained with regards to what is legal and or ethical. The chapter invites you to think carefully about the ethical considerations of your PhD research and to comply with ethical guidelines. The chapter stresses the importance of being a responsible researcher and the need to avoid any breach of UK or EU data protection laws.

By the end of the chapter, you will have a better understanding of

- the importance of ethics in research,
- ethical principles and morals in PhD research,
- applying for and obtaining ethical approvals for your research,
- key ethical issues in research involving vulnerable people and
- essential information regarding GDPR and other legal issues regarding the collection, storage and use of personal data.

Ethics and morality in research

Ethics in research are the moral and legal principles that guide the design, conduct and dissemination of research in the social sciences. Research ethics define what are morally and or legally acceptable practices. They set out the role and responsibilities of a researcher. Your research participants have legal rights that must be respected. A code of research ethics provides an agreed-on standard of activity for researchers, which is designed to protect participants' moral and legal rights at every stage of the research. Ethics codes of research seek to promote quality in research by ensuring they are conducted in an ethical way so as to gain public trust. They also ensure that research activities do not negatively impact participants and society in general. Also, by demanding researchers conform to codes of research, ethics help protect against harmful, poor or dishonest research practice and provide safeguards against misrepresentation or abuse of research data and results.

Examples of unethical research

Cases of unethical research are very well documented. Notable examples and reviews on this are the following:

- Exposing Unethical Human Research: The Transatlantic Correspondence of Beecher and Pappworth. Annals of Internal Medicine https://doi.org/10.7326/0003-4819-156-2-201201170-00012
- 20 Most Unethical Experiments in Psychology www.onlinepsychology degree.info/unethical-experiements-psychology/
- Research Unethical www.encyclopedia.com/science/encyclopedias-almanacs-transcripts-and-maps/research-unethical

Historical and contemporary unethical research has led to the development of ethics codes, protocols, guidelines and laws that all researchers are now expected to or required to comply with. Ethics codes vary across the world and different universities and organisations have varying sets of rules governing research. Different disciplines also have standards of ethics to which research in those disciplines or subjects must comply. Ethics guidelines are very well developed within medical research compared to any other areas of study. Hence, contemporary research ethics have developed mostly from medical research. In the social sciences, there are diversities with regards to subjects and focus of research. That means ethical issues and complexities associated with social science research vary from those in the medical sciences. Nevertheless, most ethics codes have general principles that are now applicable regardless of the subject of study.

Ethics codes and regulatory guidelines

Historically, decisions on research ethics have been made by individual researchers. In the last two decades, however, there has been an increasing emphasis on ethics with self-regulation being replaced with institutional, organisational and professional regulations. Also, ethics is no longer an internal matter within a university or research institute. It has become a national, international and societal issue to uphold ethics standards in scientific studies. Hence, most ethics codes now have international applicability. While the research environment and level of research activities may differ from one country to another, the fundamental principles of upholding ethical values in research have become a universal concern.

Ethical principles for medical research involving human subjects: the Helsinki Declaration

The first attempt at developing an International ethics standard was made by the World Medical Association (WDA, 2020). Known as the Helsinki Declaration, the first version was adopted in 1964 in Helsinki. The declaration sets out an international ethics standard for good practice, especially in medical research. Amongst other things, the declaration identified four main principles to which all medical research must comply:

- beneficence – research should be conducted with the aim of doing 'positive good'.
- non-malfeasance – research should not be conducted to deliberately do harm to participants, individuals or society. This is a 'do no harm' principle.
- informed consent – all research should be conducted with informed consent with no coercion, entrapment or intimidation.
- confidentiality/anonymity – research participants are entitled to their anonymity and confidentiality.

Ethics framework of Economic and Social Research Council (ESRC)

In 2006, the ESRC launched a Research Ethics Framework to which all research it funds must comply. According to this framework, all research must meet the following six criteria:

- All research should be designed, reviewed and undertaken to ensure integrity and quality.
- Everyone connected with a research study, including research staff and subjects, must be informed fully about the purpose, methods and intended possible uses of the research; what their participation in the research entails; and what risks, if any, are involved.
- The confidentiality of the information supplied by research subjects and the anonymity of respondents must be respected.
- Participation in any research study must be voluntary and free from any coercion.
- Any harm to research participants must be avoided.
- The independence of research must be clear, and any conflicts of interest or partiality must be explicit.

The EU and the GDPR

If you are a PhD student doing research in a UK university, the two main ethics guidelines you need to follow are the GDPR and the UK Data Protection Act (DPA; 2018). Both the GDPR and the UK DPA legislation apply to all research projects that process personal data and inform on how personal data and the privacy of participants should be managed. The GDPR outlines the rules and regulations governing the processing (holding or using) of personal data in the UK and across the European Union (EU, 2016, 2018).

Under the GDPR, personal data is defined as

> any information relating to an identified or identifiable natural person ('data subject'); an identifiable natural person is one who can be identified, directly or indirectly, in particular by reference to an identifier such as a name, an identification number, location data, an online identifier or to one or more factors specific to the physical, physiological, genetic, mental, economic, cultural or social identity of that natural person.
>
> (Regulation (EU) 2016/679, Chapter 1, Article 4)

Within the GDPR framework, there are special categories of data that are considered more sensitive and therefore require greater protection. These include data relating to a person's race, ethnic origin, sex life, sexual orientation, health, genetics, religion, trade union membership and politics, amongst others. The main focus of GDPR is to protect these and other data or information which can be used to identify people or participants in a research study, especially if those people or participants are still alive. If your research involves the collection of data that are entirely anonymised, then GDPR may not apply. However, under the GDPR you still have the responsibility to keep your research data safe. If you are dealing with any identifiable information and there is any data safety breach, your data subjects need to be informed and the breach needs to be reported.

The UK and the DPA 2018

The DPA 2018, which went into effect on 25 May 2018, sets out the guidelines for data protection law in the UK. It replaces and updates the DPA of 1998. It spells out how the GDPR should be applied in the UK. The new regulation provides the framework for good practice in research and demands that information and data collected and processed for research should be lawful, fair and transparent.

To ensure compliance with this regulation, the Information Commissioners Office (ICO) was set up as an independent regulatory office. The ICO is the UK's independent authority set up primarily to uphold information rights in the public interest, promote openness by public bodies and enforce data privacy for individuals (Information Commissioner's Office, 2020). As an independent authority, the ICO has the power to carry out investigations into any breach of data protection laws and can issue fines as well as provide advisory service to organisations on how to comply with the GDPR. Essentially, the ICO promotes a culture of openness by public institutions and ensures adherence to data protection and privacy regulations in the UK.

Professional bodies and ethics guidelines

In addition to national and international ethics guidelines, many professional bodies and institutions such as the British Sociological Association, the American Sociological Association, the American Anthropological Association, the British Psychological Society, the UK National Health Service, the National Probation Service and others have developed their own bespoke ethics codes. If your PhD research relates to any of these professional bodies, you may need to ensure that you comply with their professional/institutional ethics codes. Each university also has its own ethics requirements and ethics approval process that you may need to follow before you commence your data collection.

Ethics and online research

Social media such as Twitter, Facebook, Google, and other social network sites (SNSs) provide an important source of data and information for research. Researchers from many disciplines such as politics, sociology, anthropology, business management, accounting, marketing and computer science, to name a few, are increasingly using these digital platforms to collect essential data. Alongside the growing use of SNSs and online platforms for research is the potential ethical concerns that come with these sites, as they often contain sensitive data (Henderson et al., 2012).

Amongst the key ethical issues and questions relating to the use of SNSs are the following:

- Do academic researchers need to take more care on using social media data?
- To what extent are SNS providers responsible for the ethical use of information and data on their platforms?
- When it comes to research using underage children's or adolescents' data on SNSs, is informed consent required? If so, how is that to be obtained?
- Is it right and ethical for a researcher to just take and use people's data that are shared on social media?

- What responsibility does a researcher have to protect data collected from SNSs that have already been publicly shared?
- Given that there are complex connections between SNSs users and their friends, families and people from their social networks, how can these people be protected even when a user agreed to or gave their consent to take part in a research study?

These and many other ethical concerns have led to the development of special online codes of ethics to ensure online research meets ethical standards. An example is the online research ethics codes developed by the Association of Internet Researchers (AOIR; see Franzke et al., 2020).

An overview of ethics considerations in your PhD research

From the foregoing, it is apparent that complying with formal ethical guidelines is an essential requirement in your PhD research. Those requirements could be those stated by your university or faculty and/or any other organisations or institutions connected with your research. Differences may exist between universities in relation to specific ethics requirements; however, all universities in the UK require their PhD students to comply with the EU's GDPR with regards to processing personal data belonging to EU citizens.

Regardless of where you are doing your PhD research, it is vitally important that you pay attention to issues of morality and ethics. Most universities will not allow you to commence your PhD research until you obtain formal ethics approval and you demonstrate that you know about and understand important ethical issues and laws relating to data protection and security (Figure 7.1).

Figure 7.1 Ethical issues relating to PhD research

Your behaviour, attitudes and approach to data collection and how you use the data or information generated through your research need to be ethically compliant. The conduct of your research also needs to meet an acceptable moral standard. Ethical and legal issues that you need to consider are not limited to the collection, storage and use of personal data that are used in your research but also include how you use other people's work and your relationship with other researchers. To give full consideration to ethics, moral and legal issues relating to your PhD research, there are 12 key questions you need to answer.

1 How do my PhD research aim and objective correlate with the notion of 'common good'?

A PhD involves different types of research, and there are as many different reasons why PhD research is initiated as there are PhD students. Whatever the purpose or aim of your study, there is a general expectation that advancement in knowledge through your PhD research should have societal benefits. In other words, there should be a positive purpose for your study. You should consider if the conduct of your research has or will lead to any positive outcome for the common good. The notion of 'common good' suggests that your research should not be conducted to cause physical or social harm to any individuals, groups or society at large.

Your PhD research should be risk-assessed to ensure that the risks involved are tolerable and do not outweigh its benefit. Doing a PhD should not put you or anyone in any danger, and no one should have to suffer as a direct result of your PhD research. Any risks involved in conducting your study must be outweighed by the social, economic, political or educational benefits of your study.

2 Have I applied for and obtained formal ethical approval to conduct my PhD research from my university and other relevant authorities or professional bodies?

Applying for and obtaining formal ethics approval for your PhD is an important step before you commence your research. Approval may be obtained from your university's ethics committee or other external regulatory agencies or professional bodies before you embark on your data collection. You may require ethics approval for different aspects of your study. It is necessary to seek advice from your supervisors, the faculty or the ethics committee of your university or external organisations or agencies that may be connected with your study.

The ethical approval required will depend largely on the nature of your study and the type and level of human participation involved. It will also depend on your university's ethics guidelines and the regulations of any external funding bodies or professional organisations. To obtain ethical approval, most universities will require that you submit your research plans and the data collection instruments you intend to use for your study. This may include the full proposal, sample copies of questionnaires or interview schedules and the consent forms or information sheets that you designed for your study participants.

Under the National Research Council (NRC) ethics guidelines, if you are conducting research involving prison staff and/or offenders in prison establishments, National Probation Service (NPS) or Community Rehabilitation Companies (CRC) or within Her Majesty's Prison and Probation Service (HMPPS), you will need to formally apply for research approval from the HMPPS NRC. If your research involves children or people in social care, you will also need approval from health and social care bodies, through the Integrated Research Application System (IRAS).

The IRAS is a unified system for applying for permissions and approvals for all research relating to health and social/community care in the UK. It is a single online digital platform that covers applications for permission and approval to undertake research relating to NHS (health and social care focused study) and HMPSS (crime-related study). If any aspect of your study relates to NHS, prisons and probation service (HMPPS), you will need to use IRAS and obtain approval and permission before you commence your study.

For more information on IRAS, see https://www.myresearchproject.org. uk/. Information on how to submit application for HMPPS-related research is available at https://www.myresearchproject.org.uk/help/hlphmpps.aspx and https://www.gov.uk/government/organisations/her-majestys-prison-and-probation-service/about/research.

If your PhD research requires access to National Health Service (NHS) patients, you will require an NHS Research Ethics Committee (REC) approval. The NHS has a set of criteria that will help you decide whether your research needs its ethics approval. NHS special ethics approval is needed if your study falls into any of the following categories:

- Research on patients and users of the NHS
- Research on relatives or carers of patients and users of the NHS
- Study where access to data, organs or other bodily material of past and present NHS patients are required
- Study of foetal material and in vitro fertilisation involving NHS patients
- Any study relating to the recently dead in NHS premises
- Study requiring the use of, or potential access to, NHS premises or facilities
- Research involving NHS staff recruited as research participants by virtue of their professional role

For more information on NHS Research Committee and how to apply, visit the website at www.hra-decisiontools.org.uk/ethics/. You can also find further information at https://www.hra.nhs.uk/approvals-amendments/what-approvals-do-i-need/research-ethics-committee-review/applying-research-ethics-committee/.

3 Do I have a lawful basis for collecting and processing personal data in my PhD research?

Under the GDPR and the DPA, you will need to have a legitimate reason or a valid lawful basis to process personal data. You are obliged to have an additional legal basis to process any 'Special Category' personal data, such as personal health information and criminal conviction data. The basis for using personal data in your study will depend on the purpose of your research and your relationship with the data subject. Article 6 of the GDPR outlines six lawful bases for collecting and processing personal data (Regulation (EU) 2016/679, Chapter 1, Article 6). These are consent, contract, legal obligation, vital interest, public task and legitimate interests (see Figure 7.2).

The legal basis required to justify your collection of personal data will depend on the kind of personal data your PhD research study is designed to collect, the purpose of the project and how you intend to use and store the data. Whichever data you have a legitimate or legal right to obtain, it is still essential that you don't over-collect data. Collecting data that you don't really need, or superfluous collection of random data, is considered unethical under the GDPR guidelines. So your data collection must be purposeful and limited to what is really necessary.

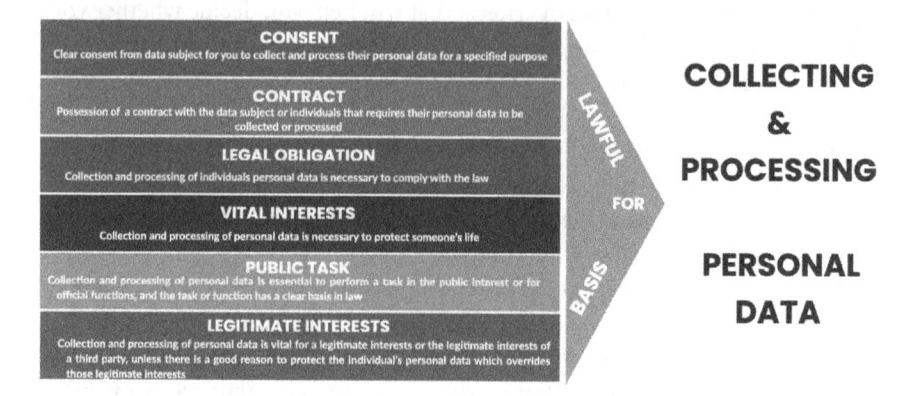

Figure 7.2 Legal basis for collecting and processing personal data

4 Have all my research participants been informed of the purpose of my study, how the data I collected will be used and my research dissemination strategy?

Your research participants need to know the purpose of your research and why they are being asked to participate in your study or provide you with data or information. They also have the rights to know how the information you collect will be processed or used. Once that is made clear to them, under no circumstances should you then use the data collected for purposes other than those stated in the research that your participants consented to. It is your responsibility to ensure that all your participants fully understand the nature of the research and expressly agree to take part without any force, coercion or manipulation.

5 Have I sought and obtained informed consent from all participants?

Ethical compliance requires that valid informed consent is obtained before any human participant is involved in your data collection. For informed consent to be meaningful, you need to have given research participants the right information to enable them to make an informed judgement or decision about whether to take part in your study. This requires that you disclose and provide, in an open and transparent way, all the information they need to make a decision. They need to be given all the facts relating to what their participation or non-participation may mean for them. If they are unable to make that decision themselves, due to their age or disability incapacity, then their carers, support workers, parents or guardian may need to be involved in the process.

None of your research participants should feel pressured or obliged to take part in your study or provide you with information. Ethical guidelines require that participants are made aware that they can refuse to answer any of your questions. It also requires that you avoid unjustifiable discrimination. Necessary and reasonable steps are taken to identify and remove any real or perceived barriers to people's participation in your study if they want to take part. Consent is usually obtained by asking your research participants to fill in a formal consent form after they have been given all the information about your study.

6 Have I taken all necessary steps to protect the rights and dignity of my research participants?

If your PhD research involves or requires contact with human subjects, it will most certainly raise some ethical questions that you will need to address.

The treatment of your participants needs to meet ethical standards. All your participants should be treated fairly and with dignity. You should avoid causing unnecessary emotional, physical or mental suffering to your participants or subjects in the course of collecting, processing your data or disseminating your research findings. You should consider the efficacy of the different data collection methods and choose the one that is most likely to not raise or have any ethical implications. You will need to ensure that your research doesn't cause personal discomfort or embarrassment to your participants. Participants' formal consent to participate in your research must be obtained and retained throughout the duration of your study. Your research participants reserve the rights to withdraw or refuse to participate in the research at any stage of your study, and those rights must be respected.

By taking part in your study, your participants should not suffer any financial loss or damage to their reputation or self-esteem. Similarly, for ethical reasons, your participants should not gain undue financial benefits as a result of their participation or non-participation in your study. While it may be necessary, in exceptional cases, to pay some participants, financial gains should not be the overriding motive for people to take part in your study.

The protection of your participants also applies if you are undertaking observational research. Observational research includes studies that require observing people or phenomenon with or without them being aware that they are being watched or observed. Usually, most observational studies take place in public spaces where people can normally expect to be observed by strangers. Others may raise an ethical issue of an invasion of privacy. Outside of the public space, any observational study involving people needs to be done only when the participants give their consent to being observed. All observational studies need to respect the privacy and dignity of the people being observed.

From an ethics perspective, you have a duty of care towards your research participants. If your study is likely to cause any emotional stress or discomfort, you need to put in place the necessary support plan for your participants. This may include providing them with contact details of helplines or counselling services or health care agencies that they may want to contact if they need support.

7 Have I taken extra measures required to safeguard vulnerable participants?

If your PhD research involves vulnerable people such as elderly people, young children, people with mental health issues, young offenders, people with learning difficulties and those under medication or receiving treatment for personality or psychological disorder, you are required to take extra safeguarding measures to protect them. It is your responsibility also to ensure that all vulnerable participants understand the purpose, scope and nature of your study and how the information they provide will be used before you involve them in your study. In some cases, you may be required to undertake criminal record check knowns as Disclosure and Barring Service before you can have unsupervised access or contact with some vulnerable research participants.

If your research deals with emotionally sensitive and distressing issues such as rape, domestic abuse, trauma and suicide, amongst others, you must ensure that you let your participants know of any support available to them and how to access the support, should they need it at any stage of their involvement with your study. If any of your participants become distressed during your interaction with them, it is essential to pause and ask them if they want to continue their participation in your study.

8 Have I given all my research participants the opportunity to withdraw from my study if they so wish at any stage?

Research should be designed in a way that all participants can exercise their rights to withdraw from the study at any stage. The rights of all participants to withdraw from the study at any stage not only must be respected but also should be explained to them before you collect their data. All your research participants should be made aware that they can change their mind at any point during your research if they so wish. All your research participants also need to know that they reserve the rights to withdraw from your study or refuse to ask any question asked of them. Your participants may also ask that their data be removed or expunged from your database after collecting their data. None of your participants should be compromised or disadvantaged in any way as a result of choosing to exercise their rights to withdraw.

It is good practice that you provide your contact details so that your participants can contact you at any stage to exercise their rights to withdraw. You may, however, wish to set a period or duration within which the right to withdraw may be exercised by your participants.

9 Have I anonymised or pseudonymised my data to protect the identity, privacy and confidentiality of my participants?

Anonymising or pseudonymnising your data will help protect the confidentiality of your research participants and reduce most ethical concerns. Anonymisation of data involves the processing of personal data by masking the identity of the data subject. Generally, personal data that are anonymysed are out of the scope of the GDPR. Pseudonymisation of data involves the processing of personal data in a way as to make the data unattributable to any participant without the use of extra or additional information. To enhance the non-attributive value of a pseudonymised personal data, the additional information required to make any connection or link with participants should be kept separate and away from the original data set. Whichever method is used, protecting the confidentiality and integrity of personal data provided by your participants is of paramount importance in your PhD research.

While the confidentiality of personal information collected needs to be protected, there are exceptional cases when you may be legally required to disclose information to the relevant authorities. If there is any likelihood of that occurring, your participants need to be made aware of your legal duty to disclose such information, if legally required. So having the foreknowledge that you may be legally required to handover or disclose personal information collected for your PhD requires that your participants are made aware of this possibility before collecting their data.

10 Have I taken all necessary steps to ensure the personal data I collected are accurate and are being stored securely?

All personal data collected from your research participants that are not yet anonymised must be treated with care and stored securely. Your research data files, containing any personal information, should be kept safe, and when you finish with them, they must be disposed of carefully. Under the DPA 2018 and the GDPR, it is an offence to hold incorrect personal data. So all personal data held or processed for your PhD should be correct and accurate. If you hold any incorrect data, you should, at the earliest possible time, attempt to correct them.

Also, the data must be appropriate for your study. As the data controller and or data processor, you are responsible for ensuring that the collection, processing and storage of personal data meet the GDPR ethics standards and guidelines (see Figure 7.3). The GDPR ethics guidelines also require that you do not store or retain personal data longer than necessary.

11 As a responsible researcher, am I satisfied that I have complied with the GDPR and all relevant laws and regulations relating to conducting my PhD research?

In terms of who is responsible for ethical compliance, the GDPR makes a distinction between the data controller and the data processor (Figure 7.3).

A data **'controller'** is anyone who makes a decision as to the type of personal data to collect, the means and purpose of collecting and processing them and the storage or retention of data. A data **'processor'** is anyone who is involved in or helping with the processing of personal data. This can be done by the data originator or by a third party on behalf of the originator. Data

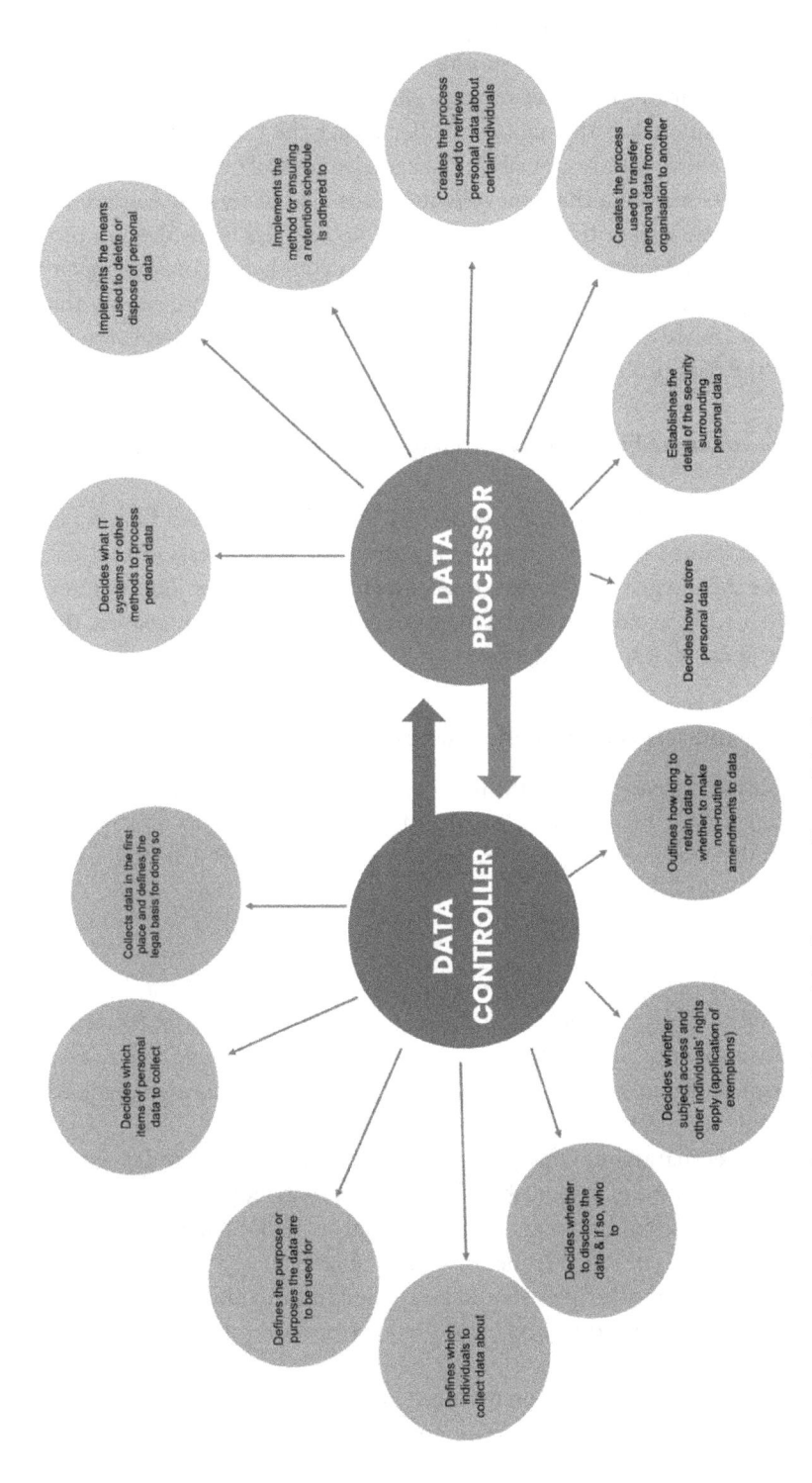

Figure 7.3 GDPR – roles and responsibilities of the data controller and the data processor

processing may involve data handling, statistical or qualitative analysis, data synthesis, storage, retention or disposal.

As the initiator or originator of your PhD independent research, you are effectively considered as the data controller under the GDPR ethics regulation. It is, therefore, your responsibility to exercise control over the processing and use of personal data that you collected. It is also likely that you are the data processor as well as the data controller if no one else is involved in processing your data. However, if anyone is acting on your behalf, in any capacity relating to your data collection and processing, it is your responsibility that they are also aware of the GDPR regulations as you will still be liable for any breach of the data protection regulations.

12 Have I conducted my PhD research in an open and honest way?

Your research should be beyond reproach. It must be conducted in an open and honest way as to avoid any ethical, moral or legal question that can undermine the integrity of your study. As much as possible, conflicts of interest should also be avoided in your PhD research. Where, for any reason, this cannot be avoided, it must be declared.

Protecting and respecting intellectual property rights

Besides ethical consideration outlined earlier, you need to understand the intellectual property rights and copyright policies relating to any written work and the use of other people's work in your study (see Chapter 11 on Writing Up Your Thesis).

Key messages

- You need to apply for and obtain formal ethics approval from the ethics committee of your university and or from other external regulatory agencies or professional bodies connected with your study before you embark on your data collection.
- It is absolutely paramount that your PhD is ethically compliant and meets the standards expected of responsible research that contributes to knowledge.
- Your research should not cause any personal or social harm to yourself, your participants or any member of society at large.
- Ethical and moral principles should be applied in the conduct of your PhD research, and you need to understand your responsibilities towards your research participants.
- Extra safeguarding arrangements need to be put in place if your PhD research involves vulnerable participants.

- Your approach to data collection and how you process and use the data or information generated through your research need to be informed by appropriate ethics guidelines and regulations.
- Ethics should not be treated as an afterthought or an add-on to your research. It ought to and should constitute an integral part of your research design and a key element of your overall research strategy.
- It is essential that you acknowledge and respect the intellectual property rights of authors of materials used in your study.

Further reading

Alderson, P., and Marrow, V. (2011). *The Ethics of Research with Children and Young People: A Practical Handbook*. London: Sage.

European Union. (2016). *Regulation (EU) 2016/679 of the European Parliament and of the Council of 27 April 2016 on the Protection of Natural Persons with Regard to the Processing of Personal Data and on the Free Movement of Such Data and Repealing Directive 95/46/EC*. General Data Protection Regulation.

European Union. (2018). *General Data Protection Regulation*. Available at: https://gdpr-info.eu/. Accessed on 19th August 2020.

Franzke, A. S., Bechmann, A., Zimmer, M., Ess, C. M., and the Association of Internet Researchers. (2020). *Internet Research: Ethical Guidelines 3.0*. Available at: https://aoir.org/reports/e

Gaw, A. (2020). Exposing unethical human research: The transatlantic correspondence of Beecher and Pappworth. *Annals of Internal Medicine* [Online]. Available at: https://doi.org/10.7326/0003-4819-156-2-201201170-00012. Accessed on 18th August 2020.

Hausman, D., McPherson, M., and Satz, D. (2016). Appendix: How could ethics matter to economics? In *Economic Analysis, Moral Philosophy, and Public Policy* (pp. 337–352). Cambridge: Cambridge University Press.

Henderson, T., Hutton, L., and McNeilly, S. (2012). Ethics and online social network research – Developing best practices. *Proceedings of BCS HCI 2012 Workshops HCI Research in Sensitive Contexts: Ethical Considerations* [Online]. Available at: www.scienceopen.com/hosted-document?doi=10.14236/ewic/HCI2012.74. Accessed on 19th August 2020.

Information Commissioner's Office (ICO): Blog: Data Protection and Brexit – ICO Advice for Organisations [Online]. Available at: https://ico.org.uk/about-the-ico/news-and-events/news-and-blogs/2018/12/data-protection-and-brexit-ico-advice-for-organisations/. Accessed on 16th August 2020.

Information Commissioner's Office (ICO): Consent at a Glance [Online]. Available at: https://ico.org.uk/for-organisations/guide-to-data-protection/guide-to-the-general-data-protection-regulation-gdpr/lawful-basis-for-processing/consent/. Accessed on 16th August 2020.

Information Commissioner's Office. (2020). *Guide to Data Protection* [Online]. Available at: https://ico.org.uk/for-organisations/guide-to-data-protection/. Accessed on 19th August 2020.

Israel, M. (2015). *Research Ethics and Integrity for Social Scientists: Beyond Regulatory Compliance*, (2nd ed). London: Sage.

Jegede, F., et al. (2020). *Writing Successful Undergraduate Dissertations in Social Sciences: A Student's Handbook*, 2nd ed. Chapter 8. London: Routledge.

Kara, H. (2018). *Research Ethics in the Real World*. Bristol: Policy Press.

Moreno, M. A., Fost, N. C., and Christakis, D. A. (2008). Research ethics in the MySpace era. *Pediatrics*, 121, pp. 157–161.

Neuhaus, F., and Webmoor, T. (2012). Agile ethics for massified research and visualization. *Information, Communication & Society*, 15, pp. 43–65.

NHS. (2018). GDPR – Guidance for researchers. Health Research Authority. *National Health Services (NHS)* [Online]. Available at: www.hra.nhs.uk/about-us/news-updates/gdpr-guidance-researchers/. Accessed on 16th August 2020.

NHS. (2018). Using confidential patient information without consent. *National Health Services (NHS)* [Online]. Available at: www.hra.nhs.uk/planning-and-improving-research/policies-standards-legislation/data-protection-and-information-governance/gdpr-guidance/gdpr-and-use-confidential-patient-information-without-consent/. Accessed on 16th August 2020.

Traer, R. (2008). *Doing Ethics in A Diverse World*. Abingdon, Oxon, UK: Routledge, Taylor & Francis. Available at: VitalSource Bookshelf.

UK Government. (2018). *Data Protection Act 2018*. Available at: www.gov.uk/data-protection. Accessed on 19th August 2020.

UKRI. (2018). *GDPR and Research: An Overview for Researchers*. Available at: www.ukri.org/files/about/policy/ukri-gdpr-faqs-pdf/. Accessed on 16th August 2020.

World Medical Association (WDA). (2020). World Medical Association declaration of Helsinki ethical principles for medical research involving Human subjects. *Special Communication* [Online]. Available at: www.wma.net/wp-content/uploads/2016/11/DoH-Oct2013-JAMA.pdf. Accessed on 18th August 2020.

Zimmer, M. (2010). "But the data is already public": On the ethics of research in Facebook. *Ethics and Information Technology*, 12, pp. 313–325.

CHAPTER 8

Owning and driving your own PhD research

Introduction

This chapter provides essential information on how you can drive your own research forward through personal motivation and a general sense of ownership. It shows how you can map your own journey and channel your resources and energy to achieving your aims. Using examples, it highlights some personal attributes required to succeed as a researcher in a multi- or interdisciplinary area. It underlines the need for you to gather the necessary tools and training required to reflect on, synthesise, evaluate and document information to support the key arguments of your research.

By the end of this chapter, you will have a better understanding of

- the importance of time management, self-discipline, motivation and drive in PhD research,
- the need to map your own PhD research journey,
- getting the necessary tools and training required to work on a multidisciplinary research project and
- how to navigate through your PhD journey while staying focused on your research questions.

Take ownership of your PhD

With all the support you may get from your supervisors, faculty, friends, families and others, you may still not succeed in your PhD if you don't own and drive your PhD to success yourself. Your supervisors and all the support networks discussed in Chapter 4 are there to support and guide you through your study. However, the real driving force for your success has to be you. After all, it's your own PhD. You should take pride in working for it and owning it. Unlike an honorary award, getting a PhD through research and making an original contribution to knowledge requires a great deal of hard work. By the time you come to the end of your doctoral study, you should be one of the leading experts, if not the leading expert in the world, on your topic or field of investigation. This can only be achieved with a great sense of responsibility and dedication. As you approach the end of your first year, if you are a full-time student, or your second year if you are a part-time student, the enormity of the tasks involved in doing a PhD may become clearer to you, hence the need for you to buckle down, arm yourself with the necessary tools and focus on the work to be done. Being a doctoral student means a commitment to conduct independent research in an original work and embracing all the challenges this may entail.

Set goals, get organised and map your own research journey

It is essential that you set yourself achievable goals and map your research journey (see Figure 8.1). Progress monitoring is essential to ensure you are meeting all the necessary milestones. To succeed in a PhD, you will need to have self-discipline and possess a great sense of motivation. You don't do a PhD because somebody said you have to do it. You do a PhD because you really want to do it and you understand the intrinsic value of doing it for you and by you. So, you need to get organised and plan for the rigorous tasks you need to undertake to achieve your goal. Not only do you need to know the complexity of the work you need to do but also the processes that you need to go through in order to get your PhD. You need to know about your university's regulatory framework for PhD, your role and responsibility as a PGR student and any extra tasks you may need to carry out as part of your studentship or scholarship. All these require some self-organisation. By setting yourself specific goals and organising yourself to meeting those goals would give you an opportunity to monitor your own progress at every stage of

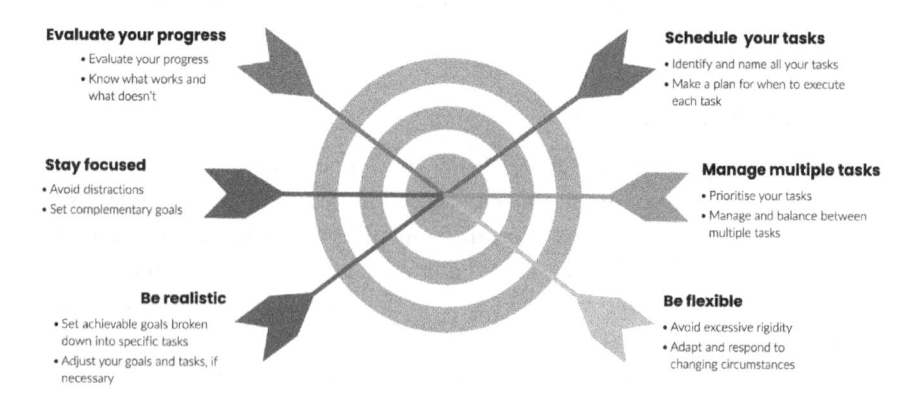

Figure 8.1 Setting an effective goal for your PhD

your doctoral journey. Creating an effective Gantt chart could help you plan your key activities and show the timeline for your key milestones.

You need to know where you are at in every stage of your PhD journey and understand what you need to do to get to where you need to be. It is always helpful to have a well-defined work schedule so that you know when you are most productive and which tasks to do at what time to maximise your efficiency and productivity. Understanding your work schedule will also help you work towards your target thesis submission date. If for any reasons, you're falling behind, you will know why you are behind your schedule and what you need to do to catch up with the outstanding tasks. Success in a PhD requires a great deal of planning. Plan for your own success.

Factors influencing the completion of a PhD

It is one thing to start a PhD, but it is another thing entirely to see it through to completion. While almost everyone who starts a PhD would like to complete it, not everyone who embarks on a PhD journey gets to reach the destination or achieves that completion target. Doctoral studies completion rates have always been a subject of interest not only to prospective PhD students but also to universities and research-funding organisations and agencies. Apart from yourself, there are other stakeholders who have an interest in the completion of your PhD. It is in the interest of all universities that their PhD students successfully complete their doctoral study in a good time. Yet PhD completion rates vary across subjects and between universities, and many students who did complete it did so with more time than originally anticipated. While it is sometimes difficult to unpick and fully understand and explain the complex reasons why many who started a PhD never complete, it is important to note that there are certain factors that could enhance your success and timely completion of a doctoral programme.

It has been suggested that PhD students' innate behaviours and attitudes towards their studies, the quality and level of supervisory support they received and the project management and writing approach adopted have significant effects on their completion (Lindsay, 2015). Other studies have identified the quality of doctoral training program received, the type and structure of the program and the research environment of the university as the key factors in determining completion or dropout rates amongst PhD students (Kyvik and Olsen, 2014).

It could be argued, that the chances of successfully completing a PhD programme and the time it takes for the completion will depend on a multitude of factors. Some of these are personal – for example age, gender, motivational, work ethics, aptitude, experience and the like. Others are institutional – relating to the faculty or the university's research environment, training opportunities, supervisory support and so on, while others may be external factors such as general life pressure, health issues, access to funding or scholarships, social and economic support network and domestic/living arrangements, amongst many others. While it may be difficult to control all the factors that may have an impact on your doctoral studies, you have absolute control over others.

For example, you have much control over your own motivation, commitment and personal dedication to your PhD study. It is, therefore, in your own interest to do all you can in order to succeed in your PhD. By setting your mind on completion and putting the work in to get your PhD finished in good time, you'll increase your chances of success. If you are self-funding or your studentship is time-limited, you may have extra pressure or 'incentive' to get your PhD completed in good time. As most scholarships or sponsorships are time-limited, it is essential that you complete your PhD before your funding sources run out. Most universities also have a maximum registration period beyond which your PhD study is due to expire. The maximum registration for a full-time student is usually set at 8 years.

Give your PhD your dedication and commitment

Success in a PhD requires dedication and commitment. Possessing or developing personal attributes such as self-drive, self-belief, adaptability and agility, coupled with a conscientious attitude towards work, will greatly enhance your chances of success in your PhD. For the 3 to 4 years of your PhD, you need to focus and show commitment, self-motivation and dedication to your research. The level of commitment you give to your PhD will be reflected in the effort you put into the research itself and how you conduct yourself throughout your doctoral programme. Availing yourself of training opportunities made available to you is a good way of showing your commitment. Also, the way you manage and navigate the relationship between you and your supervisors, how you respond and use feedback provided on your work and your general sense of engagement with your own research will all indicate the degree of your commitment.

The expectation is for you to complete your PhD within 3 to 4 years if you are studying full-time. This period includes the time required to submit and defend your thesis in a viva. So you need to have a sustained period of commitment, self-motivation and dedication if you were to complete within this period. You also need to give allowance for any unforeseen circumstances that may slow down your progress and factor that into your work plan. Most PhD students overrun their completion target. According to a study of PhD students' completion rates in 30 universities in the UK, 70% to 87% of full-time students completed in 7 years (Fuller, 2015). While this provides a general picture, it is important to note that completion rates vary across disciplines.

If you have studentships and you are required to do some teaching while doing your research, it is important that you do not let the teaching take over your time to the detriment of your PhD research. Getting the balance right among your research, your teaching engagements or your work commitments is key to making good and sustained progress with your PhD.

Evaluate your personal and professional skills and get trained

It is important that you undertake regular self-assessment of inter-personal and professional skills essential for success in your PhD. Through these regular assessments, you will know which skills you need to develop and which new skills you need to acquire. Doing a PhD is essentially about doing a research project. So you need basic knowledge in project management. It is also important that you get the necessary research training in order for you to succeed. Research training is particularly important in your first year to prepare you for the rest of your study. However, training and continuous professional development could be done at any stage of your doctoral programme. Your research training should be subject-specific and relevant to your own project. This will help you in acquiring the necessary tools you need to get through your study. Some of the key skills that could help you with your PhD include writing skills, presentations skills, analytical skills, logical argument and theoretical analytical skills, business analysis skills, organisational skills and many others.

Identifying your skills gaps and targeting your training to close those gaps will significantly enhance your chances of success in your PhD (Figure 8.2). By continuously developing essential skills together with other interpersonal and transferable skills as part of your professional development while doing your PhD, you will acquire the necessary tools to complete your doctoral study. Those tools will enable you to think critically, methodically and logically. Armed with the right tools, you will be able to challenge disciplinary boundaries, undertake effective critique and create new knowledge or ideas that could add value to existing knowledge.

Make the most of what your university offers

Doing your PhD at a university that has a good track record for PhD completions and an established research programme may significantly enhance your rate of success and completion of your PhD. The research funding model in the UK tends to use a block grant and cohort funding model in which some high-ranking universities attract more government funding than other less prestigious universities. Also, research culture, outputs and infrastructures are significantly different between universities in the UK. Russel

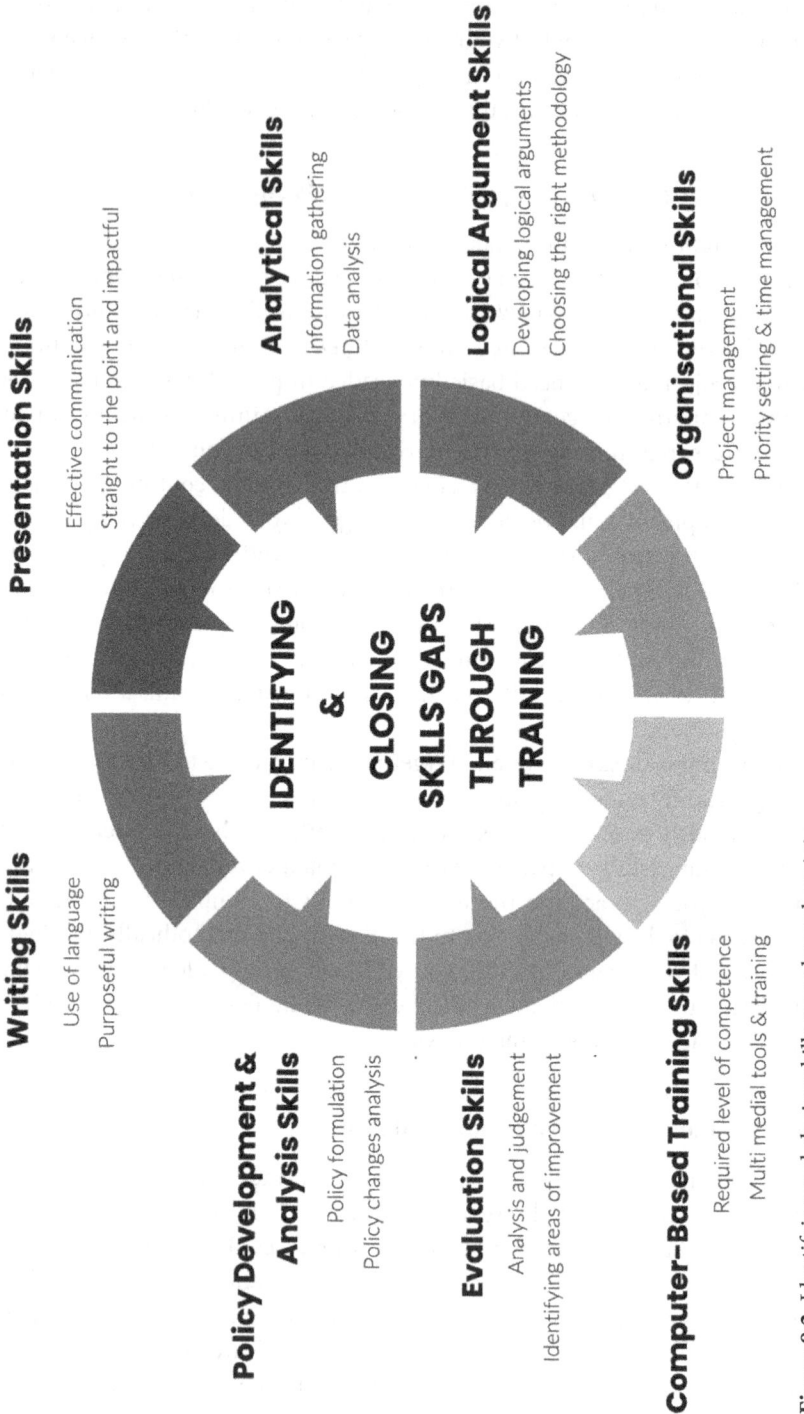

Figure 8.2 Identifying and closing skills gaps through training

Table 8.1 UK Russel Group universities

University of Birmingham	London School of Economics and Political Science
University of Bristol	University of Manchester
University of Cambridge	Newcastle University
Cardiff University	University of Nottingham
Durham University	University of Oxford
University of Edinburgh	Queen Mary University of London
University of Exeter	Queen's University Belfast
University of Glasgow	University of Sheffield
Imperial College London	University of Southampton
King's College London	University College London
University of Leeds	University of Warwick
University of Liverpool	University of York

Group universities comprising 24 world-class research-intensive universities (Table 8.1) produce two-thirds of the UK's world-leading research, with an annual economic output of more than £32 billion. The disproportionate influence of these universities in the UK research landscape could mean that students who do their PhD in these high-ranking universities have an undue advantage over students from non–Russel Group universities. While access to research infrastructure is not a sole determinant of completion rates, it is arguably, an important factor in creating a better experience for PhD students.

Nevertheless, you can work for and earn your PhD regardless of the university you are studying in. Not everyone will be able to attend or want to go to a Russel Group university. Indeed, for some people, these prestigious, high ranking university may not always be the most suitable for your research. Regardless of which university you are doing your doctoral study in, your personal motivation, self-discipline and dedication could make a difference between success and failure in your PhD study.

Develop your writing and communication skills

You need to develop your creative writing skills. Writing is a craft and art. The more you write, the better you will get at writing. Writing a thesis for a PhD requires some special skills. Understanding what you want to write about and how to write it is key to a good thesis (see Chapter 12). Developing your writing skills involves knowing what to say and how to say it. Some people have great things to say but fail to communicate them well in writing. Clarity should underpin whatever you write. Whether you are an experienced writer or new to academic writing, getting your message across to your reading audience in an effective way is critical. Through your writing, you can communicate your ideas to make them understood. Your style of writing will dictate how your message is interpreted or received by your audience. By its nature, academic writing is not only informative and factual; it could also be imaginative. By learning the skills of writing in an imaginative way, you can make your PhD study a great literary or calligraphic experience.

Practice your presentation skills

Presentation skills are also essential for success in your PhD. This can be particularly important if your viva involves some oral presentation (see Chapter 13). Good presentation skills can also help you in your career after completing your doctorate. Presenting papers in academic conferences and taking part in seminars, workshops and other public academic discussions offer great opportunities to practice your presentation skills. Public fora that offer the opportunity to share your research ideas and findings and to receive feedback from others are essential training grounds for developing presentation skills. An effective presentation skill will not only enable you to communicate your idea, but it can also help develop your self-confidence.

Three Minute Thesis (3MT)

For example, taking part in a global initiative, such as 3MT, could help you sharpen your presentation skills and help your PhD. The 3MT competitions are held in over 200 universities, across more than 18 countries worldwide. Aimed at PhD students and developed by the University of Queensland, the 3MT challenges students to present a compelling presentation on their thesis and the significance of their study in just 3 minutes. This strictly time-limited presentation needs to be done in 3 minutes and in language appropriate to a non-specialist audience. As a PhD student, taking part in the 3MT competition and other similar initiatives will not only help boost your confidence and presentation skills; it could also provide the only opportunity you have to share your study with a diverse audience. To be able to present your thesis in just 3 minutes to a non-specialist audience, you will need to have a great deal of creativity and ingenuity. It is believed that an 80,000 words thesis will normally take up to 9 hours to present, and you are required to do this in just 3 minutes according to the 3MT competition rule (Vitae, 2020a). This requires you to be able to filter, summarise, synthesise and condense your research ideas and discoveries into something concrete that you can communicate in a clear and engaging way. Even if you don't win, although that may be a bonus, mere taking part in a 3MT competition has its advantage, and it can help you think through and crystallise your research ideas.

Expand your horizons and develop some generic and transferrable skills

In addition to the key training outlined earlier, you may also need to expand your horizons and undertake generic skills training that could be helpful to you while doing your PhD and useful when you complete your doctoral study. Generic skills training, such as conference presentation, could also help you at a later stage in your career development. Less than 20% of PhD students end up working in academia. So the transferable skills that you acquire during your doctoral study may well be the cornerstone on which you build your future career. Take the whole of your PhD experience as a form of training for your future.

Explore new ideas/techniques and show your creativity

PhD research is about the development of new knowledge and ideas to add to an existing body of knowledge. It is therefore essential that you explore new ideas, techniques, methods of analysis and so on through your research that will show your creativity and originality. Consider doing an internship or going on a placement. Depending on your PhD research, you may benefit from partnerships and internship opportunities if available at your university or the partner institutions or universities. Taking advantage of such opportunities could greatly enhance your academic mobility and experience. If you have the opportunity and you are able to spend some time abroad or in an industry that is related to your research that could be very helpful to your success. It should go without saying, however, that if embarking on any of these activities, they do not compromise the progress of your own research and data collection. In all cases ensure that you have the full approval of your supervisor(s).

Self-evaluate and monitor your own progress

An effective way of driving your own success is knowing where you are at with your PhD and knowing what is going well and what needs to be improved. This requires periodic and honest progress monitoring (Figure 8.3). Done either as part of your university requirements or as a personal initiative, regular evaluation or monitoring of your PhD progress will help you move your study forward when you are hit stumbling blocks or face challenges. As part of their regulations for PhD students' progress monitoring, some universities require an annual or quarterly report to be submitted by directors of studies or supervisors.

Completing an annual progress report, which may be mandatory for your university and conditional upon your re-enrolment every year, is an opportunity for you and your supervisors to work together to assess your progress against your research milestones and timelines. It gives the opportunity to

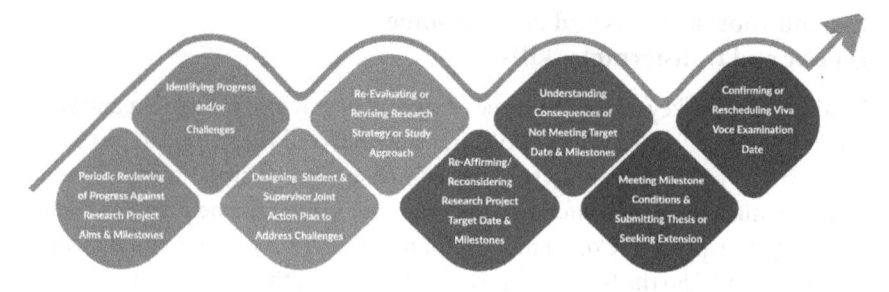

Figure 8.3 PhD progress monitoring

look back on the previous year or quarter year to understand what went well and what didn't go so well. Through such reports, you and your supervisors can agree on an action plan to address any challenges you may be facing in your PhD research. A regular progress report provides the opportunity not only for you to reflect on your own work but also for your supervisors to have an oversight and be sure that you are progressing against the specified milestones and timelines. Assessing your progress against the Gantt chart you drew up for your research plan will allow you to know where you are and where you need to be at any given time.

The completion of an annual report, if done properly, could help identify your achievements and pinpoint any area of concern or challenges that need to be addressed and planned for in the next year or phase of your study. It is important that your annual report provides a realistic and accurate assessment of your progress.

Both you and your supervisors should have input into any annual report and should contain specific and detailed progress you've made since you started your study or since the last report. Progress made against the research project timeline as originally shown in your Gantt chart should be clear. Specific actions can then be drawn up to deal with areas of concern or challenges that need to be addressed. Following the annual report, you may need to review your work plan or research strategy. The review process may also help you identify any training needs or support plan to help you progress your study. If necessary, you may need to revise your research plan, update your research dissemination strategy or even adjust or redraw your Gantt chart to fit into a more realistic time frame.

Be resilient and sustain your interest in your study when the 'PhD Blues' sets in

You probably started your PhD with a high degree of enthusiasm. You may find that the novelty of enrolling in and doing a PhD may begin to fade as you progress through your doctoral study. This feeling is very common amongst PhD students, and it is generally known as the 'PhD Blues'. The PhD Blues generally set in in the second year of a doctoral programme. For some, this period may come sooner rather than later, but many PhD students do have these feelings. However, most students rise above this and find a renewed energy and enthusiasm to press on with their doctoral study. It has been suggested that PhD students are six times more likely to experience depression or anxiety than the rest of the general population (Evans et al., 2018).

When the real pressure of doing a PhD begins to set in and you start having moments of doubts, that is when you may need to draw on your support networks. You also need to be resilient and try to keep yourself focused. It is at this time you need to remember why you wanted to do a PhD in the first place. The passion and enthusiasm you started with originally may have begun to wane, and you may find that you are struggling to sustain the interest in your research.

You may even feel that the PhD you signed up for is not what you thought it was. Your personal circumstances may have changed. You may be facing some difficulties with regards to your personal or domestic situation and something is not going well. Or it could be that you are not getting on with your supervisors, or you have just begun to find doing a PhD too demanding and onerous for your liking. Other personal issues such as financial difficulties may also have added to or compounded your feelings to the point that you are becoming disillusioned. Disillusionment is one major reason why some students drop out of doctoral studies. Doing a PhD involves a lot of challenges. You have to manage many tasks. Who says doing a PhD is easy? The road to success in a doctoral study is full of obstacles and hurdles. You may have moments of doubts, times you may feel you need to quit as PhD, by their nature, can be unruly (Peabody, 2014). Yes, it could be tough and challenging, but it is not impossible. It can be done.

With some degree of resilience and commitment, you can overcome most obstacles and challenges that doing a PhD may present. Seek help if you need to (see Chapter 4 on getting support for your PhD). Don't give up easily. A PhD requires a great deal of resilience, and you need to do all you can to maintain and sustain the interest in your study. Keep the fire burning and set your eyes on the goal. Remember the saying 'no pain, no gain'. Your success depends on you not giving up easily. You need to stay optimistic while you set realistic expectations for yourself. You also need to look after your mental well-being.

Seek help or advice and act on feedback

One of the best things you could do to help yourself with your PhD research is to seek advice when you get stuck. Rather than spending endless hours worrying about how to get things done, good advice on how to navigate the hurdles may save you some headaches. Doing a PhD can be an isolating experience. Many students do feel lost and disconnected. That is the very critical time that you need to connect with others and draw strength and support from those who understand what you may be going through (See Chapter 4). Seeking advice from people with experience in doing a PhD such as other PhD students, supervisors and examiners and others may save you some headaches and stress.

Find a healthy balance and stay sane

Doing a PhD will most certainly take a lot out of you during the 3 to 4 years or 6 to 7 years of your study, depending on whether you are a full-time or part-time student. Doctoral study can be overwhelming and exhausting. You will need to juggle so many balls and manage multiple commitments. Some manage without dropping any balls. Others are not so lucky as they drop a few balls along the way. Whichever category you think you fall in, it is important that you put your PhD into some perspective and try to strike a healthy balance in your life. Yes, getting a PhD is great, but far more important is for you to stay sane and healthy after your PhD. It has been suggested that success depends on finding a healthy balance amongst all our competing priorities (Helmut, 2019). It is when we get this balance right that we will begin to experience an increase in our engagement, our productivity, our performance and our satisfaction.

Stay creative and flexible, even in times of uncertainty

As a researcher, there are times when, due to unforeseen circumstances, you may have to work under extremely difficult situations and uncertain times. An example of such a time of uncertainty is when the world was hit by the coronavirus pandemic named COVID-19. The global health emergency, which started in the latter part of 2019 in China and later spread to all parts of the world, not only caused considerable fatalities around the world but also caused a great deal of disruption to social, economic, educational and professional lives of people around the world. With schools, colleges and universities closed and restrictions imposed on movements and face-to-face contact between people as part of the government's strategies to control the infection, doing research became particularly challenging. Physical access to library resources became impossible, and data collection and field surveys were severely disrupted. The unprecedented situation such as the COVID-19 pandemic provides an example of when you as a PhD student could be creative and flexible and still drive your research forward in spite of the difficult situation.

New ideas and initiatives could be developed in times like this to keep your research and scholarship going. Difficult times sometimes bring opportunities. In spite of the unprecedented disruption to scholarships and access to physical resources, adapting to an off-campus-based research experience could be a creative way of driving your research forward even in a difficult time such as the COVID-19 pandemic.

Seek an extension or suspension rather than termination

If you do struggle after you have put in all the efforts to drive your PhD forward and you are still not making any progress, you may consider seeking suspension of your study or an extension to your target submission dates. It is reasonable to consider applying for an extension with regards to your milestones if you really struggle to meet them, about 2 to 3 months before the deadlines. Some universities will work with their students to mitigate the impact of any unforeseen circumstances and support them through difficult times. Explore what support you could get and come up with a plan with your supervisors to keep your studentships live. It is important you check your university's guidelines on policy regarding requests for extensions, exceptional extenuating circumstances and authorised break of study that you may be entitled to if you are going through a difficult time.

Applications for support may be considered on a case-by-case basis, so it is important you present a strong case and evidence to support your request.

Key messages

- To succeed in your PhD, you need to take ownership of your study and drive it forward with a real sense of dedication and commitment.
- Set yourself specific goals for your PhD. Stay focused and work towards completion in a timely manner.
- Regularly self-evaluate your skills and identify any skills gap you need to fill to support your doctoral study.
- Avail yourself of training opportunities that may be available to support your PhD and to help your own personal and professional development.
- Periodic PhD progress reports provide an opportunity for you and your supervisor to monitor and review your progress against your milestones or timelines that were set for your study.
- Through your progress report, you can identify challenges and plans for the next phase of your study.

- Design and update your Gantt chart to reflect realistic progress towards meeting your research project milestones.
- When things become tough and you suffer from the 'PhD Blues', get help and tap into your support networks.
- If necessary, seek suspension or extension of deadlines rather than termination of your study.

Further reading

Churchill, H., and Sanders, T. (2007). *Getting Your PhD: A Practical Insider's Guide*. London: SAGE.

Evans, T., Bira, L., Gastelum, J., et al. (2018). Evidence for a mental health crisis in graduate education. *Nature Biotechnology*, 36, pp. 282–284. https://doi.org/10.1038/nbt.4089

Fuller, M. (2015). Doctoral education in the UK: Ideal models and the stark reality. *Presentation at the Australian DDOGS Meeting, Sydney, April 19–20* [Online]. Available at: www.researchgate.net/publication/275640304_Doctoral_education_in_the_UK_ideal_models_and_the_stark_reality. Accessed on 21st August 2020.

Gallagher, P., and Gallagher, A. (2020). *The Portable PhD. Taking Your Psychology Career Beyond Academia*. Washington, DC: American Psychological Association.

Helmut, L. (2019). *How to Set Goals and Achieve Balance – in and Outside the Classroom: Learn How Solid Goals and Time Management Can Help You Achieve Success* [Online]. Available at: https://blog.dce.harvard.edu/extension/how-set-goals-achieve-balance-outside-classroom. Accessed on 22nd August 2020.

Kyvik, S., and Olsen, T. B. (2014). Increasing completion rates in Norwegian doctoral training: Multiple causes for efficiency improvements. *Studies in Higher Education*, 39(9), pp. 1668–1682.

Lindsay, S. (2015). What works for doctoral students in completing their thesis? *Teaching in Higher Education*, 20(2), pp. 183–196.

Morris, C., and Murphy, C. (2011). *Getting a PhD in Law*. Oxford and Portland, OR: Hart Publishing Ltd.

Peabody, R. (2014). *The Unruly PhD: Doubts, Detours, Departures, and Other Success Stories*. Basingstoke, UK: Palgrave Macmillan.

Russel Group. (2020). *Our Universities* [Online]. Available at: https://russellgroup.ac.uk/about/our-universities. Accessed on 21st August 2020.

Spronken-Smith, R., Cameron, C., and Quigg, R. (2018). Factors contributing to high PhD completion rates: A case study in a research-intensive university in New Zealand. *Assessment & Evaluation in Higher Education*, 43(1), pp. 94–109.

Vitae. (2020a). Realising the potentials of researchers. *Careers Research and Advisory Centre (CRAC) Limited*. https://www.vitae.ac.uk/about-us

CHAPTER 9

Conducting fieldwork and collecting your data

Introduction

This chapter discusses fieldwork and data collection strategies for your PhD research. Covering qualitative, quantitative and mixed-methods approaches, it uses examples from both primary and secondary sources to illustrate data collection schemes that could be used in your PhD research. It focuses on how to undertake original work involving fieldwork and collecting necessary data to answer specific research questions. Using examples, the chapter provides practical advice and guidance on how to organise and collect your data through interviews, focus groups, questionnaires, panel studies and the like.

By the end of the chapter, you will have a better understanding of

- deciding on appropriate data collection strategy for your PhD,
- how to collect and evaluate qualitative data,
- how to conduct interviews and focus group study,
- how to conduct field observations and recordings and
- how to collect data through field measurements and surveys.

Getting the right data for your PhD research

Whether it is new data generated by yourself or secondary data that need sourcing, getting the right data for your PhD is, arguably, one of the most important aspects of your PhD. Any progress with your PhD depends largely on how successful you are in generating, collecting or sourcing the necessary data to answer your research question(s). Doing research at a PhD level requires that you have an in-depth understanding of the nature and type of data that you need for your study. You need to know how to source or gain access to essential information or data, without which you cannot make any appreciable progress with your research. Getting the required data that are of relevance and of highest quality possible (no data are perfect) will enable you to interrogate and add value to existing knowledge. It is also essential that you have access to particular information sources that are critical to your study aims and objectives. The type and nature of data collected will, to a large extent, influence and shape your analyses, inferences and conclusions (see Chapter 10).

Conducting fieldwork and collecting data – issues for consideration

The term *fieldwork* is often used to mean or denote investigation or search for data or information in the 'field' as opposed to the data collected in the library, classroom or laboratories. However, fieldwork can also be used to refer to all types or manners of data gathering in various social and geographical settings. While fieldwork in disciplines such as geology or geography often requires field investigations that may involve travels to specific geographic locations, collection of data for social science research can be done at a range of different settings using different methods. These range from interviewing participants in their homes or places of residence, conducting focus groups in an office or elderly people's homes, just trawling through archive materials in a library or analysing financial data on company's websites. Any space that allows social interaction and enables collection of data is a 'field' in social sciences. So your fieldwork may involve attending political rallies, interviewing government officials or talking to inmates in a prison or interviewing ex-offenders. You may also spend most your time surfing the internet or querying databases or searching through historical records or archives. Whichever form it takes, it has been suggested that fieldwork or the process of data gathering constitutes the focus of doctoral research projects (Naveed et al., 2017).

Giving the importance of fieldwork and data collection in PhD research, you will need to devote a great deal of your time, energy and resources to this process of data gathering. It is critical that you constantly reflect on your field work strategy and your data collection processes to ensure you get the best information you can possibly get to answer your research questions. The type of fieldwork you undertake, and your data collection strategy will be influenced, to a large extent, by the theoretical and ideological underpinnings of your research. While collecting your data, you also need to keep in view the planned process of analysis. The key issues that you need to be aware of with regards to conducting fieldwork and collecting your data for your PhD are summarised in the following subsections.

Allow sufficient time to generate or collect your data

Your fieldwork may take longer than you expected. More often than not, fieldwork tends to overrun the originally time allocated or anticipated. It is, therefore, important that you leave yourself sufficient time to set up your fieldwork and to generate or collect the necessary data for your PhD. It is not uncommon for people to go back to the field to collect more data, if the original fieldwork failed to generate sufficient information for a thesis. So, to avoid a return to the field, always ensure you give yourself enough time to collect sufficient data and obtain essential information that is critical to your analysis. It is sometimes difficult to judge how long your fieldwork will take as this depends on so many factors some of which may be outside your control. The process of data generation or data collection is often fraught with challenges. The key issue is to be prepared to face the challenges and to have the will and the means to overcome any obstacles you may face while doing your fieldwork. Perseverance and an ability to navigate through obstacles in a thoughtful way are essential requirements for success in a PhD fieldwork.

Work towards gaining the trust of people, especially your data 'gatekeepers'

Doing fieldwork is one of those situations where you may need to rely on other people to gain access to your data. In that case, it is important that you gain the trust and support of those people in order to have access to or obtain critical data you may require for your PhD. In some countries, getting information depends on personal contacts and networks as there may be no official or legal framework to make information readily available to people. If you are doing your fieldwork and collecting data in countries where data are not made freely available and there is no legal provision or requirement for freedom of information that you can use to gain access to public data, the only way open to you is to use every connection and contacts you have to effect, as your access to essential data may depend entirely on the goodwill and relationships you are able to build with the people who control the data. These 'data controller' or 'data gatekeepers' may arbitrarily grant or deny you access to essential data in which case you may not be able to make progress until you navigate through these human barriers. In such situation, you may need to use your interpersonal skills of social relations and diplomacy to persuade people to give you access to the data. The need to build rapport and trust between yourself and the data 'gatekeepers' in order to obtain some essential data is, therefore, an essential issue to consider while doing your fieldwork.

Try different methods or ways of collecting your data

There are many different ways of achieving an objective. Fieldwork requires some degree of creativity. If you are unable to collect your data using one method, you may want to consider if the same data can be collected using other means or approaches. There may be different ways of getting information that you require, and you should not be too rigid in your approach or give up too readily if one approach at collecting data is not working well for you (see Figure 9.2).

Research methods are non-static. There are constant changes in the methods and approaches to conducting research. Also, an approach that proved useful in one discipline may be tried in another discipline to see if it works. An interdisciplinary approach to your fieldwork and data collection could be considered. The rapid change in methods and technology used in conducting research means that you need to be aware of methodological changes and advancement and how you can use these to your advantage. So try what works and what is scientifically defensible, no matter how different.

Be aware of cultural sensitivity around your study

Besides the general ethical issues relating to conducting research as discussed in Chapter 7, you also need to be aware of other social and cultural issues that may affect your ability to generate or collect essential data for your research. The way other people perceive you may influence or affect your success on the field and your ability to generate or gain access to some data. Your own perception of other people may influence the way you approach them and the method of obtaining information from them. As a PhD student, you need to be aware of and think carefully about how to guard against any negative perception or stereotypes in your study. Depending on your cultural background, you may also need to reflect on the perceived power relations between yourself and your data subjects. This is particularly important if you are doing a multicultural research and your study involves collecting culturally sensitive data. It has been suggested that researchers from Western society are generally considered to have a relatively privileged background compared with other non-Western and often marginalised groups that they may be studying (McEwan, 2011). So you may need to think carefully about your own values and how those values sit within the general frame of your PhD research. You may also consider how your position of privilege may influence your research methodology and how others may perceive or relate to you while collecting your data. Consider carefully whether your data subjects are telling you what they think you want to hear rather than what they really feel.

Understand country differences in ethics, data protection and compliance

If you are conducting your fieldwork overseas, especially in a non-Western society, you may need to be aware of differing standards and diverse guidelines on ethics. The UK/EU research ethics guidelines may not always or necessarily work or apply in other non-EU countries. This may cause you some difficulty, especially with regards to deciding which ethics guidelines to follow if the local ethics regulations on research do not tally or are incompatible with the EU GDPR or the UK DPA of 2018 (see Chapter 7).

Doing fieldwork overseas may also require that you cover the full spectrum of ethical issues not only in the EU/UK but also in the country where your fieldwork is based. This may require some of the ethics regulations not only in the UK but also in the country where you are collecting your data. Also, collecting data in some countries may present some practical problems as not every country is freely open to the free flow of information with regards to gathering or collecting research data. Political sensitivity to national data is one issue you may also need to consider if you are doing fieldwork overseas. What you consider as innocuous data may be seen as nationally sensitive or classified information in other countries, which may lead to an accusation of espionage. Be very careful with photography – photographing seemingly innocuous things like railways or hospitals can be fraught as these are seen as strategic and/or militarily vulnerable assets. So you need to understand the cultural, political and economic settings of the country in which your fieldwork is based and obtain the necessary clearances or approvals before you start your data collection. University research is generally considered as strategic political, cultural and economic importance for many nations. It is therefore necessary that you are aware of the national significance of your PhD research and how your study fits into the socio-political context of the country in which your fieldwork is based (Brew and Lucas, 2009).

Doing your fieldwork overseas may also require that you put in place the necessary measures and widen your risk assessment to mitigate or reduce any risks that may be associated with your fieldwork. Collecting primary data in some countries can also be time-consuming and can be fraught with a range of unforeseen problems or difficulties. If your fieldwork is based in remote locations, issues such as accessibility, transportation, adverse weather condition and language barriers, amongst others, may need to be considered. It is, therefore, important to have a contingency plan in place for your fieldwork or data collection strategy just in case things don't work out or go according to your original plan or schedule.

Understand your data population and ensure your sample is representative of the population

For any of your analysis to have any degree of generalisability and validity, you need to understand the population on which your research is based and ensure that you select a representative sample. If your PhD research is based on surveys, the chances are that you will need to consider taking representative samples from a population. In general terms, a sample is a subset taken from a population that is used to represent the larger population from which it is drawn. It is often impracticable or too expensive in terms of time and resources to study the whole population relating to your study; hence, samples are used as substitutes or surrogates for the population of interest. Regardless of whether your research is qualitative or quantitative, collecting data requires a careful consideration of the representativeness of your samples. Equally important is the process of selecting samples from your target population, as there are many different ways or methods of sample selection. Notable amongst these are random, stratified, clustering and probability sampling methods, to mention a few. Whichever sampling method you use, the essential point is to ensure that your sample is selected in a way as to represent the characters of the general population from which they are drawn and there is no inherent bias in the way the samples were chosen. Where that is not possible, those biases should be kept to a minimum.

Approaches to fieldwork and data collection

Having thought through and considered the social, cultural, geographic and political settings of your fieldwork, the next step is to initiate and launch your data collection strategies. There are many different approaches to research design and data collection in a PhD project. Some PhDs in the social sciences rely purely on primary data. Others use secondary sources while others use a combination of both primary and secondary sources.

Primary data

If you base your PhD research on information or data that you generated or created yourself and which has not previously been presented, published or analysed, then you are using primary data. This could be any form of data that you collected through your own field observations, interviews or any structured surveys. Generally, primary sources of data are considered more reliable than secondary data because you have absolute control over what type of primary data to generate and how to collect such data and the form or units in which they are collected. Primary data can be collected in many ways such as surveys, interviews, focus groups and workshops. These could be done face-to-face, over the telephone or online. In much social science research, questionnaire surveys are commonly used for the purpose of collecting information directly from people; hence, this method of collecting data constitutes an important primary source of data.

Secondary data

Secondary data are data generated by people or institutions other than yourself. They include data or information obtainable from sources such as government publications, statistical agencies, books, press reports, data banks, archives, journals, conference papers and newspapers (Figure 9.1). In general terms, secondary sources of data refer to existing stocks of information which you are reusing, reinterpreting or repurposing for your own study. Consider carefully the original source of the data that you are intending to use. For example data presented in books and newspapers are unlikely to be original in source but rather taken from some other institutions research – always refer to the original data source when using secondary data.

While it is possible to base your PhD entirely on secondary sources of data, it is essential that the source of such data is credible and the integrity or accuracy of the data is not in doubt. By its nature, secondary data are essentially 'secondhand' information that you may be using in your PhD. The credibility of your research rests heavily on the accuracy or reliability of such data. Extra care should be taken to ensure you understand the secondary data that you are using for your PhD and any limitations that the data may contain. The key issue with using secondary data in PhD research is knowing how to make existing data fit your research aims and objectives. Most PhD research studies tend to combine different forms of data, primary and secondary, and use various approaches and methods to obtain data. As a general rule, make use of all the secondary data

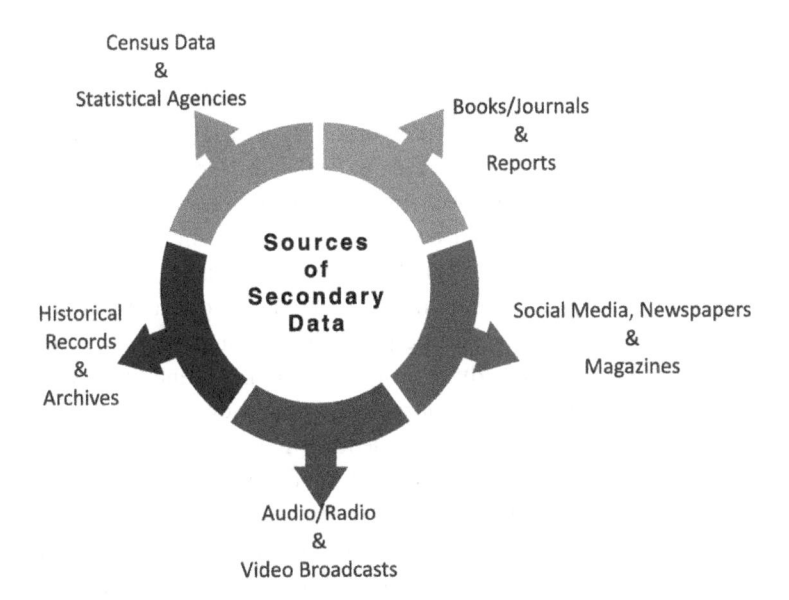

Figure 9.1 Typical sources of secondary data

available in your chosen area and then decide what primary data collection is needed. There is no point in reinventing the wheel by collecting data which have already been collected and analysed in other research.

Methods of obtaining data

There are several commonly used methods or approaches for gathering or collecting data. These, amongst others, include the following:

- Observations
- Experiments
- Participatory action research
- Ethnographic study
- Surveys
- Interviews
- Focus group

These categories are neither mutually exclusive nor exhaustive as different variations or combinations of data collecting strategies may be used in your PhD research (Figure 9.2).

Observational study

Observational studies involve the collection of data by observing a physical or social phenomenon. This method relies on your ability to observe and record events as they occur. It also relies on your observational skills and ability to record and document what you've observed. The recording can be done electronically or through non-electronic means. Observation research is a form of qualitative research method. It could be used if, for example, you are interested in studying people's behaviour in their natural environment. The idea is to collect information or gather data with minimal or non-intervention or manipulation of the observed. Your data collection, using this approach, is based purely on what you observed rather than what people tell you or say to you. Observational research could be participatory or non-participatory. A participatory observational study requires that you intervene in the environment of the observed by inserting yourself into the group or the environment. This insertion enables you to gather inside information that you will not otherwise be able to collect as a researcher looking from the outside.

In a non-participatory observation, you may decide to study the group or phenomenon from the outside, albeit, the group or phenomenon being studied is still in their natural environment. Observational studies tend to be generally subjective as the information collected is based purely on what you considered important to you as an observer. If other people were to observe

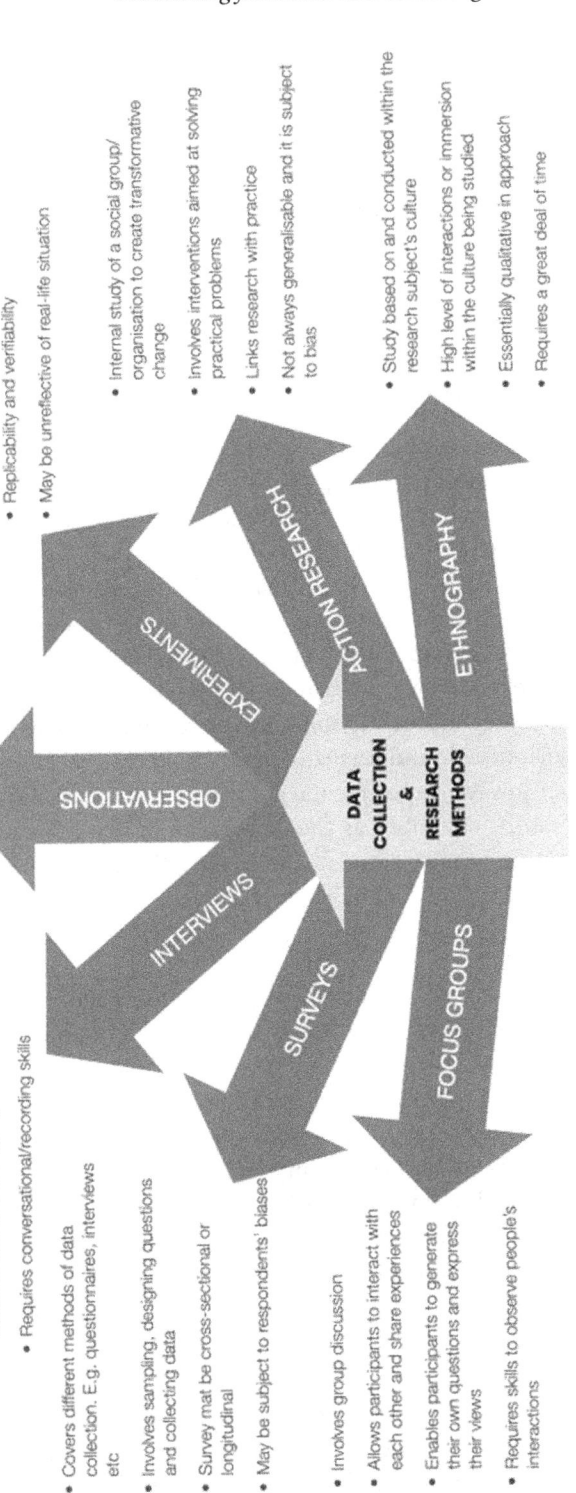

Figure 9.2 Common methods of data collection

the same event, the information they collect may be different from yours. What is observed may mean different things to different people depending on their observational skills, attention to details and note-taking ability, amongst many other factors. If you are using this method of data collection for your PhD research, you need to guard against any implicit or explicit bias or prejudices in your observation and recordings. You also need to ensure that you get your recordings right the first time as the event being observed may not be replicated and you may never have the opportunity to record the event or transaction again.

Experiments

Although not exclusively, experimental studies are often conducted in a controlled laboratory setting. These often follow some logical scientific principles involving the drawing of inferences and reasoning. Experimental research strategy is particularly useful if the main purpose of your study is to demonstrate the existence of a cause-and-effect relationship between two sets of variables. It is a scientific approach to research and data collection in which you could manipulate a set of independent variables and applied them to some dependent variables in order for you to determine or measure the effect of the independent variables on the dependent variables. This form of study is generalisable and verifiable, and it tends to generate strong internally valid data. However experimental study may not always have general applicability to real-life situations as the complexity of real-life situation means that not everything can be simulated in a controlled environment.

Participatory action research

Action research, also known as participatory action research (PAR) is a form of interventionist study which allows you to be embedded within an organisation or social group in order to generate data that could be used to create change or improve the organisation's practices and procedures. Commonly used in the social sciences, especially in health care practice, PAR involves studies that aim at collecting data in order to bring about a transformative change within an organisation or practice through research and interventions. PAR requires some degree of careful planning, observation, listening, critical evaluation and reflection (Koshy et al., 2010).

Ethnographic study

Ethnographic study is based essentially on data gathering within the context of the research subject's culture. It involves a high level of engagement with the research participants. Collecting data through ethnographic study requires observation of the daily life of the subjects being studied. Commonly used in social sciences, especially in anthropology and sociology, ethnographic study requires some level of immersion within the culture being studied in order to gain knowledge about their behaviour and to understand their way of life.

From its traditional approach of ethnographic study involving observation of people within their culture in person, technological advancement has enabled digital ethnography. Through social media and online blogs, it is possible to conduct an ethnographic study digitally.

Surveys

Data collected through survey methods can take several forms such as questionnaires or interviews. Conducting a survey requires some degrees of skills and knowledge of social survey techniques. Collecting data through field surveys is an important method of research in social sciences. This method of data collection is particularly useful if your objective is to measure a set of dependent and independent variables in order to test for any correlation or relationship between these variables. Surveys can take two main forms – cross-sectional or longitudinal – depending on the time and sequence of collection of your data. In a cross-sectional study, data relating to your independent and dependent variables need to be collected at the same point in time using a single data collection instrument such as a questionnaire. This gives you a snapshot of the phenomenon or issue of investigation. In a longitudinal study, your data may be collected over a longer period such that data relating to dependent variables could be collected at a later point in time than the independent variables. This allows a series of snapshots of the phenomenon or situation over a longer time. For example, if you interview a new sample of people every time you carry out your survey, then your study is cross-sectional. If, instead, you decide to interview the same cohort or sample of people at different periods over time, your study is essentially longitudinal. Whether cross-sectional or longitudinal, collecting data through surveys provides an opportunity to gather a large quantity of information or data from a large number of people. The method, however, has the disadvantage of being prone to respondents' biases as information provided may not necessarily be accurate as they are based on respondent's feelings and views on the subject.

Interviews

Interviews are essential ways of collecting data in social sciences. This form of data collection allows conversation between you and your research participants. Whether done on a one-to-one or group basis, interviews provide flexible engagement with respondents. Using interview methods to collect your data could enable you to discuss sensitive issues with your participants, which you may not be able to do through other methods. Interviews may be structured, semi-structured or unstructured. Interviews allow research participants to provide information or express information which may not be possible just by asking preset questions. Data collected through interviews tend to be qualitative in nature. Collecting data through interviews often requires that you build up some trust and rapport with your participants. In most cases, you only have one chance to interview your participant. It is therefore essential that you make the most of that opportunity as a follow-up interview may not be possible. With the consent of your participants, you may need to audio record your interviews to ensure you are able to transcribe or analyse the information collected. Collecting data through interviews requires an ability to take notes and listening carefully to and engaging with your research participants in an effective way to generate the data you require. It also requires that you have some degree of empathy. Your ability to empathise with your participants could go a long way in making them feel comfortable talking to you about your research.

Focus groups

Focus groups allow data to be collected from many people in one session. This method of data collection is particularly useful in exploratory research, where you may want to gauge people's feelings or views on issues. The method involves bringing a small number of selected people together to discuss specific issues. The main purpose of focus groups is to gather essential information on participants' views, experiences, or comments on the topic of discussion. It is a form of group discussion in which participants are encouraged or facilitated to express their views or ideas. This method of data collection allows participants to share their views, knowledge or experiences on the issue of discussion. Data collected through focus groups tend to be qualitative in nature. Focus group research is widely used in the social sciences, especially in anthropology, health research and cultural/media studies. While this approach of data collection allows participants to be involved and express their views, the small number of people often involved in a focus group makes any generalisation of the results problematic. The quality of data generated through focus groups may also be influenced by the way the focus group is managed or facilitated.

Case studies

If your PhD requires an in-depth analysis or investigation of a problem over a long period in order to gain a full understanding of issues relating to the problem, using a case study approach may be a useful way to generate your data. Case studies require an in-depth study into a particular subject or area of investigation using a combination of techniques such as interviews, observations and analysis of other materials or documents relating to that subject or area. Data collected through case studies, generally lend themselves more to qualitative rather than quantitative analysis as they tend to involve a wide range of information on a specific issue or aspect of investigation. However, the main issue with this method of data collection is that of generalisability. A study based on one or two case studies may not be reflective of the situation being studies as those cases studies may not be replicable or applicable in many settings or cases.

Pilot study and seeking advice from others

One of the decisions you may need to make before fully launching your fieldwork is whether to conduct a pilot study before your main field study. A pilot study is a mini test study that precedes the main study usually carried out to test how the main survey is likely to work. Conducting a pilot study before launching your main study can help you identify any potential issues or problems before you embark on a costly study. A pilot study can be used to test your research design and could form the basis for any planning or modification of your research instruments, such as your questionnaires, focus group study and so on. For example, a pilot study will enable you to test your data collection methodology or your interview techniques. It can also help you establish the reliability of your data sources and whether the variables you've selected for your study are appropriate and are measured correctly. A pilot can also give you an idea of the sampling techniques that could work for well your main study.

Conducting a pilot study will also enable you to ascertain whether your data collection instrument is sufficient in generating the required details to answer your research questions. A pilot study will save you a lot of time as you would be able to adjust your data collection instruments and make necessary changes, if necessary, before launching your full study. It is also a good idea to seek advice from anyone you know who has done similar work relating to your study. Advice from other researchers who have done similar work could be beneficial especially with regards to learning about how they conducted their fieldwork and the pitfalls you need to avoid. You could then learn about what other researchers did, what they achieved in terms of data collection, and what they learned that could help you in your own study.

Conducting fieldwork remotely

There may be times when it is not practicable or feasible to collect data in real time or face-to-face. The COVID-19 health epidemic that hits the world in

2020, is a classic example when research plans may be disrupted making it difficult if not impossible to collect data face-to-face or in real life. For example, conducting social research at a time of social distancing and restrictions on people's movement presents a great deal of challenges.

By its nature, social research is an academic and social activity that requires interactions between the researcher and the participants. It involves building trust and rapport between the researcher and the researched. Under normal circumstances, social researchers need to meet people, listen to them, ask them questions and observe them as they go about their daily business and finding out information about them. All these activities and practices become disrupted, impossible or difficult to carry out in a lockdown situation with strict limits to social interactions. This means traditional social research methods are being reconsidered and alternative ways of collecting data have become necessary, due to what has been described as the shifting of space-time, that no one knows for how long it will go on (Fuchs, 2020).

In circumstances such as this, conducting fieldwork virtually may be the only solution. Virtual fieldwork is becoming popular in disciplines such as geography, where engagement with the world is essential but real fieldwork is not possible. While conducting fieldwork remotely may have its challenges, it also has some opportunities or advantages. Online data collection instrument could be designed in a way as to avoid ethical and regulatory problems that may occur if you need to collect data in different political jurisdiction with different laws of data collection and protection. However, it needs to be emphasised that not every PhD research could be conducted using data that are sourced virtually.

Using your fieldwork to refine or redefine your research question

Whichever method you used to source your data, conducting fieldwork gives you an opportunity to refine or redefine your research question. Sometimes there is a disconnect between theory and practice which means what could be considered an excellent research design before you start your fieldwork may not necessarily work in practice in the field. So making changes to a preplanned schedule could be necessary during your fieldwork. You may also need to change your methodological approach, your research instrument or even your research question, if necessary. New ideas may emerge during your data collection process that may demand that you look again at your research focus. If, for any reason, you are unable to gain access to critical data for your PhD, you may need to reconsider your original research plans and think of alternatives.

Fieldwork provides an opportunity not only to collect your data but also to reflect on your PhD in general. For many PhD students, fieldwork provides opportunities for new experiences. Through the fieldwork, you may acquire new knowledge or develop a new approach towards your investigation. Fieldwork also provides the opportunity for you to adapt to and deal with changing situations and any unexpected scenarios that may occur while you are in the field.

Data collection, objectivity and biases

Whichever types of data you collected for your PhD research, it is important that you avoid bias and misrepresentation. Your data should be truthful and as accurate as practically possible. Recorded information collected through interviews must be transcribed as truthfully as possible and should be devoid of prejudices or bias. If there is any bias in your study, such as in your selection of participants, case studies, choice of field study location, case studies and the like, it is essential that you state these biases in your report to enable your reader to make a judgement whether the degree of bias is tolerable.

Key messages

- Fieldwork provides an opportunity to generate, collect essential data for your PhD.
- Your fieldwork could offer an opportunity to refine or redefine your research question.
- Overseas fieldwork and data collection may have potential risks and ethical challenges that need to be acknowledged and managed.
- If your PhD requires conducting fieldwork or collecting data overseas, cultural or political differences may mean a conflict or tension in ethics regulations and varying expectations regarding your role as a researcher.
- Not every country is open to freedom of information, and strict national control of data may mean that you need a special clearance or permit to undertake your data collection.
- Understanding the cultural, political and economic settings of your fieldwork is central to your success in collecting the essential data for your PhD.
- Depending on your fieldwork location, you may need to widen your risk assessment and put in necessary control measures to mitigate or reduce any risks that may be associated with collecting data in a non-EU country.
- Conducting a pilot study before launching your main study could help sharpen your data collection instruments and identify any potential issues that could form the basis for any planning or modification of your study.

Further reading

Bhattacherjee, A. (2012). *Social Science Research: Principles, Methods, and Practices*, 2nd ed. Tampa, FL: University of South Florida.
Brew, A., and Lucas, L. (2009). *Academic Research and Researchers*. Maidenhead, UK: McGraw-Hill Open University Press.

Fuchs, C. (2020). Everyday life and everyday communication in coronavirus capitalism. *Triple C: Communication, Capitalism & Critique*, 18(1), pp. 375–399.

Greenfield, T., and Greener, S. (2016). *Research Methods for Postgraduates*, 3rd ed. Hoboken, US: Wiley Blackwell.

Hine, C. (2015). *Ethnography for the Internet: Embedded, Embodied and Everyday.* London: Bloomsbury

Koshy, E., Koshy, V., and Waterman, H. (2010). What is action research? In *Action Research in Healthcare*. Sage Books [Online]. Available at: www.sagepub.com/sites/default/files/upm-binaries/36584_01_Koshy_et_al_Ch_01.pdf. Accessed on 5th September 2020.

McEwan, C. (2011). Development and fieldwork. *Geography*, 96(1), pp. 22–26.

Naveed, A., Sakata, N., Kefallinou, A., Young, S., and Anand, K. (2017). Understanding, embracing and reflecting upon the messiness of doctoral fieldwork. *Compare: A Journal of Comparative and International Education*, 47(5), pp. 773–792. http://doi.org/10.1080/03057925.2017.1344031

QSR International. (2020). Discover how researchers are innovating, rethinking research, and teaching in a remote world. *Remote Research Center* [Online]. Available at: www.qsrinternational.com/nvivo-qualitative-data-analysis-software/resources/remote-research-center. Accessed on 8th June 2020.

CHAPTER 10

Analysing your research data
Quantitative and qualitative approaches

Introduction

This chapter focuses on the analysis of your PhD research data. The chapter invites you to think critically about different ways of analysing your data and choosing the method that is appropriate to your study and your research objective(s). The chapter does not pretend to, nor can it possibly, cover all analytical techniques and methods that could be used in PhD research. However, it provides an essential pointer to common quantitative and qualitative data analysis methods which you may wish to explore further and apply to your own study. Where appropriate, the chapter directs you to where you can get further information and training on developing your quantitative and qualitative data analytical skills. The chapter also offers some tips on assumptions on which most univariate, bivariate and multivariate analyses of data are based and suggest conditions under which you may use them in your study. Given the complexity of many of the qualitative and quantitative methods discussed in this chapter, it is recommended that you consult relevant sources for detailed information on each of the methods discussed as no single chapter would nor could suffice as an entire guide for data analysis at the PhD level.

However, by the end of the chapter, you will have a better understanding of

- different types of data and the scales at which they are measured;
- factors to consider in choosing between quantitative and qualitative analysis;
- how to prepare your data for analysis;
- choosing appropriate analytical techniques that can be used to synthesise, summarise or organise your research data; and
- how to draw inferences or conclusions from statistical analysis of your data.

Understanding data measurement scales and preparing your data for analysis

Whatever data you have collected during your fieldwork (Chapter 9), these may have been measured using a variety of scales and methods. Measurement could be defined as the assignment of numerals to objects or events according to some scientific or logical rules. All data are measured using one scale or the other to make them intelligible. The scales with which your data are measured will indicate what type of analysis you can carry out on the data. There are four main levels of measurement of data. These are nominal, ordinal, interval and ratio scales.

Nominal scale: This is the weakest level of data measurement, commonly used to name or classify objects. This form of measurement only assigns names or labels to objects and does not assume any numerical or hierarchical differences between the classes; hence, no mathematical or statistical operations can be carried out on these types of data. They are useful for identification or classificatory purposes. Examples of data measures on nominal scales are gender categorisation, occupational categories and colour labelling. As data measured on nominal scaling have no mathematical power, they are generally used for identification, meaning that standard arithmetic operations such as addition, subtraction, multiplication and division cannot be carried out meaningfully on such data.

Ordinal scale: The next level up in the measurement scale is ordinal. This often involves the ranking of events from the highest to the smallest or from most to least based on the order of their magnitude. Although higher than the nominal scales, data measures on an interval scale may still not provide full information on the magnitude between the ranks. For instance, if a set of objects is ranked from 1 to 50, the rankings may not necessarily show how much the object in the 1st rank is different from that in the 20th or 50th rank. An example of data measured on an ordinal scale is the UN listing of countries based on their Human Development Index.

Interval scale: Data measured in a way as to allow a comparison of how far apart each of the data sets are from each other based on an arbitrary scale, such as temperature measurement in Fahrenheit and Centigrade scales are known to be measured at interval scale. Although it is possible to determine how far apart the magnitudes are from each other in interval scales, the fact that such scales may not have a natural origin on 0 makes an in-depth analysis of comparison a bit difficult. For example, it may not make statistical sense to suggest that 60 °C is twice as hot as 30 °C. The best that can be deduced from these data is that 60 °C is hotter than 30 °C. Generally, data measured on an interval scale have a higher level of analytical properties than those measured on nominal and ordinal scales.

Ratio scale: The ratio scale is the highest level of data measurement. This form of data calibration allows comparison, not only on the basis of the intervals between the data but also on the actual values or magnitude of the data. Examples of data measure on a ratio scale are the ages of respondents, number of visits to the hospital, calorie consumption and so on. Other measurements, such as weight, distance and volume, also fall into this category. As the most commonly used measurement scale, data measured on ratio scales have the highest analytical properties as all standard arithmetic operations can be performed on such data. Hence, they lend themselves to more rigorous analysis.

Checking and organising your data

Regardless of the scales of measurement of your data, it is important that you check your data for accuracy before starting your analysis. The validity of your analysis and your conclusions depend largely on the accuracy and reliability of your data. So, before launching into full data analysis, try to search for any anomalies, irregularities or inconsistencies in your data set. Any anomalies or weaknesses in your data must be identified and rectified before you begin your analysis.

Data checking and organisation may also involve sorting, labelling or counting the data you have collected with a view of bringing some kind of order into the data and ensuring that you have collected the right data and that your sample size is large enough to make any analysis meaningful. This initial data-checking process is useful, especially if you are dealing with complex or large data sets. Date checking could also provide the basis for deciding on the best way to enter your data onto a computer ready for any statistical analysis. If questionnaires are used, you may need to check for accuracy of the responses and consistency and code these responses accordingly to make your analysis meaningful. Once the data-checking and computer entry procedures are completed, the next step is to choose or select the appropriate methods or approaches to analysing your data.

Analysing your data – qualitative approach

There are two main approaches to analysing your data. One is based on the quantitative tradition of statistical analysis and the other relies on explaining social phenomena using a qualitative method with emphasis on non-statistical data. It is common in most PhD research to use either or a combination of these approaches depending on the data and the study objective.

Qualitative data analysis – a general principle

Qualitative research is an approach to inquiry or study in social science research that explores social or human problems using specific methodological techniques (see Chapter 6). Qualitative analyses generally involve building a complex and holistic picture of a problem or issue by analysing and synthesising texts, words, reports, interviews and other information obtained in a natural/social setting (Srivastava and Thomson, 2009).

Qualitative analysis generally involves a non-statistical approach as most of your data may not be quantitative in nature. Rather than collecting quantitative data, your research objective may be to describe events or social phenomena in a way that makes them more comprehensible without relying on any statistical methods. A qualitative approach is most desirable when your data or information you've collected do not allow for a quantitative analysis.

Other factors that may influence your choice of whether to use qualitative or quantitative approaches include the following (Figure 10.1):

- Epistemological and ontological considerations
- The nature and amount of data that you need to collect
- Ethical values associated with your research
- Your knowledge and understanding of data analytical methods

Some studies, such as those relating to understanding people's experience, in terms of their personal, social or cultural values and environment, may involve the collection of data that are not quantifiable. In this case, a descriptive and non-statistical method of evaluation is required. Qualitative analysis often starts with the transcribing of any field notes, scribbled or written notes, audio files, photographs and other visual data you may have collected during your fieldwork. Transcribing refers, essentially, to the process of getting spoken words, ideas, thoughts, speeches and so on transferred into a written or printed form to make them more comprehensible.

Qualitative analysis requires a high level of interaction with your data in order to dig deep into the data in order to draw out essential findings and meanings that may not be obvious. It is a time-consuming process that will involve many hours of transcribing, reading through recordings, watching video clips, interviews recordings and the like and cross-checking them with your field notes. The more you immerse yourself in the data, the more you will be able to make an evaluative judgement and critical assessment of what the data are saying.

A key aspect of qualitative analysis involves the identification or definition of key issues or themes in your data. These themes or issues are essentially what you considered important or essential findings in your data or text based on your research questions and your study objectives. Having identified what you think is relevant, which could be issues, words, phrases or sentences, amongst others, you may then decide to categorise or classify them into groups of related ideas. The process of classification may involve

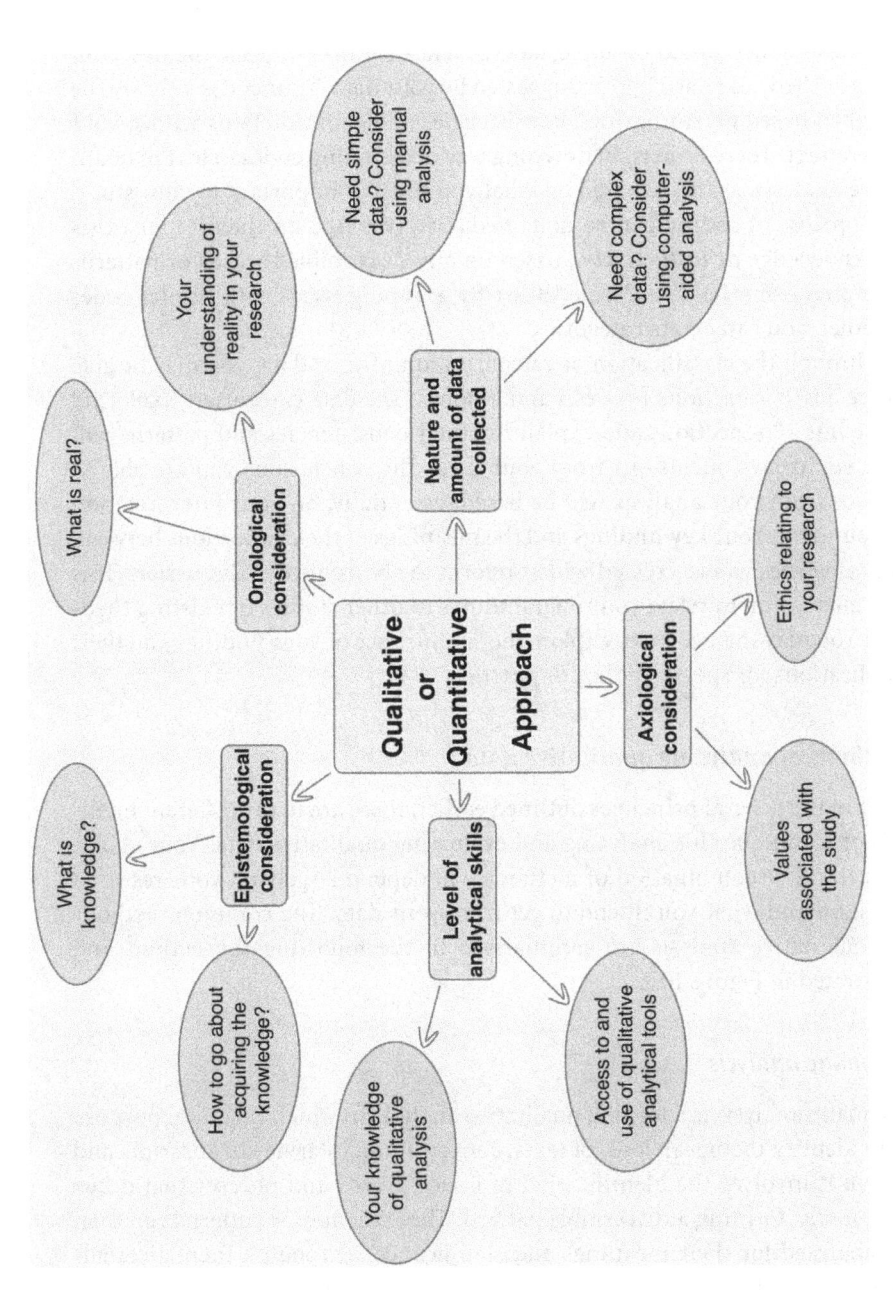

Figure 10.1 Deciding on a qualitative or quantitative analytical approach

the use of coding. Coding, also known as indexing, involves picking out parts of related issues in your data that you consider important or significant and then attaching codes or colour labels to them to make them stand out. Codes may be assigned based on topic, story, events, signifiers, ideas, themes, concepts or theories relating to or suggested by your data. Your codes may also be assigned based on similarities, consistencies and contradictions within your data or text. There is no right or wrong way of assigning codes to text in qualitative analysis, as this is based on what you think is important to your study. The process of coding can be done ***deductively***, based on theories, or existing knowledge **or *inductively*** , based on any discernible threads or patterns emerging from the data (Neale, 2016). By grouping issues with similar codes together, you can create categories.

Through the classification or categorisation of your data, you may be able to see any connections between and amongst the data categories. Exploring these inter-connections and explaining their consistencies and patterns will help you draw conclusions from your data. The conclusions you are able to deduce from your analysis will be based, essentially, on your interpretation of your data. Your key findings and the meanings of the connections between the categories you've created will also form the basis of your discussion. This will enable you to relate your own findings to other studies or existing theories. You may then go on to explore the significance of your findings and their implications for specific policy or practice.

Methods of analysing qualitative data

Within the general principles outlined earlier, there are many different methods or techniques for analysing and evaluating qualitative data. Your choice of method or combination of methods will depend largely on your research question and what you intend to get from your data. The common methods for qualitative analysis are summarised in the following subsections and illustrated in Figure 10.2.

Thematic analysis

Thematic analysis is a form of qualitative analysis in which the main purpose is to identify themes in a set of texts, conversation, interview transcripts and so on. It involves the identification of issues, words and phrases that occur repeatedly, forming a discernible pattern. These themes or patterns can then be analysed for their meanings and significance. Through a thematic analysis of your data, you can identify themes in the data set that are relevant to your research question. Identified themes can then be analysed for their significance. Thematic analysis can be carried out in three main ways. First,

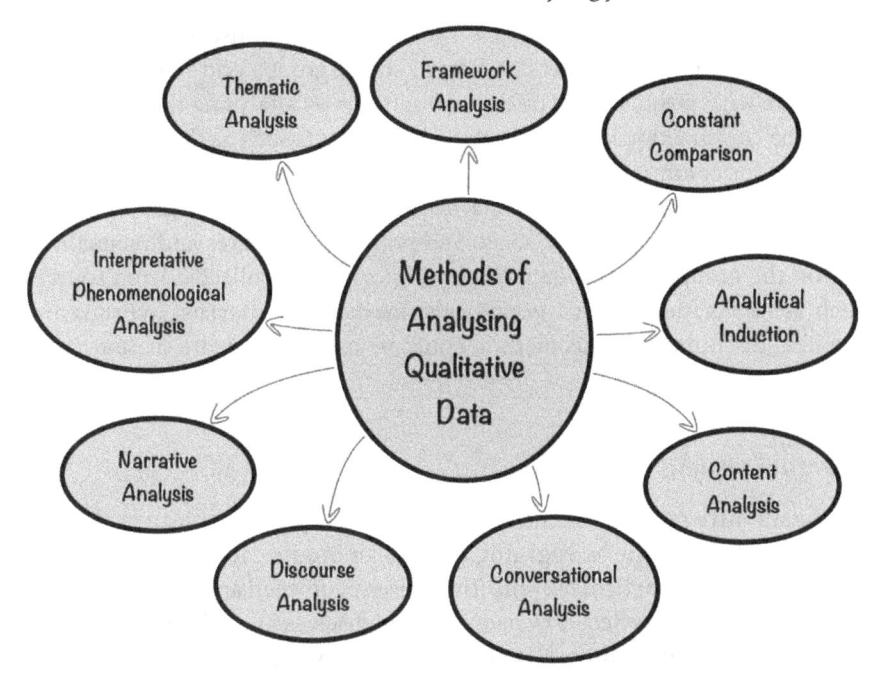

Figure 10.2 Methods of analysing qualitative data

thematic analysis can be done inductively by identifying themes based on the content of the data or text. Second, it can also be done deductively by identifying themes based on existing theories, concepts or ideas. Third, it can be done in a semantic way by identifying themes that are based on explicit content or connotation of the text. Whichever way it is done, thematic analysis provides an opportunity for qualitative analysis of your data by identifying common themes that may be repeatable.

Discourse analysis

Discourse analysis is a generic terminology used to refer to different ways of analysing written, audio, vocal or spoken text and sign language. This method of communication analysis is very common in social science disciplines, especially in sociology, psychology, cultural studies, linguistics and anthropology, amongst others. Texts and communications used in everyday social settings, such as in schools, businesses, workplace, courtrooms, police stations or others, could be subjected to discourse analysis. This involves an examination of how language is used and how meanings are created through communication in different social contexts. It is an ethnography of communication that covers written or oral language, as well as non-verbal aspects of communication such as sign language and gestures. The main focus of discourse analysis is, essentially, gaining an understanding of social groups and how they communicate within their social or cultural settings by analysing their conversation. The conversational analysis can include aspects such as the use or choice of words for communication. Also, it may relate to how the use of language reflects power relations within social groups, and these power relations could be manifest in the economic, social and political structures and inequalities within the groups. If your data relate to information collected from sources such as books, newspapers, periodicals, marketing materials, websites and the like, discourse analysis method could be used to evaluate these texts or contents.

Narrative analysis

As a qualitative research method, narrative analysis focuses on an evaluation of stories people create by engaging them in an inquiry of asking them questions relating to a particular event. The stories people tell and the way the stories are told tend to reflect how people see themselves and others within their worlds. A narrative approach is generally used to evaluate biographical and life-story accounts. This often consists of an analysis of what is said (theme), how it was said or communicated (structure), the exchanges between the storyteller and listener (interaction) and how the story is initiated or constituted (Bryman, 2004).

Interpretative phenomenological analysis

Interpretative phenomenological analysis (IPA) is a method of qualitative analysis commonly used in social sciences especially in psychology, health and related disciplines. It seeks to analyse texts within the context of the creator's lived experiences, and the meanings they attach to their experiences. It is an ethnographic approach concerned with understanding the meanings which people attach to phenomena within their social worlds. It relates to understanding people's actions, decisions, beliefs, values etc. and how these shape the way they interpret their social world. This approach is based on the assumption that the researcher and the social world have an impact on each other in a complex and interactive way and that facts and values cannot be separated from each other (Ritchie et al., 2014).

Constant comparison analysis

The constant comparative method is a qualitative approach often used to, inductively, code or categorise data for the purpose of comparison. For example, if you interviewed two different groups of people in your study, you may decide to deal with or analyse the responses separately as distinct groups or integrate the two groups and then identify similarities and differences between them within a more thematic framework (Ritchie et al., 2014). The constant comparison approach underlies the importance of drawing comparisons between groups. It suggests that if evidence from different populations is obtained separately, it should be compared and contrasted in order to gain a general overview and understanding of the groups being studied. In general terms, the constant comparison approach suggests that each interpretation and finding in your study should be compared with existing findings, theories and concepts in order to provide some perspectives.

Framework analysis

Framework analysis is an approach to qualitative analysis that is commonly used in policy research. It is mostly applicable to an empirical study with a specific research question that is carried out within a specific or limited time frame. It is usually used with a predesigned sample such as a group of workers, workforce or professional (Srivastava and Thomson, 2009). Framework analysis involves a careful screening of data that are then synthesised and categorised into key issues and themes. The categorisation are generally based on five main principles. These are the researcher's familiarisation with the data/issue, identification of appropriate thematic framework, data coding or indexing, charting or graphing of the data and the evaluation and interpretation of the results. The outcome or results of this analysis can then be used to inform or change policies within an organisation or institution to ensure efficiency of operation.

Familiarisation with the data requires that you spend time listening to audio recordings or reading through the data, texts or transcripts of interviews or focus groups in order to gain an insight into the nature of the data and its essential features. Through the process of familiarisation, key themes can then be identified. Identification of key themes may be derived entirely from the data or established on a preconceived theme based on theories or concepts. The key issues and themes that have been expressed by the data or participants could now form the basis for creating a thematic framework. The logically derived thematic framework will reflect not only the key issues but also the meanings, significance and importance of these issues. Coding refers to the process of indexing the key issues within the thematic framework and linking common issues or ideas together. The connections or linkages can then be visually displayed using charts. The process of charting the data may require showing which theme a particular idea connects with. Each of the charts could be carefully labelled and annotated with headings and subheadings. These charts can then be analysed and interpreted using their key characteristics.

The process for undertaking framework analysis as described earlier has been suggested to reflect the key or essential features of qualitative analysis, which are the definitions of concepts, the appraisal or evaluation of a phenomenon, the creation of typologies or classification, the identification of connections and association, the provision of explanations and the application of findings to inform policy or strategies (Ritchie and Spencer, 1994).

Content analysis

Content analysis is a qualitative analytical approach to analysing texts, transcripts of interviews or focus group studies or other audio materials. It involves a systemic coding and categorisation of contents or texts in order to determine any trends or patterns of words used, the frequency of usage, the relationship between the patterns and the general structures and discourses of the communication. The main objective of content analysis is to analyse the general characteristics of a document based entirely on its contents. It is a form of analysis that requires an examination of what is said or written in a document, who said what, to whom was it said and what is the effect of what is said. This approach to qualitative analysis seeks to deconstruct the communicative exchanges by breaking texts or conversation into small units of content and then analysing or interpreting those contents within the framework of the issue or problem. Every form of your research data, which could consist of texts, images, recordings, expressions and the like, can be subject to content analysis in order to establish their meanings.

Conversational analysis

Conversational analysis is an approach to the study of human and social interaction that involves verbal and non-verbal communication and exchanges in an everyday-life setting. The main objective in a conversational analysis is to explore how participants understand and respond to one another in a communicative exchange. This method is increasingly used in the social sciences, especially as a practical way of understanding people's conversation or talk in their everyday interactions. The approach focuses on how social actions are performance with language. That is, the way we do things through what we say or talk about. For example, when we ask questions, respond to questions, greet someone and so on. Conversation analysts often need to be in close proximity to where the conversation is taking place in order to gain a detail view of the conversation in terms of what is said and how it is said. As communicative exchanges occur naturally, conversation analysts are able to obtain naturally occurring data. It can also involve an analysis of transcripts of interviews to explore all verbal and non-verbal interactions and symbols such as intonation, vocal and non-vocal. The method of analysis is based on the assumption that a conversation or talk between people is orderly. It assumes a sequential order of conversation. Conversation analysis can cover ordinary talks between private individual, talks within social groups in an informal environment or talks that take place in an institutional setting such as places of work, school, hospital, prison, religious centres and places of worship, amongst others. Undertaking conversational analysis may require that you obtain a recording or transcribing of the conversation using some digital tools.

Regardless of the method you use for analysing your data, qualitative approaches share a common goal – which is to explore or understand a particular phenomenon from the perspective or standpoint of those experiencing it. You may need to decide which of the qualitative techniques is best suited to your data, participants and main research questions. Your choice of method of analysis may also be influenced by the level of description and qualitative analysis you want to obtain or generate from your data.

Essential tools for qualitative data analysis

To help with your qualitative analysis, there are a number of specialist tools and software that could aid the process of coding, classification and categorisation of your data or text. Amongst the commonly used software for analysing qualitative data are NVivo, ATLAS.ti, HyperRESEARCH, MAXQDA, The Ethnograph and Transana. You may choose to use any of these computer-aided qualitative analytical packages to analyse different types of data, such as audio recordings, graphic or visual data, text documents and written notes. NVivo is generally very widely used as an analytical tool for qualitative data, especially where a large set of data is involved. Using, NVivo, you can identify themes and common patterns within your data set which are stored as *Nodes*. If you are planning to use NVivo or any analytical tools for your analysis, it is advisable to get some training on how the software works before you get onto the stage of your analysis.

There are many other specialist programmes for analysing survey data such as Qualitrics, which is mostly used in psychology research. Your supervisor or information technology support staff in your university may be able to advise on the options available to you based on the software license held by your university.

Analysing your data – quantitative approach

The main purpose of statistical data analysis is to help explore your data more critically so as to reveal the essential information or meanings conveyed or hidden in the data. Statistical analysis provides the opportunity to describe your data, draw inferences from your results and evaluate and explain your research findings. Analysing your data can take different forms, ranging from simple descriptive statistics to a much more complex analysis of relationships to those advanced analytical techniques that can be used in prediction and modelling. Knowing your data and using appropriate statistical techniques to analyse the data can help reveal or generate key findings of your research. Choosing the right technique for analysing your data, drawing correct inferences from your analysis and presenting your results in a coherent and logical way could significantly improve the quality of your thesis (see Chapter 11).

There are two main types of statistics in relation to quantitative data analysis. These are **descriptive statistics** and **inferential statistics**.

Exploring your data through descriptive statistics

Descriptive statistics are used generally to explore or describe sample data through the computation of a number of statistical measures of central tendencies or measures of dispersion. Both measures of central tendency and dispersion relate to the inherent distribution of the data set and the degree to which they are close to or farther away from the mean or an assumed mean value. A descriptive exploration of your data may involve manual or computer-generated statistics that measure central tendency and other characteristics, such as the average value, variability, skewness or kurtosis.

Using averages and measures of central tendency

Averages

An average is the one value that best represents an entire group of scores or values in your dataset. There are three forms of averages. These are the **mean**, the **median** and the **mode**. While all these three measures describe and reflect the central tendency of your data, they also provide different types of information about your data.

Mean

Often referred to as the **arithmetic mean**, the mean is the most commonly used type of statistical averages computed in the social sciences. It is obtained by summing all the values in your data set and then dividing the sum by the number of values or cases in your data set. If your data set involves more than one value, a **weighted mean** score could be obtained by multiplying each value by the frequency of its occurrence (frequency), adding the total of all the occurrences and then dividing the sum by the total number of occurrences.

There is also the **geometric mean**, used when the data set is highly skewed, that is distorted by extreme values and for which the arithmetic mean would not be a realistic measure of central tendency. It computed by taking the **nth** root of a product of **n** numbers (data values). Expressed symbolically, for data values, $a_1, a_2, a_3, \ldots, a_n$, the arithmetic mean is

$$\frac{1}{n}(a_1 + a_2 + a_3 + \ldots + a_n),$$

and the geometric mean is

$$\sqrt[n]{(a_1 \times a_2 \times a_3 \times \ldots \times a_n)}.$$

Median

In a set of values or scores, the median is the midpoint that divides the values or scores into two equal halves such that one-half, or 50%, of the scores or values in your data set falls above the median point and the other half or 50% falls below the median point. The median value can be obtained by listing all the values in order, either from highest to lowest or lowest to highest, and then picking the middle-most score. In cases where the number of values is even, then a median value can be picked by averaging the two middle values.

Mode

The value or score that occurs most frequently, in your data set is referred to as the **mode**. Modal value or score can be computed by listing all the values in your data set or distribution (each value or score should be listed once), tallying the number of times that each value occurs and then picking the value that occurs most often. It is possible to have a data set that has no mode or modal value. This can occur if every value in the distribution contains the same number of occurrences. **Multimodal** is the statistical term used to refer to cases where more than one value appears with equal frequency. Similarly, your distribution is **bimodal** if there are two modes in your set of data or scores.

Percentile

A **percentile** is a statistical measure of distribution that shows the value below which a given percentage of observations in a set of data or group of observation fall. Less commonly used than the averages, percentiles can be used to define the percentage of cases equal to and below a certain point in a distribution or a set of scores. If a score is at the 75th percentile, it means that the score is at or above 75% of the other scores in your data set or sample. The median is the 50th percentile, that is the point below which 50% of your data sample fall. The 25th percentile is known as the **First Quartile (Q_1)** which is the middle number between the smallest number and the median of your data set. The 50th percentile is the **Second Quartile (Q_2)** which is also the median of the data. The 75th percentile is referred to as the **Third Quartile (Q_3)** which is the middle value between the median and the highest value of your data sample.

Variance and measures of variability

Variance and variability refer to statistical measures of spread or dispersion. These show how scores differ from one another. Statistically, variability is a measure of how much each score in a group of scores or data set differs from the mean. There are four most commonly used measures of variability: *range, standard deviation (SD), variance and mean deviation.*

Range

The *range* gives an idea of how spread out or wide apart scores are from one another. As a statistical measure, it can be obtained either of two ways: (a) by subtracting the lowest score in a distribution or data set from the highest score (*inclusive range*) or (b) by subtracting the lowest score in a distribution or data set from the highest score and then adding 1 (*exclusive range*).

SD

The **SD** is a statistical measure of the average amount of variability in a set of scores or data. Technically, the SD is a measure of the average distance from the mean value. The larger the standard deviation, the larger the average distance each data point is from the mean of the distribution. The procedure for manually computing the SD for your data set involves

a   obtaining the difference between each individual score or value in your data and the mean value,
b   squaring each difference and summing them all together,
c   dividing the sum by the size of the sample (minus 1) and
d   then taking the square root of the results.

Variance

As a statistical measure of variability, *variance* is obtained by squaring the SD, obtained as described earlier.

Mean deviation

Also known as the ***mean absolute deviation,*** the ***mean deviation*** is the sum of the absolute value of the deviations from the mean divided by the number of data points. The sum of the deviations from the mean is always equal to 0.

Exploring and analysing your data using graphs and plots

Graphical representation of data using graphs, plots and other visual aids are an important part of data exploration and analysis. Graphs and plots can help make sense of your data. Through graphs and plots, you can summarise, highlight and reveal essential features of your data. Your graphs or plots may also reveal key areas or issues that may need further analysis or investigation.

Different types of graphs can be used to show different things and to make your data more visually intelligible and comprehensible. Amongst the most commonly used graphs and plots for presenting data in social sciences are ***frequency distributions, stem-and-leaf plots, normal probability plot, scatter plots, histograms, bar graphs, line graphs, pie charts*** and ***box plots***.

Frequency distributions

Plotting ***frequency distributions*** offers a useful way of presenting your data graphically. Frequency distribution shows the number of occurrences for each case or value or category of scores or values in your data set. Frequency distributions can be used to present all types of data measured at nominal, ordinal, interval or ratio scales. The presentation of your frequency distribution will depend on the type of data being analysed. Frequencies can be presented using tables or graphs. Whichever way they are presented, frequencies could reveal a great deal about your data and any trends which may not otherwise be visible in the raw data. Frequencies are particularly useful in questionnaire surveys in which responses to questions could be examined against the number of people that responded one way or the other. Such simple analysis could also serve as a pointer to further analysis.

Histogram

The ***histogram*** is a simple statistical technique used to represent data graphically. In this method, the range of observed values is divided into equal intervals and the number of cases in each interval is obtained. The vertical axis is usually used to indicate the number of cases while the horizontal axis is used to show the midpoints of value ranges. Histograms are also very useful to show whether your data is normally distributed about the mean to within a reasonable approximation.

The stem-and-leaf plot

Providing a bit more information on the actual values in your data set than a histogram, the **stem-and-leaf plot** represents each case or score with a numeric value that corresponds to the actual observed value. In this technique, observed values are divided into two components, comprising (a) the leading digit or digits called the **stem** and (b) the trailing digit called the **leaf**, hence the name – stem-and-leaf plot. In a stem-and-leaf plot, the length of each row corresponds to the number of cases that fall into a particular interval. Compared to other forms of plots and graphs, using stem-and-leaf plot to analyse your data offers some advantages. First, the technique provides useful information about the distribution of observed values in your data. Second, it will show how tightly cases cluster together in your data set or sample. Third, any peak or peaks in the distribution (i.e. extreme values) will be shown in the plot.

The boxplot

The **boxplot** is a useful graphical technique for comparing the distribution of values in several groups or categories. The technique displays summary statistics for each distribution by plotting the following:

a   The median represented by the horizontal line inside the box
b   The 25th percentile which is indicated by the lower boundary of the box
c   The 75th percentile shown by the upper boundary of the box
d   Extreme values that are far removed from the rest, commonly referred to as **extreme values** or **outliers**

In statistical terminologies, the 25th and 75th percentiles are usually referred to as **Tukey's hinges**.

It is important to note that if you use boxplot in your analysis, 50% of the cases, that is your data distribution, will have values within the box. The length of the box will correspond to the interquartile range, which is the difference between the 75th and 25th percentiles.

Depending on your data, two types of extreme values can be plotted in your boxplot. First are the plot of cases with values that are more than 3-box lengths from the upper or lower edge of the box. These are generally referred to as **extreme values** and are shown in a boxplot by an asterisk (*). Second are cases with values that are between 1.5- and 3-box lengths from the upper or lower edge of the box. These are known as **outliers** and designated with a circle. In addition to these, the boxplot also shows the largest and smallest observed values that are not outliers. These are usually represented by lines drawn from the ends of the box to these values. The lines that depict these largest and smallest values are often referred to as **whiskers**. That's why box-plots are also known as **box-and-whiskers plots**.

If used and interpreted correctly, a boxplot could offer a very useful graphical summary and overview of your data. The length of the box generally indicates the spread, or variability, of the observations or scores in your data set. As a matter of general rule, 50% of cases have values within the box. If the horizontal line inside the box (i.e. the median) is not in the centre of the box, then it means that the observed values of your data are skewed. If the median line is closer to the bottom of the box than to the top, that means that your data set is positively skewed. Similarly, if the median line is closer to the top of the box rather than to the bottom, then it means your data are negatively skewed. The length of the tail is shown by the number of whiskers and the outlying and extreme values. Boxplots are particularly useful when used to compare different distribution or data sets, with a boxplot generated for each set.

Normal probability plot

The **normal probability plot** is a form of statistical graph commonly used to examine if a data set is normally distributed. Many statistical tests work under the assumption that the data being analysed is normally distributed. To test this assumption, a normal probability plot can be used to plot each observed value against the expected value from the normal distribution. If the observed values or sample is from a normal distribution, we expect that the plots or points will fall more or less on a straight line. The more clustered around a straight line the points or plots are, the closer your data are to a normal distribution. The presence of any pattern in the points will indicate that your data are not normally distributed. In order to show clearly the degree of deviation from the normal distribution of your data, a **detrended normal plot** could be used. The detrended normal plot will show the actual deviations of each point from a normal distribution or a straight line.

Scatter plots

As a way of exploring relationships in your data set, it is sometimes useful to show graphically the relationship between two variables using **scatter plots** or **scatter graph**, as it is sometimes known. Scatter-graph can be obtained by plotting one variable (Y) against another variable (X). In a scatter-plot, a cluster of data points around a straight line indicates a very strong association between variable Y and variable X, while a dispersed or random distribution indicates a weak association between the two variables.

Understanding data distribution with curves and skewness

Normal distribution curves and skewness

Curves and skewness are, respectively, graphical and statistical measures used to describe the shape of a data distribution. Most statistical analysis assumes a normal distribution of data with a symmetrical bell-shaped pattern. Skewness measures are based on the degree by which the distribution of a data set deviates from the normal symmetric bell-shaped pattern and the direction of deviation (***positive skew*** or ***negative skew***). Generally, the direction of skewness in your data will depend on the location of the mean value of the data in relation to the median value of the data. On one hand, if the mean value of your data is greater than the median value, the distribution of your data is positively skewed. On the other hand, if the median is greater than the mean, then your data distribution is negatively skewed.

In statistical terms, skewness is computed by subtracting the value of the median from the mean. For the purpose of illustration, if your data set has the mean value 75 and a median is 67, then the skewness value for your data is 8, that is (75 – 67). This suggests that the distribution is positively skewed. By the same token, if the mean value of your data distribution is 72 and the median is 83, the skewness value is –11, that is (72 – 83). That will suggest that the distribution is negatively skewed.

Kurtosis

In graphical terms, ***kurtosis*** relates to how flat or peaked a distribution appears when plotted in a graph in comparison to a normal symmetric bell-shaped curve. Different data distributions produce different kurtosis. A normal bell-shaped distribution is described as *'mesokurtic'*. A distribution curve that is relatively flat is generally referred to as *'platykurtic'*. If the shape of your distribution is relatively peaked compared to a bell-shaped distribution, then your data distribution is *'leptokurtic'* (see Figure 10.3). Generally, data sets that are platykurtic are relatively more dispersed or variable than those that are leptokurtic. Distributions that are leptokurtic are relatively more compact and less dispersed or variable. Skewness and kurtosis are often used in graphical and descriptive terms; however, mathematical indicators or measures can also be computed to indicate how skewed or kurtotic your data distribution is.

Common statistical/analytical techniques

In addition to the descriptive statistics and various graphical and visual presentation of data described earlier, there are several statistical techniques and tools available to analyse quantitative data. Most of these statistical techniques, go beyond just describing your data to providing the basis for

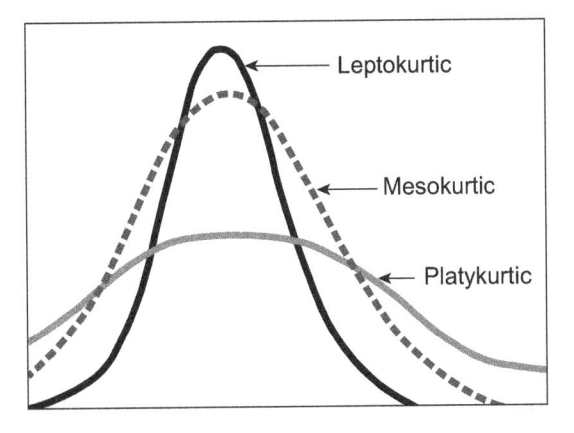

Figure 10.3 Data distribution – curves and kurtosis

explaining connections and relationships between variables in your data or making predictions using your data. Most important, these statistics offer a scientific basis for validating your hypotheses and enabling you to draw inferences from your data. Hence, these types of statistics are commonly referred to as *inferential statistics*. There are two main categories of inferential statistics: *parametric* and *non-parametric* statistics.

Parametric statistics are generally used to analyse data that are drawn or assumed to be drawn from a normally distributed population (a typical bell-shaped curve). A non-parametric statistic is used, generally, in situations in which the data distribution is not or is assumed to be not normally distributed, in which case this may be positively or negatively skewed. Non-parametric statistics are also used if the distribution is unknown or if there is a presence of extreme values in terms of range in the data set. Where the sample is too small to verify the distribution of your data; for example if you are using a sample size of less than 30, then a non-parametric statistic should be used. A decision on whether to use a parametric or non-parametric statistic should be based on the nature of your data, the scale of measurement of the data and the power efficiency of the test statistics. Generally, parametric statistics are more powerful than non-parametric statistics. Examples of some parametric statistics used for explaining, describing or testing hypotheses in social sciences are summarised next.

Hypotheses and hypotheses testing

Formulating, testing or validating *hypotheses* around your research questions is an important aspect of your data analysis. A hypothesis is a proposition or statement put forward concerning your guess or intuition concerning the strength, direction or nature of the relationship between a specified set of variables. Such guess may be based on theories or your own ideas regarding the problem of investigation. Whatever the bases, hypotheses need to be subjected to a scientific (statistical) test in order to have any validity. It is only when a hypothesis is tested and proved to be true or false that it is of any scientific value.

Types of hypotheses

There are two types of statistical hypotheses. The **null hypothesis** often indicated as (H_0), and the **alternative hypothesis** usually represented by (H_1). The null hypothesis is usually stated in the form of the exact opposite of what you want to prove. For example, if you are interested in showing that two variables or samples A and B are different, you may pose a null and an alternative hypothesis, as follows:

(H_0): There is no significant difference between variables or samples A and B.
(H_1): There is a significant difference between variables or samples A and B.

As only one of these two statements or hypotheses can be true at any given time, accepting one means rejecting the other, and vice versa. Therefore, the aim of testing the null hypothesis is to see whether it can be rejected or accepted. If, on the basis of a statistical test, a null hypothesis is rejected because it is untrue, then the alternative hypothesis must be accepted. Conversely, if the null hypothesis is accepted as true, then its alternative hypothesis must be false and should be rejected.

One-tailed and two-tailed tests

In testing your hypothesis, you may use appropriate statistical techniques as described next. You also need to decide on whether to use a **one-tailed** or a **two-tailed** test. The way your null hypothesis is stated will determine whether you need a one-tailed or two-tailed test. In the example of the null hypothesis earlier, there is no indication of the direction of difference between variables or samples A and B. So, a two-tailed test will be most appropriate in this case. If the null hypothesis were to be restated or reformulated to read as

H_0: Variable or sample A is significantly greater than variable or sample B.

Then, a direction of difference has been introduced. This will then require a one-tailed test.

Hypothesis testing and significance level

To test your hypotheses, you need to state the required **level of significance** for the test. The level of significance is the statistical basis on which your decision to accept or reject the hypothesis is predicated. In statistical terms, the level of significance of a hypothesis test is the maximum probability with which you are prepared to risk committing an error of judgement in your test. An error of judgement (***type 1 error***) is committed by rejecting a null hypothesis that you should have accepted. Similarly, an error of judgement is equally committed if you accept a null hypothesis that you should have rejected (***type 2 error***). Technically, the significance level is the maximum probability of committing, a type I error and it is often denoted by the Greek letter (***alpha*** $\propto$). In most studies in social sciences, the significance level is often specified at 95%. That is an alpha ($\propto$) level = 0.05. This means there are 5 chances in 100 (or 1 chance in 20) of rejecting the null hypothesis when it should have been accepted. An alpha level of 0.05 suggests you are 95 % confident that the right decision will be made in the rejection or acceptance of your stated null hypothesis. This is generally referred to as the ***confidence level*** in statistical tests.

For purposes of clarity, it is essential that you understand the statistical process of testing a hypothesis around your research question and how to present your result in a consistent and logical fashion for the readers to make sense of your analysis. As a guide, the essential steps and procedures for testing your hypotheses and presenting your results are discussed next and are illustrated in Figure 10.4.

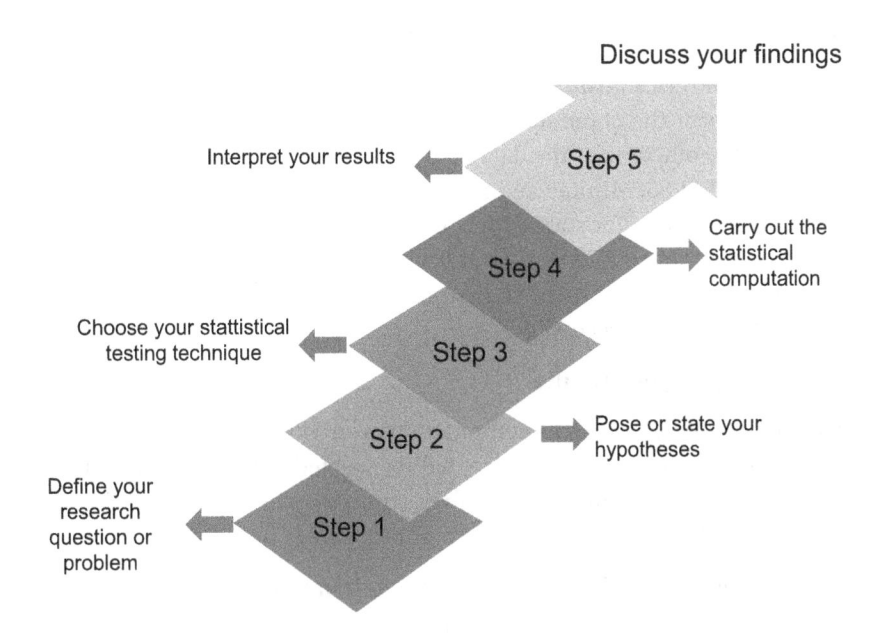

Figure 10.4 Key steps in statistical tests of hypotheses

Step 1: Defining your research question or problem

You need to understand your research question and establish the context for the use of any statistical test that may be required. A brief statement which clearly details why a test is required and for what purpose could be essential here. This could help define the problem and what you intend to achieve using a test statistic.

Step 2: Pose or state your hypotheses

Here both the null and the alternative hypotheses must be fully stated in order to make clear what statistical test you are trying to achieve. The statement of hypotheses should be posed in light of and with reference to your research question.

Step 3: Choose your statistical testing technique

It is important to provide a brief justification for choosing a particular statistical test. Usually, the choice of statistical test depends on three main factors. These are (a) the type of or nature of your data and the scale at which they are measured (e.g. nominal, ordinal, interval, ratio), (b) your research question and whether your aim is to carry out a test of difference or association or relationship test between variables or phenomena and (c) the way you state or pose your hypotheses and whether a one-tailed or two-tailed test is required. It is also necessary to state the level of statistical significance you intend to use in the test, that is 95% or 99% being the most usual.

Step 4: Carry out the statistical computation

Computing the test statistics will almost certainly require computer analysis. Whichever form the computation takes, the data set must be entered correctly, and the outcome of the data analysis presented, usually as a computer printout. IBM-SPSS, Minitab and Stata are some of the most widely used programmes as software for statistical computation. These programmes provide a complete and integrated statistical package that you can use for your data analysis and management. The statistical package on Microsoft Excel can also be used and is readily accessible.

Step 5: Interpret your results

From the result of your test computation, you would need to make clear whether the null hypothesis is accepted or rejected and state why. You may also need to state the implications of rejecting or accepting the null hypothesis in terms of your research question or problem.

Testing hypotheses – inferential parametric statistics

There are many statistical techniques that you can use to analyse your data and test your hypotheses. Examples of commonly used statistics are summarised in the following sections. It is practically impossible to cover all possible statistics in this book. So you may need to consult relevant texts to gain in-depth understanding and training on how to apply these techniques to your own study (see further reading).

Tests of difference

1 Student's t-test statistics

If one of your research objectives is to establish differences between sets of variables, **Student's t-test statistics** may be used depending on your data. The technique is applicable to samples of all sizes, and it is particularly useful when dealing with a small sample ($n < 30$). It is a parametric test of difference commonly used in social science research. The test is used to establish whether two samples could have been drawn from the same population. It is useful in a situation where you need to test a hypothesis concerning the difference between a sample mean and a specified value. An example is when you have an assumed mean or standard mean or when you have two samples and you wish to test a hypothesis about the difference. Generally, the null hypothesis of Student's t test is that two sets of data are random samples from a common, normally distributed population.

The Student's t-test statistics work under the assumptions that

a your data are measured on an interval or ratio scale,
b the samples are normally distributed and
c the sample variances are drawn from the same population.

2 Analysis of variance

If your objective is to establish any difference between just two samples, the Student's t test is an appropriate parametric statistic to use. However, if you need to compare more than two samples. For example, if you have a set of measurements taken from different locations or different social groups and you want to establish any significant differences within and between the locations or social groups, then an **analysis of variance** (ANOVA) could be an appropriate technique to use. The method is used to test the null hypothesis that several population means are equal. The technique examines variability in the samples and determines whether there are reasons to believe the population means are equal.

In order to determine any significant difference between two or more samples, the ANOVA statistic normally identifies two types of variations in the samples. These are (a) the variability of the observations within a group (i.e. around the group mean) and (b) the variability between the group means themselves. **Within-group variability** is a measure of how much the scores or observations within a group vary. It is the variance of the observations within a group that the technique uses to estimate the variance within a group in the population. Using the sample mean for each of the groups the technique then computes how much these means vary, that is the between-group variability. The ANOVA statistic works under two major assumptions: (a) each of the groups must be a random sample from a normal population, and (b) the variances in all groups must be equal in the population.

Test of association or relationship – correlation statistics

Correlation statistics are used to test the relationship between two variables. As these statistics show the degree of association between two variables, they are sometimes referred to as tests of association. Correlation techniques show how two variables behave together. For example, if your research aim is to examine the relationship between variables A and variable B or two sets of samples or phenomena, then the technique could be used. Two variables are said to be related if knowing the value of one variable tells you something about the other variable. Every correlation statistic involves the computation of a coefficient, known as the **correlation coefficient**. A correlation coefficient is a mathematical measure of the degree of association between two paired variables. There are various methods of computing a correlation coefficient. Whichever method is used, the statistics work in a way that when one variable increases in exact proportion to the other, the coefficient will be +1. Similarly, if one variable decreases in exact proportion to the other, the coefficient will be –1. If there is no relationship, whatsoever, between the two variables, the coefficient will be 0 or close to 0. In statistical terms, correlation analysis shows the extent of **co-variability** between two sets of variables, that is how one variable varies in relation to the other. Because the correlation coefficient describes the degree of association between two variables, it is also a useful method of comparison between variables.

Depending on the nature of your data, you may use either of the two main methods of correlation analysis. These are (a) **parametric methods of correlation** and (b) **non-parametric methods of correlation**. An example of a parametric correlation statistic is the **Pearson product-moment correlation**. This technique could be used under the following assumptions or conditions:

a Your data set has been collected or drawn from normally distributed populations.
b Your data are measured on interval or ratio scales.
c The populations from where your data was drawn have the same variance or a known ratio of variances.

d The values or observations of each of your data set are independent in their respective population; that is the selection of one value or observation from the population does not influence the selection of another.

Explaining and predicting relationships – regression analysis

Besides just testing hypotheses regarding relationships, regression analysis provides other essential tools for explaining and predicting social phenomena. There are different types of regression analysis.

Simple linear regression

The *simple linear regression* analysis is one of the most widely used analytical tools in social science research. Not only does the technique explores any relationship between variables, but it also measures the degree or magnitude of that relationship. The technique shows how changes in one variable affect the other variable. It enables you to determine how much a variable is affected by other variables or factors. In other words, if two variables X and Y are related and there is a unit change in variable X, the regression analysis technique could tell you how much variable Y is likely or expected to change.

One of the objectives of the simple linear regression model is to help determine the best line through the data points in a scatter plot. This line, which runs through the middle of the points in a scatter plot, is sometimes referred to as the *regression line*. The regression technique determines this *line of best fit* through the method of least squares; hence, the regression line is also known as the *least squares line*. The underlying principle of the least squares method is that the line of best fit which runs through the scatter plots such that the sum of the squares of the deviations from the points to the line is a minimum. In graphical terms, a correlation statistic shows how closely the data points are distributed around a straight line. Regression analysis involves the computation of the statistics and the fitting of the regression line.

In mathematical terms, the simple linear regression model is stated as

$$Y = a + bx + e,$$

where
Y is the dependent variable,
a is the intercept (the point at which the regression line touches the y axis),
x is the independent variable,
b is the slope of the regression line and
e is the error term (that is the stochastic disturbance or the residuals).

The regression technique is a powerful statistical tool for describing, drawing inferences, predicting and explaining social phenomena. The linear regression analysis technique works under the following conditions and assumptions:

a   Your data has no measurement error.
b   The relationship between your dependent variable (y) and independent variable (x) is linear.
c   The data in the variables used in your simple linear regression analysis are normally distributed.
d   The regression residuals (that is the error term of the regression equation) should be randomly distributed and should have a mean value of 0.
e   The variance of the distribution of the residual should be constant for all values of x.
f   The distribution of the residual should not show any serial or spatial autocorrelation.
g   Your number of cases should be more than the number of variables.

Multiple linear regression

While simple linear regression is used to analyse a problem using only one independent variable (X), **multiple linear regression** analysis offers the opportunity to examine an issue using more than one independent (explanatory) variables. The multiple regression technique is more useful in a real-life situation in which many factors may account for the existence of a problem. The technique provides a higher level of explanation than the simple linear regression that uses only one predictor or explanatory variable.

The multiple linear regression model is mathematically stated as

$$Y = a + b_1 X_1 + b_2 X_2 + b_3 X_3 + \ldots b_n X_n + e,$$

where Y is the dependent variable,
a is constant,
$b_1, b_2, \ldots, b_n$ are partial regression coefficients or slope coefficients for each of the explanatory variables,
$X_1, X_2, \ldots, X_n$ are the independent (predictor) or explanatory variables (can be either continuous
or categorical),
e is the model's error term (also known as the residuals). .

The multiple regression analysis operates under a similar assumption as simple linear regression with an additional criterion that there should be minimal multicollinearity between the independent or predictors variables.

Logistic regression analysis

Unlike simple linear regression and multiple linear regression, logistic regression analysis is used to analyse dichotomous and categorical data. You may be conducting research where your dependent variable may not meet the general condition of normal distribution required for simple or multiple linear regression, as discussed earlier, or your data are not continuous. In that case, logistic regression could be most suitable for your analysis.

The logistic regression analysis technique requires your dependent variable to be categorical. So if you are analysing a dependent variable that is dichotomous and categorical such as a questionnaire survey with Yes or No, Good or Bad, Leave or Remain responses and so on, then a logistic regression analysis would be more appropriate for your data. There are generally no strict data requirements or conditions for using logistic regression other than that you need a larger sample size than used in ordinary regression analysis to increase the validity of your results.

Binary logistic regression

As a form of regression analysis, the binary logistic regression could be used to analyse your data if your dependent variable (y) has only one of two outcomes, such as Yes = 1 or No = 0. The method determines the impact of one or more independent variable(s) on predicting membership of one or other of the two dependent variable categories. In technical terms, the binary logistic regression determines the probability of realising a 'Yes' outcome.

Non-linear regression analysis

The relationship between a dependent variable (y) and independent variables $(X_1, X_2, \ldots, X_n)$ may not necessarily be linear. If your data exhibit a non-linear relationship, the appropriate regression analysis to consider is a **non-linear regression** technique. It is therefore important to check your data carefully in order to determine if non-linear regression analysis would be more suitable or appropriate for your analysis. This is most easily done by doing a scatterplot of the two variables in question which will readily show the nature of any relationship. The scatter plot may show quadratic, cubic, power, exponential or logarithmic relationships between the two variables.

Testing hypotheses – inferential non-parametric statistics

Test of difference – chi-square statistic

Chi-square is a non-parametric test of difference or independence that is widely used in social science research. It is not as powerful as the parametric t test. It is important to note that t tests and chi-square tests are for totally different research hypotheses: the former tests differences in group means, the latter in data distributions and no assumptions are made concerning the form of the distribution being tested. Basically, the chi-square tests whether the observed frequencies; that is data distributions of a given phenomenon differ significantly from frequencies which might be expected according to some assumed hypothesis. Although the chi-square test has the advantage of using very simple data requirements, it has certain limitations which restrict its usefulness. The technique can be used when the following criteria are met:

a Your data set is expressed in frequencies counted in each of a number of categories.
b As a matter of rule, no more than 20% of the cells used in chi-square computation should have an expected frequency of less than 5.
c None of your cells should have an expected frequency of less than 1.
d The sets of variables or observations being compared must be independent; for example one observation must not influence another.

Depending on the number of samples you want to test, you can use two main types of chi-square test analysis. These are (a) the **one-sample chi-square test**, usually used to test the difference between an observed distribution and the expected distribution; the expected distribution could be any theoretical distribution, for example normal or Poisson distribution or any other forms of observed distribution; and (b) the **two- (or more) sample chi-square test**, which is used to test whether two or more samples follow the same distribution.

Test of difference – Mann-Whitney U test statistic

Mann-Whitney U test, also known as the **Wilcoxon** test, is a non-parametric test of difference commonly used in social sciences. It is the non-parametric version of the t test. The technique is used to test the hypothesis that two independent samples come from populations having the same distribution. Unlike Student's t test which requires data to be measured on an interval or ratio scale, Mann-Whitney U test technique can be applied to data measured either on ratio, interval or ordinal scales. The only condition necessary to apply this statistical technique to your study is that the samples used in your data should be randomly selected and the values should lend themselves to some sorts of ordering. The statistical technique works under the following assumptions:

a The two samples used in your analysis should be independent and random.
b Your data or variables should be continuous variable in terms of how they are measured.
c At least one of your variables should be measured using an ordinal scale.

The computation of the Mann-Whitney U test statistic requires the ranking of your data, usually from the smallest to the largest value.

Apart from the analytical techniques mentioned previously, there are many other statistical tests that could be used to analyse your data. For a list of commonly used statistical tests and hypotheses validation techniques in social sciences, see Appendix 1. Some of the most widely used techniques for analysing quantitative data are also shown in Figure 10.5.

Discussing your findings

It is essential to remember that statistics are tools to aid your analysis and help make sense of your data. Whichever analytical approach or technique you use, it is still essential that you are able to interpret the results in the context of your own research question. Discussion and evaluation of your findings are also critical to your understanding of whether your data have answered your research question or whether you need to collect more data or conduct further investigation.

It is equally necessary to discuss your test results and findings in the context of the existing literature, concepts, paradigms or prevailing knowledge. The value of your analysis and conclusions can only be evaluated in the context of, and in relation to, your study aims and objectives. A major weakness of most PhD theses is for students to present their data analysis results without a full and detailed critical evaluation of what the results mean for their studies. Every conclusion you arrived at, as a matter of necessity, needs to be informed by your data. Similarly, your conclusions about specific findings in your research need to be related back to the literature so as to set them in a wider context.

Key messages

- Before commencing your data analysis, it is important you understand the nature of your data and the scales at which they have been measured.
- The nature and scale of measurement will dictate the type of analysis that you can carry out on your data.
- Data measured on interval or ratio scales lend themselves readily to quantitative analysis while data measured on a nominal or ordinal scale are best suited for qualitative analysis.

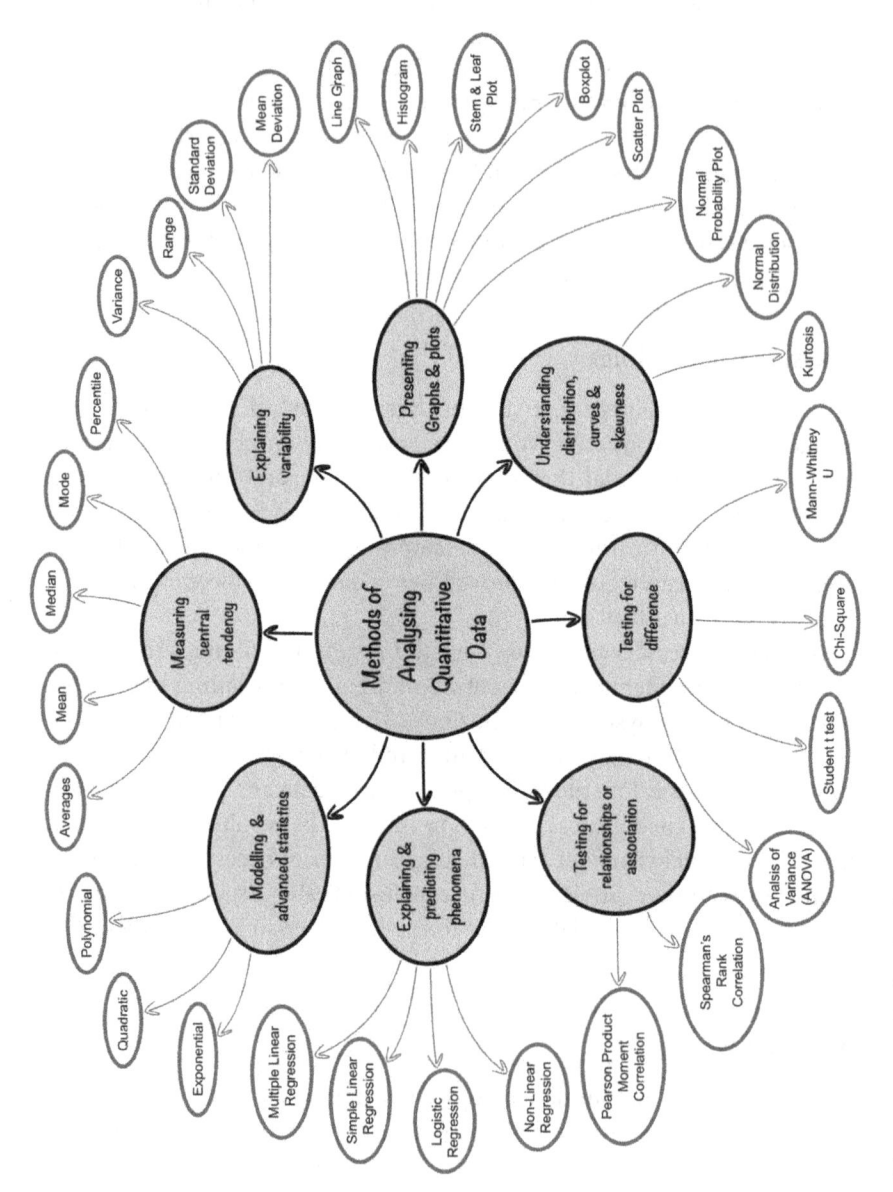

Figure 10.5 Methods of analysing quantitative data

- Quantitative methods follow the tradition of statistical analysis while qualitative methods rely on explaining social phenomena using non-statistical data.
- Within the general qualitative or quantitative traditions, there are several methods of analyses.
- Many qualitative methods have common features such as problem definition, data classification, coding or indexing, making connections, discussing results and relating findings to theory and/or policy.
- Quantitative techniques place emphasis on quantitative data that can be statistically analysed in order to draw conclusions or inferences from the data.
- Statistics are tools to aid your analysis and help make sense of your data. Whichever analytical technique you use, it is still essential that you interpret the results in the context of your research question.
- It is also important that you evaluate your research findings and analysis with regards to the existing literature, concepts, paradigms or prevailing knowledge.
- Through your analysis and discussion of your results you should know whether you need to collect more data or conduct further investigation.

Further reading

Adcock, R., and Collier, D. (2001). Measurement validity: A shared standard for qualitative and quantitative research. *American Political Science Review*, 95(3), pp. 529–546.

American Ethnographic Society. (2020). [Online]. Available at: https://american ethnologist.org/. Accessed on 23rd October 2020.

Beins, B., and McCarthy, M. (2018). Advanced research and data analysis. In *Research Methods and Statistics in Psychology* (pp. 251–252). Cambridge: Cambridge University Press.

Bryman, A. (2004). *Social Science Research Methods*, 2nd ed. Oxford: Oxford University Press.

Creswell, J. W., and Poth, C. N. (2018). *Qualitative Inquiry and Research Design: Choosing Among Five Approaches*, 4th ed. London: Sage.

Denzin, N. K., and Lincoln, Y. S. (2011). *The Sage Handbook of Qualitative Research*, 4th ed. London: Sage.

Field, A. (2018). *Discovering Statistics Using IBM SPSS Statistics*. London: SAGE Publications Limited.

Kellstedt, P., and Whitten, G. (2020). *An SPSS Companion for the Third Edition of the Fundamentals of Political Science Research*. Cambridge: Cambridge University Press.

Leech, N. L., Barrett, K. C., and Morgan, G. A. (eds.). (2015). *IBM SPSS for Intermediate Statistics: Use and Interpretation*, 5th ed. New York and London: Routledge.

Lemahieu, W., Vanden Broucke, S., and Baesens, B. (2018). Analytics. In *Principles of Database Management: The Practical Guide to Storing, Managing and Analyzing Big and Small Data* (pp. 664–730). Cambridge: Cambridge University Press.

Marchant-Shapiro, T. (2015). *Statistics for Political Analysis.* London: Sage.

Marinac, A., Simpson, B., Hart, C., Chisholm, R., Nielsen, J., and Brogan, M. (2017). Analysing and persuading. In *Learning Law* (pp. 186–208). Cambridge: Cambridge University Press.

Neale, J. (2016). Iterative categorization (IC): A systematic technique for analysing qualitative data. *Addiction,* 111(6), pp. 1096–1106, Published by John Wiley & Sons on behalf of the Society for the Study of Addiction, 9th May 2016.

Odden, D. (2013). Doing an analysis. In *Introducing Phonology.* Cambridge Introductions to Language and Linguistics (pp. 147–204). Cambridge: Cambridge University Press.

Packer, M. (2017). The analysis of qualitative interviews. In *The Science of Qualitative Research* (pp. 71–95). Cambridge: Cambridge University Press.

Ritchie, J., Lewis, J., Nicholls, C. M., and Ormston, R. (2014). *Qualitative Research Practice: A Guide for Social Science Students & Researchers,* 2nd ed. London: Sage.

Ritchie, J., and Spencer, L. (1994). Qualitative data analysis for applied policy research. In A. Bryman and R. G. Burgess (eds.), *Analyzing Qualitative Data* (pp. 173–194). London: Routledge.

Silverman, D. (2014). *Interpreting Qualitative Data,* 5th ed. London: Sage.

Smith, A. (2009). *Interpretative Phenomenological Analysis: Theory, Method and Research.* London: Sage.

Snijders, T. A. B., and Bosker, R. J. (2011). *Multilevel Analysis: An Introduction to Basic and Advanced Multilevel Modelling,* 2nd ed. London: Sage.

Srivastava, A., and Thomson, S. B. (2009). Framework analysis: A qualitative methodology for applied policy research. Research note. *JOAAG,* 4(2), pp. 72–79.

Warne, R. (2017). Applying statistics to research, and advanced statistical methods. In *Statistics for the Social Sciences: A General Linear Model Approach* (pp. 443–484). Cambridge: Cambridge University Press.

CHAPTER 11

Writing up your PhD thesis

Introduction

This chapter provides an essential guide on the art and craft of thesis writing. It explains how research ideas can be communicated on paper through a structured and logically presented thesis. It considers PhD thesis writing as an activity that requires a great deal of imagination and creativity. It provides essential information on designing the synopsis of a PhD thesis and key issues to consider while writing your PhD thesis. Issues such as originality, style, spelling, effective referencing, punctuation, clarity, coherence. etc. are discussed with reference to each of your thesis chapters. The chapter explains the use of diagrams, tables, figures and illustrations in a thesis and provides a useful guide on how to navigate the process of drafting, redrafting and editing your thesis and proofreading it before you submit the final document for your viva voce examination. The chapter also provides information on issues relating to referencing, citations, using quotations, paraphrasing and acknowledging other people's work in your thesis.

By the end of the chapter, you will have a better understanding of

- key features of a PhD thesis and what should be included in a thesis;
- how to structure, draft, redraft and edit your PhD thesis;
- making effective use of diagrams, illustrations and figures in your thesis;
- how to overcome 'writer's block' if and when you do get stalled in your thesis writing;
- working on your referencing and citations; and
- the checklist for preparing your thesis for submission.

Preparing for writing up your thesis

Most of the materials covered in this chapter will be relevant to most PhD theses across disciplines such as the social sciences, business, law, the humanities, the arts, health and related disciplines. However, before you start writing up your thesis, it is crucial that you are familiar with your university's requirements regarding PhD theses. Every university is different and has its own style and requirements with respect to PhD theses. Not only are there differences in university requirements for a PhD thesis, but there are also differences in style depending on the discipline. Your director of studies or supervisors should be able to guide you through this important phase of your PhD journey. Given the institutional or disciplinary variations that may be involved in thesis structure, presentation and submission, the advice is to adhere to and comply with your university's guidelines for your subject or discipline. It is better not to assume anything but to ask for guidance as to specific requirements for thesis writing and submission for your university.

Generally, writing a thesis requires that you pull together all the essential materials from your proposal, your review of literature, your research methodology, your fieldwork, your data analysis, your discussion of results, your conclusions and so on and present these in a single document in form of a research report. Regardless of your discipline, you need to be mindful that your thesis is an academic report. It is also an essential part of your examination, as this report will be scrutinised during your viva voce examination (see Chapter 12). Your thesis will be read, dissected, and subject to scrutiny by your internal and external examiners and everyone else involved in your examination. Your thesis, if passed, will also become a public reference material that the academic community may want to read and peruse long after you have finished your PhD. It is therefore essential that you get it right. As your thesis is a fundamental aspect of your examination, it is doubly important that you put everything you've got into writing it.

As an original piece of work for your PhD, your thesis has to serve the purpose for which it is intended. It has to meet the high expectations required at a PhD level in terms of the quality and standard of its content, structure and presentation. So you need to bear all these in mind while writing your thesis. It is not just any other report or document you have written before. Whether you are full-time or part-time, your thesis is the product, irrespective of 4 or 7 years of work. The better thesis you write, the greater your chances of sailing through your viva and getting that outcome you have been working hard for all these years. Also, you are more likely to get publications out of your thesis if it is potent and impactful (see Chapter 13).

Seeking help with academic writing

If you are an international student and English is not your first language, you may need to seek extra support from your supervisors or your university towards developing your academic writing skills. Different universities have different ways they support their international students through their PhD journey (see Chapter 4). Part of this support could well be through the provision of training in academic writing. Before writing your thesis, it is advisable you discuss any academic writing training or support needs or issues with your supervisors.

Doing a PhD and writing up a thesis of about 10,000 words in a language that is not your natural language may pose some challenges for some students. These challenges become even more amplified with the pressure to write to the strict requirements and standards befitting a PhD award.

It must be said, however, that the language difficulty and the challenges of effective academic writing are not limited or confined to international students or non-native English speakers, as some home students may also struggle with academic writing even though English is their first language. So the main issue is about understanding the conventions and what is required of you in a thesis and ensuring you write to the required and expected standards regardless of whether you are a native or non-native English speaker. For more information on writing a thesis as a non-English speaker, see Bitchener (2017).

Writing style

Your style of writing needs to be clear and scientific in relation to the use of language and communication of ideas in your thesis. Paragraphs should not be so long as to make the flow of ideas unintelligible. There should be consistent and coherent links between chapters to ensure that your ideas flow in a reasoned and logical fashion. There is a huge difference between writing a thesis and writing a paper for an academic journal, not only in terms of the nature of the content of an academic paper and a thesis but also in terms of the size, structure and purpose of these two academic writings. However, if you have already published parts of your PhD in a peer-reviewed academic journal, the chances are that you have already developed and acquired essential writing skills through your published work that could be beneficial to you in writing your thesis. The general mistake that some students new to writing a thesis make is in their thinking that a PhD thesis is just an extended version of their master's dissertation. You should not fall into that trap: far from it.

A PhD thesis is a unique type of academic writing, and your thesis needs to be written to meet specific standards. Just as gaining a doctorate is a distinct learning process from doing an undergraduate or master's degrees, a master's dissertation is essentially different from a PhD thesis. A PhD thesis, for all intents and purposes, is quite unique and should be written with a great degree of care and attention. The level of critical analysis required for a PhD thesis is far higher than those required for any master's degree programme. More than a master's dissertation, your PhD thesis will most certainly be subject to a much more rigorous and critical evaluation. So you need to be able to demonstrate a far higher level of knowledge. By the time you finish your PhD, you are expected to know a great deal about your research, and you may be regarded as one of the world's experts, if not the world expert, on the topic. Your thesis, therefore, needs to be an outstanding piece of work that evidences your contribution to knowledge in the area of your research. As a unique piece of academic writing and a research report, your thesis should be evidence-based and written in a way as to communicate your findings and your contribution to knowledge effectively to the readers or your audience.

Also, your thesis needs to have a strong methodological foundation on which your whole argument and conclusions are predicated. The stronger your methodological foundation, the better the structure of arguments and conclusions you can build on it. There are three main interrelated elements of writing a thesis. These are content, structure and argument. Content relates to all the materials and information you need to pull together to create a thesis of about 10,000 or so words. This will include your reviews of literature, analysis of your data and creation of 'values', for example new tables, figures, illustrations and so on. The structure relates to how you put these materials together in an intelligible and coherent way. The argument relates to your interpretation, explanation, claims, justification and conclusions you drew from all the materials you presented to build a convincing and forceful argument of the contribution of your thesis to existing knowledge. These interacting features are illustrated in what could be referred to as a **'PhD thesis writing triangle'** (Figure 11.1).

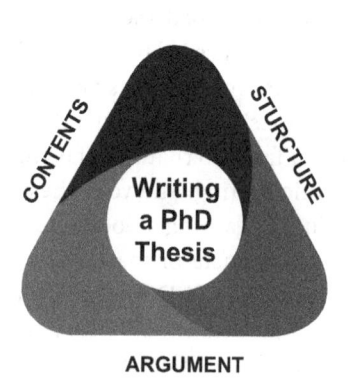

Content
- Reviews of literature
- Analyses of data
- Added value to knowledge. E. g. new ideas, new tables, illustratio

Structure
- Coherence
- Logic
- Flow

Argument
- Explanation
- Interpretation
- Claims and justifications
- Conclusion

CONTENTS   STURCTURE

Writing a PhD Thesis

ARGUMENT

Figure 11.1 PhD Thesis writing triangle – argument–content–structure

General contents and structure of a thesis

Most PhD theses in the social sciences commonly consist of six key sections or chapters in terms of structure:

- Introduction
- Literature review
- Methodology
- Analysis and Findings
- Discussion
- Conclusion

While these main features are very common, especially, in PhD theses that are essentially quantitative in nature, other theses that follow the qualitative approach may have a rather different structure with different emphasis with regards to analysis and discussion and findings sections. Regardless of whether your research is quantitative or qualitative, your thesis needs to be coherent and easy to follow and navigate. Each chapter of your thesis needs to be built on a solid foundation.

Title, acknowledgements, table of contents, and list of figures and tables

As a matter of convention, your thesis should have a title that reflects the document and what your research is about. It is advisable to keep the title brief and focused but broad enough to give the reader a good idea of what the thesis is about. Titles often reflect the main focus of the study and the study's target population, research participants or case study. This is often followed by acknowledgements, which gives formal recognition to the support you may have received from individuals, organisations, institutions, supervisors and all those who have helped you along the way in your PhD journey. Writing an acknowledgement is a personal preference as not everyone may want to be named or listed as having helped with your thesis. The acknowledgements page is usually followed by a table of contents that helps readers navigate through the document and to dip in and out and move to different sections of your thesis with ease. Your table of contents should, essentially, reflect the structure of your thesis. It is also conventional to have all your tables and figures listed in order of presentation in your thesis under a list of tables and a list of figures, respectively. These are then followed by your abstracts.

The abstract

An abstract is a short summary of what your thesis and research are all about. This usually covers the background to your study, the purpose of your research and your research question, methodology, findings, conclusions and limitations. Your abstract should set the scene for the rest of your thesis and gives the reader a foretaste of what is in your thesis menu. A good abstract should encapsulate the main features of the thesis and leave the reader wanting to read more about your study. An abstract is rarely more than 200 words – check your university regulations on this.

Writing your introductory chapter

Your introductory chapter is, arguably, one of the most important chapters in your thesis as it sets out the scene and lays the foundation for subsequent chapters. The chapter should provide the general background to your study and set out your study's context, aim(s) and objectives. It is where you need to introduce your research topic to your reader and highlight the specific area of investigation your research was focused on. The background information about the issue or problem of investigation should be clearly explained in this chapter. It is usual to make reference to previous research or works that have already been done in your areas of investigation and what your own study is bringing to the table to add to the existing stock of knowledge in the area. It would be helpful also to your readers to provide some definitions or clarifications of any technical terms you may be using in subsequent chapters in your thesis. Usually, the structure of the rest of the thesis should be explained in the introductory chapter to help readers navigate through your thesis. This is the chapter where you need to tease out what is to follow in your thesis. It should be written in a clear, logical way as to invite your readers to want to read more about your thesis. While you don't necessarily want to go into too much detail in this chapter, you need to provide enough information and context for your study to be understood and what you set out to achieve in your research. Readers of your introductory chapter should be made to feel they want to read the rest of your thesis. So write your introductory section in a way as to invite rather than turn off your readers. Write clearly, logically, intelligibly and convincingly.

Writing your literature review/theoretical framework chapter

The purpose of the literature review is to help situate your research in the context of current knowledge or what is known about your study (see Chapter 5). In writing your literature review chapter it is important that you use and cite all necessary and relevant sources to inform your reader of the importance of your study, what other studies have shown about similar research, how pertinent your research question is and the justification for your own research and the knowledge gap you intend to fill through your study. In some theses, the literature review is presented as a standalone chapter while in other theses the literature review is woven throughout several chapters in the theses. Whether presented as a standalone chapter or embedded throughout the chapters, your thesis should have a strong literature review and a theoretical dimension.

Writing your methodology chapter

Your methodology section should provide detailed information on how and why you have conducted your research the way you did it. Also, a justification for choosing a particular method of investigation or method of analysis is required. It is essential to recognise and acknowledge the limitations of your study and any inherent weaknesses in the methodologies or techniques you have used. The purpose of your methodology chapter is to demonstrate the robustness of your research strategy. Your methodology chapter should clearly demonstrate that you have a deep knowledge of the methodologies and any issues relating to the use of those methodologies and techniques in your study. How your chosen methods fit in the general methodological discourse in your particular field of study needs to be clearly shown as well as your rationale or justification for using or applying a particular method to your study. If you are making any claim to a new contribution to knowledge, in terms of methodology, this needs to be highlighted and justified.

Your methodology chapter should also provide essential information on your data collection and measurement strategy, sampling frame and sample selection. A detailed description of your data collection instruments and procedures you adopted or followed in gathering your data such as the use of questionnaires, focus groups, interviews, tests, treatments and the like need to be covered in your methodology chapter. The assumptions underlying your choice of method or use of a particular technique in your research need to be made clear. This chapter should give your reader all the information they need to make a judgement on how you have carried out your study and the science or thinking behind your approach.

Writing your analysis and findings chapter

Your analysis section of your thesis should provide the analytical framework for your study and discussions on specific techniques used in synthesising and analysing your data (see Chapter 10). The section on findings should contain detailed information on the outcomes of your investigation and essential results with regards to what exactly your study has produced. There should be a connection between the main findings of your statistical analysis and the overall argument you are making in the thesis. The depth of your analysis needs to reflect the standard of work required for a PhD thesis, where critical analysis and rigorous interrogation of data are expected. If your analysis is quantitative, it is usual to present the results of any statistical test that you have used, using tables and figures, together with the interpretation of the results. Your statistical tests of your hypotheses need to be clearly explained. The statistical hypothesis testing approach you used to validate or verify your hypotheses needs to be explained in relation to how your data support or disprove your hypotheses.

If, however, you have adopted a qualitative analysis approach, you will need to describe in detail the way you classify, code or index your qualitative data obtained interviews, transcriptions, audio and video recordings and other sources. Your analysis and findings chapter should also show the patterns, themes and connections that emerged from your qualitative data analysis. This should also include any direct quotations from your research participants that may be necessary for your discussion.

Writing your discussion chapter

The discussion section should explain and evaluate your research findings in the context of existing knowledge and the knowledge gap that your PhD was designed to fill. Your discussion chapter or section also requires that you construct a coherent, strongly reasoned and substantiated argument about your research findings. A detailed and proficient discussion of your findings should be undertaken with regards to your analysis and conclusions. The chapter gives you the opportunity to reflect on your research finding and the degree to which your findings have answered or not answered your research question.

In writing the discussion section, it is essential that you clearly state and point out how your study has contributed to and advanced knowledge in your area of study. This is not the section you want to be modest about your findings or what those finding means. Every incremental addition or increase to existing knowledge that your study has enabled or uncovered should be highlighted and discussed. Your discussion chapter should not only discuss your results, but it should also cover the significance of your results. The implications of your findings for further research, current or future policy, professional practice and so on need to be discussed. The chapter needs to be forceful as to how your PhD research has produced a new understanding and what this means for the advancement of knowledge in the area of your study. This chapter should clearly show how your data and the conclusions you arrived at from your analysis both support your narrative of the contribution your study has made to knowledge. You also need to appraise the value of your contribution in relation to existing knowledge, theory or paradigm. It is also important to link your discussion back to the key research question that you set out to answer in your study. Furthermore, the chapter should contain a discussion of your overall research approach, noting any limitations or weaknesses in your research.

Writing your concluding chapter

It must be stated that all chapters and sections of your thesis are important as they focus on different aspects of your research. Nevertheless, apart from your introduction, your concluding chapter is, arguably, one of the most important chapters in your thesis. It should bring together every important element from your study into a relatively short chapter that readers will take away with them from reading your thesis. Some readers have the habits of reading the abstract, introduction and the conclusion of an academic thesis and then forming an opinion about the work. While this is not likely to be the case with your examiners, as your thesis will most certainly be closely scrutinised, your concluding chapter should be thoughtfully written. It should be sharp, succinct and very punchy as to highlighting and summarising the essential feature of your study. Your conclusion needs to be strong, forceful, convincing and persuasive. After reading your thesis and your conclusion, readers should be left in no doubt that your research and contribution to knowledge is of PhD level. If necessary, this chapter is where you can make recommendations and suggest how other researchers might pick up the baton from where you left the study. A brief summary of the implications of your study for theory, your professional practice or development of new theories or methods could be included in your concluding chapter.

Writing your reference list or bibliography

Your reference list or bibliography should contain all the sources you used for your research and which are cited in the text of the thesis. It is customary to list all your references in alphabetical order. As there are several ways of referencing, it is important that you check the requirements for your university and your discipline. While in some disciplines or profession, students are required to use Harvard referencing style; others may prefer Oxford Standard for the Citation of Legal Authorities (OSCOLA), American Psychological Association (APA) or Oxford Referencing. Whichever style of referencing you use it is critical that all the sources and materials used in your thesis are properly referenced and listed in your bibliography.

Adding an appendix to your thesis

If you have additional information that you don't want to put in the body of your thesis to avoid any distraction, then you may decide to put these at the very end of your thesis after your list of reference. Any non-essential data or material that is not critical to your thesis but nevertheless could provide context or background information such as raw data, interview transcripts, sample questionnaires, large tables or figures and the like should be put at the back of your thesis as an appendix. It is most likely that you will have more than one appendix. If that's the case, it is important you label them alphabetically, for example Appendix A, Appendix B, Appendix C and so on or number each appendix as Appendix 1, Appendix 2, Appendix 3 and so on. The appendix label or number should be indicated in the body of your thesis when you make reference to them in your text.

Other general thesis writing up tips

Writing a PhD thesis is probably one of the biggest document or report that you will have to write in your lifetime. Writing is an art as well as a skill to be learned and perfected. The more you write the better you are at writing. A PhD thesis is usually about 10,000 words, but some variation of this is sometimes permitted. So it will take time to put everything together. Write more often and stay motivated. So it is advisable that as you write, you should also remember to create backups of your data, texts and essential information in case you lose your computer or storage device. The use of a cloud file storage facility, such as Shared Drive, One Drive or Dropbox, is strongly recommended.

Using figures, tables, diagrams and visual aids in your thesis

Used effectively, figures, diagrams and visual aids could significantly enhance the quality of your thesis and add value to your discussion. However, due attention should be paid to how these could be used effectively to enhance your thesis. Tables could be very useful in summarising information and figures and, when used correctly, could serve as essential tools to illustrate and present your ideas in a visually intelligible way. Where necessary and appropriate, figures, diagrams and other visual aids should be used to support the points being made in your thesis. However, tables, figures and diagrams should not be used frivolously and should only be used when they complement or emphasise the key points or arguments being made. When used, figures and diagrams should add value to your discussion and should not be too laboured or complex as to distract readers from your central argument.

Making a convincing argument in your thesis

For your thesis to stand out as an original piece of work with elements of internal consistencies that can be scientifically verified or proved, the flow of the arguments in your thesis needs to be logically and lucidly presented.

Writing a well-seasoned thesis based on a lucid argument with strong evidence of scientific data and analytical rigour will set you up on the road to success for your viva. Not only do you need to show in your thesis that you have done enough original work to merit an award of a PhD, but your thesis also needs to be credible, convincing and demonstrative of the importance of your work and contribution to knowledge. Through your thesis, you need to show that you possess sufficient knowledge of your field and that your thesis offers an important and significant addition or contribution to the existing body of knowledge. Your thesis provides the medium through which you can demonstrate your explicit ability to apply research methods efficiently and competently to generate results in line with your research aims.

Engaging with theories and concepts

Your thesis should contain evidence of your engagement with existing theories or concepts that are critical to the development of your argument and your conclusions. A clear explanation as to how these theories or concepts validate your findings or how your results deviate from, change or confirm existing theories and knowledge needs to be provided with examples in your thesis.

Thesis with a creative or professional work element

If your PhD involves a creative or professional work element, your thesis may not necessarily follow the general structure outlined earlier. Some DProf or Professional Doctorates require their students to write a thesis that comprises both written and practice elements which are examined together as a single document. Others prefer a thesis with two separate documents one comprising the academic research element and the other focusing on the practice or research implications for practice. Your university and supervisors will provide you with guidelines if your PhD falls into this category.

Understanding and overcoming writer's block

Drafting and writing a thesis is rarely a smooth-sailing process for many people. There are setbacks, challenges and difficult moments that you may face in the course of writing your thesis. Putting ideas on paper, in form of a thesis, and making it coherent, intelligible, comprehensible, convincing, compelling and admissible is a huge task. Even when you have all the facts, knowledge and information from your research, there may come a time when you suffer partial or total blackout as to what to write. This experience is what is generally referred to as *'writer's block'*. If this happens to you, the advice is to either take a short break from writing, change your writing routine or find and deal with the cause or causes of your creative writing blockage, which could be due to stress, fear of failure, a general lack of motivation; amongst other factors.

Checking your first draft and redrafting

Writing a thesis may take several drafts before it fits together and reads as a coherent document.

So you may have a couple of iterations of your draft thesis, and the process of drafting and redrafting will, hopefully, lead to a better thesis. It is important that you give yourself enough time to rewrite or revise your draft thesis until you are fully satisfied that it meets the standard required. There is no point submitting a substandard thesis or a thesis that is not fully ready for examination. It is better to wait and get it done properly first time rather than put it and yourself through the viva only to come back again to do what you know you should have done in the first place.

Most theses often require some amendments or revisions after examination (see Chapter 12). Any such amendments could be kept to a minimum if you submit a well-written thesis the first time. As much as possible, you should avoid a situation in which you may be required to undertake a substantive revision of your thesis or even fail your viva voce examination as a result of your thesis not being up to standard or having significant errors. The more time you give to yourself in drafting and redrafting and perfecting your thesis, the better for a successful outcome. It is a good idea to agree with your supervisors as to when they think your thesis should be ready for submission. Working with your supervisor at this critical stage in your PhD journey is particularly important to ensure you have a smooth transition to the final phase which is your viva examination.

Understanding why some thesis fail

There are so many possible reasons why a thesis may fail that it is practically impossible to list them all in this chapter. Also, every thesis is different, just as every viva examination experience is unique to the PhD candidate. Also, there are institutional and disciplinary variations in the yardsticks used to measure what constitutes a good thesis and what should be considered a failed thesis. Institutional and disciplinary differences in requirement mean that there is no universally agreed-on template against which theses could be assessed.

While most submitted theses do pass following a viva, others have to go through a process of rewriting and resubmission. Even with the opportunity to rewrite and resubmit some theses still fail to make the mark. Some of the common reasons why a thesis may fail to pass through a viva voce examination can be identified. These, amongst others, include the following:

- A lack of clarity in the thesis as to the aim, focus and purpose of the study and how the study fits into current knowledge
- Weak evidence of the thesis's contribution to knowledge and scholarship
- A poor explanation of or absence of vital underpinning of relevant concepts and theories
- A general lack of coherence and focus on explaining the study aims and significance of the study and its findings
- A poorly argued or feeble argument not backed up with facts, data or analysis, leading to weak conclusions
- Poor or inappropriate use of visual aids, diagrams and illustrations that distract from, rather than enhance or support, the arguments
- Poor engagement with the literature and or a lack of critical evaluation of existing ideas, theories or practice
- A general lack of or weak explanation or understanding of the research processes leading up to thesis conclusions
- Weak analysis or a general lack of rigour in the synthesis of quantitative and/or qualitative data underpinning the thesis
- A generally flawed analysis that neglects facts and shows a poor understanding of causes and effects
- Use of an inappropriate research design, methodology and techniques that may not fit the study aims and objectives
- A lack of proficiency in written communication, with the thesis riddled with grammatical errors and spelling mistakes
- A poorly structured thesis and lacking in logic and substance falling short of the standard expected for a PhD

Ensuring that your thesis is written in a way as to avoid or address many of these and other issues will help you towards submitting a well-grounded thesis that is fit for purpose and that could command the examiners' confidence in your work. Barring some minor or sometimes major corrections after viva, if your thesis is well written and covers all these and other essential issues, your thesis should succeed in convincing the examiners of a strong case for a PhD award.

Checking your final draft and submitting your thesis

Before submitting your thesis, make sure you check it over. It is important that you are satisfied with the contribution you are making to knowledge through your research and that this has been fully reflected or highlighted in your thesis. Remember, your thesis will go through a rigorous process of examination, and every bit of your thesis will be subject to scrutiny by your internal and external examiners. You may want to get someone with extensive editorial review and experience to read through your thesis before you submit it. Getting someone not connected to your PhD to read through and critique your thesis before you submit could help you identify areas that may need tweaking before you submit.

Some universities will require that you give about 3 months' notice before you submit your thesis. It is essential you check your university's requirements for its intention-to-submit-thesis notice period and work towards its timetable. The intention-to-submit notice period usually takes account of the time it will take your university to arrange examination package, appoint your internal and external examiners, schedule your viva and carry out other administrative tasks before you are examined. It will also take account of your maximum registration date, which is the last date you are expected by your university to have completed and finish your PhD. If you are an international student on a Student Route (Tier 4) visa arrangement, you may need to ensure that you submit your thesis in good time so that you can do your viva and have time to do any corrections or revision to your thesis before your visa runs out. It may be possible, in exceptional circumstances, to apply for an extension to your student visa beyond the period originally granted. However, there is no guarantee that such an application for an extension of the visa will be granted. If your student visa runs out and you still have not completed your PhD and you are unable to secure an extension, you will be required by UKVI to return to your country. Your university may decide to conduct your viva examination remotely if you have to return to your country.

General advice

In concluding this chapter, the general advice in writing your PhD thesis is not to spend too much time worrying about getting things right before you start writing. Many students spend a great deal of time thinking about what to write and how to get it perfect in their head before they start writing. While this approach at writing may work for some, others may benefit from the advice of **'don't get it right, get it written'**. Rather than spending valuable time thinking of and planning a perfect thesis to write, it is far much better to write first and then spend time trying to perfect your thesis. So start your write-up as soon as practically possible, even if just a very loose draft form. There is a danger of spending too much time on data/information gathering and not leaving enough time for the write-up and rewrite, which may need to be done umpteen times! Once your draft PhD thesis is *written*, then you will have the opportunity to get it *right*. It's much easier to revise a draft than it is to write from scratch. Also, the earlier you start writing up chapters, even though just in draft form, the more it can focus your mind on what data/information is still needed.

Key messages

- Putting a report together in the form of a thesis and making it coherent, intelligible, comprehensible, convincing and compelling is a key feature of doing a PhD.
- There are differences and variations in universities' requirements as to how to structure a thesis and different disciplines, and professions have their own specifications with regards to formats, design and production of a PhD thesis. So it is important you follow your university or discipline thesis style guide.
- You may need to draft, redraft or revise sections of your thesis several times until you are fully satisfied that it meets the standard required before you submit.
- Understanding why some theses fail and avoiding the possible pitfalls could help ensure that your thesis is written in a way that is fit for purpose and that could command the examiner's confidence and respect in your work.
- Barring some minor or sometimes major corrections after viva, if your thesis is well written and covers all essential issues, as discussed in this chapter, your thesis should succeed in convincing the examiners of a strong case for a PhD award.

Further reading

Bitchener, J. (2017). A Guide to Supervising Non-native English Writers of Theses and Dissertations: Focusing on the Writing Process. London: Routledge.

Brause, R. (2012). Writing Your Doctoral Dissertation: Invisible Rules for Success. London: Routledge.

Brewer, R. (2007). Your PhD Thesis: How to Plan, Draft, Revise and Edit Your Thesis. Abergele, UK: GLMP Ltd STUDYMATES.

Burton, S., and Steane, P. (2004). Surviving Your Thesis. London: Routledge.

Carter, S., Kelly, F., and Brailsford, I. (2012). Structuring Your Research Thesis. Basingstoke, UK: Palgrave Macmillan.

Cole, T., Duval, D. T., and Shaw, G. (2012). Student's Guide to Writing Dissertations and Theses in Tourism Studies and Related Disciplines. Oxon, UK: Routledge.

Day, T. (2018). Success in Academic Writing. Palgrave Study Skills. London, UK: Palgrave Macmillan.

Dunleavy, P. (2003). Authoring a PhD: How to Plan, Draft, Write, and Finish a Doctoral Thesis or Dissertation. Basingstoke, UK: Palgrave Macmillan.

Ghauri, P., Grønhaug, K., and Strange, R. (2020). Writing the final report. In Research Methods in Business Studies (pp. 276–292). Cambridge: Cambridge University Press.

Gustavii, B. (2012). How to Prepare a Scientific Doctoral Dissertation Based on Research Articles. Cambridge: Cambridge University Press.

Kornuta, H. M., and Germaine, R. W. (2019). A Concise Guide to Writing a Thesis or Dissertation: Educational Research and Beyond, 2nd ed. Oxon, UK: Routledge.

Phillips, E. M., and Pugh, D. S. (2015). How to Get a PhD: A Handbook for Students and Their Supervisors, 6th ed. Maidenhead, Berkshire, UK: McGraw-Hill. Available at: VitalSource Bookshelf.

Pyrczak, F. (2017). Writing Empirical Research Reports: A Basic Guide for Students of the Social and Behavioral Sciences. Oxon, UK: Routledge.

Rowena, M. (2017). How to Write a Thesis. Open University Press.

Thomas, D. (2016). The PhD Writing Handbook. Basingstoke, UK: Palgrave Macmillan.

McMillan, K., and Weyers, J. (2012). How To Cite Reference Avoid Plagiarism at University. Harlow, England: Pearson Education Limited.

Williams, K., and Davis, M. (2017). Referencing and Understanding Plagiarism. London, UK: Palgrave.

CHAPTER 12

Preparing for and doing your viva voce
Oral examination

Introduction

This chapter provides essential information on the viva voce examination. It explains both the purpose of the viva as an oral examination and how to prepare yourself for this important assessment. The role of internal and external examiners in viva voce is discussed in relation to what examiners need to know from you about your PhD research and the thesis you've submitted for examination. Possible outcomes of viva voce examinations are discussed with reference to whether you get a pass without amendments, a pass with minor amendments, a pass with major amendment or, in a worst-case scenario, a fail PhD and terminate or an option for a lower award of a master's or MPhil.

By the end of the chapter, you will have a better understanding of

- what is and what a viva voce is for,
- how to prepare yourself for your viva voce examination,
- the role of internal/external examiners and chairs of viva voce examinations,
- what examiners need to know from you about your PhD research and your thesis,
- possible outcomes of your viva voce examination and
- what your next action or options are after your viva voce examination.

Getting ready for your viva voce

The general feeling after submitting your PhD thesis is most likely to be that of great relief. It is a major achievement to get that far. The submission of your thesis is the culmination of several years of toil and hard work. Now that you've submitted your thesis, you are ebbing closely to the finishing line in your PhD journey. However, your PhD journey is not finished until you've actually crossed the finish line. Your viva is the last critical phase you need to go through to cross this finishing line, by 'defending' your thesis. You cannot get a PhD until you have successfully defended your thesis in a formal viva voce examination.

The processes you need to go through could be quite daunting but will be most rewarding if you successfully defend your thesis. So you need to stay focused and keep working until your viva voce examination is over.

What is a viva voce examination, and how do you prepare for it?

A viva voce is an oral defence of your thesis. This usually takes place a few months after you've submitted your thesis. It is a process that usually involves face-to-face interaction between you (the examinee) and your examiners, who could consist of internal and external assessors. In most universities, an independent chair is appointed to oversee the conduct of the examination and to ensure proper procedures and processes are followed.

Your viva voce examination will take place after both your internal and external examiners have read your thesis and, in some cases, have sent in their initial assessment or preliminary reports to your university. These initial examiners' preliminary reports are usually kept confidential, and you may not know what your examiners think about your research or thesis until the day of your viva. Whether kept confidential or not, any preliminary reports on your thesis by your examiners often form the bases for discussion or line of enquiry during your viva.

Their initial observations could be very critical to how the tone of your viva is set. So you need to come to your viva fully prepared as your examiners will most certainly come prepared with questions they may want to ask you. Your examiners are most certainly going to be experts in your topic and will know a great deal about your area of research. It could well be that you are examined by renowned national or world experts who have extensive experience in examining PhD students whose work you may already be familiar with. It is also possible that you will have never heard of your external examiners or know them to be experts in the field. Whichever way the choice of your examiners goes, and whoever is appointed to examine you, the critical point is for you to come ready and fully prepared for your viva.

Depending on your university and their examination procedure, your viva may last from anywhere from 2 to 5 hours. In some cases, a viva could be less or more in terms of duration. However long it takes, it is usually a period of intense questioning, interrogation and academic exchanges between you and your examiners. Understanding what a viva is and what to expect will help you prepare for this important meeting with your examiners.

What to do while waiting for your viva voce examination

There are several things you could do in preparation for your viva. Knowing what to do and making effective and productive use of the time between submission and your viva could help towards good preparation.

It is essential that you keep renewing and refreshing your passion and enthusiasm for your research and understand what the main essence of your PhD research is about. You need to keep abreast of the key contributions you are making to knowledge through your research, as documented and evidenced in your thesis. Success in your viva could depend on how well you can explain your thesis and its main claims orally in a communicative exchange with the examiners. So you need to have a clear understanding of what you did in your research, how you did it, when you did it and what it means in terms of contribution to knowledge. You need to know specific ways your research has an impact on existing knowledge and why it matters that your research was conducted. All these and other essential information about your research and thesis need to be rehearsed, understood and ready to be explained to your examiners if and when asked during your viva.

Some students find it useful to do a mock viva as part of the preparation for their real viva voce examinations. A mock viva is a pretend viva aimed at second-guessing the examiners as to what their line of questioning might be during the real viva. It is a way of simulating the viva examination condition in order to establish which area that you could work on before you face the real viva. If you think a mock viva would be beneficial, you should consider asking your director of study/supervisor or an experienced researcher or academic who is familiar with the viva voce examination to help prepare you for your main viva.

It is possible that new knowledge or ideas may have emerged since you submitted your thesis. New theories or concepts may have been developed or new papers published that are central to your argument in your thesis. It could also be that an idea or hypothesis that was originally thought to be correct has now been proved to be false or that the premise of an argument in your thesis has changed as a result of new information. Whatever any new changes in knowledge and in literature may have thrown up, it is important to keep abreast with all these new developments and to continually revise your literature until you finish your viva. Your ability to demonstrate to your examiners during your viva that you know of and you are aware of recent developments in your field will inspire confidence in them that you are on top of your research. So, before your viva, take notes of and review the latest information relating to your research. This is particularly important if your research relates to a fast-moving event or phenomenon that is subject to change rapidly over a short time.

Some universities require their PhD students to give a short verbal presentation of about 15 minutes on the key features of their PhD without any visual aids during a viva. It is essential you check with your university so that you can prepare for this or any presentation that may be required.

Viva voce examination panel

It is conventional for a viva examination to consist of at least two examiners and one independent chair. One of the examiners is usually external of the university. In some cases, more than one external examiner may be involved in a viva, especially if the student being examined is also a staff member of or is closely associated with the university. The role of the chair is to ensure the examination is conducted smoothly, fairly and the integrity of the process is ensured. At the discretion of the chair and the examiners, your director of studies or supervisor may be allowed to attend your viva but only as an observer, as they are not usually part of the examination panel.

What your examiners may need to know and possible lines of their enquiry

As part of your preparation for your viva, it is essential that you understand the process of the viva examination in your university and to know what examiners do during viva voce examinations. It should be mentioned that it is impossible to state, with any degree of certainty, what might happen during your viva. Every viva voce examination is different, just as every student's experience of the viva is unique to them. There are also variations in ways different institutions, disciplines or professions organise vivas or examine their PhD students. However, it is possible to identify certain common features of viva voce examinations that could be beneficial to your preparation.

First, a viva is usually based purely on the content of a student's thesis and any other information they may provide relating to their research during the oral examination. The examiners' questions normally relate to the research, the thesis being examined and any other issues connected with the study. Therefore, your viva voce examination should be focused on your work and not on your person. You are not on trial. It is not an inquisition into you as a person in terms of your values, your politics, creed or religious or political affiliation. It is an examination of your work and your claim to advancement in knowledge. That is what a viva is and should be about.

Second, as experts in the field of your investigation, your examiners are there to scrutinise and validate the claim you are making in your thesis and to assess your contribution to knowledge. If you have more than one examiner, which is very likely as an internal and external examiner are often involved in a viva, the chances are that they would have read your thesis independently before your viva. However, they will only be able to form or confirm their recommendations on your thesis after your viva has been conducted. So you have all to play for. After meeting and asking you questions about your research and your thesis, they will most probably come to some agreement as to the strengths and weaknesses of your thesis.

Third, your thesis is the first contact that your examiners, especially your external examiners, will have with your study. It is therefore important that your thesis makes a good impression and that you provide the examiners with the confidence that you have done enough work in your thesis for them to be able to evaluate your contribution to knowledge in your chosen topic.

Fourth, your examiners may need to follow your university's guidelines in their preliminary assessment of your thesis. They may be required to submit a pre-viva confidential report on your thesis before your viva. In most cases, these preliminary confidential reports often need to be revised after the viva has taken place and the examiners now have a better and fuller picture and information about your study and your thesis. It is not uncommon for some examiners who may have been sceptical about your thesis in their preliminary reports to change their minds after listening to your response to their questions in defence of your thesis. So their preliminary reports may not have much bearing on their final recommendations.

Fifth, the examiners are not against you and should not be seen as adversaries. They have the responsibility to be thorough, forceful and rigorous in their questioning. But they are neither your enemies nor there to fail you no matter what. Many examiners actually expect or want the theses they examined to pass and the candidates to succeed. Yet they have the responsibility of ensuring that normal academic rigours are applied to their scrutiny of your thesis. Some examiners may probe and keep probing you in order to get a response to their questions. The more you are able to respond to their questions, the better for you and for a good outcome from your viva. It is possible that they may ask questions about your study to which you may have no answer. In that case, it is better to be honest that you have no answer rather than becoming unnecessarily defensive, awkward or rude. Not having answers to some of the examiners' questions doesn't mean or imply that you have failed your viva.

Sixth, most examiners would like to see a confident, well-informed and engaging PhD candidate during their viva. They also like to see a candidate who owns their thesis and demonstrates an ability to respond to questions about their work. More important, they want to see a connection between the candidate being examined and a thesis that is convincingly written with clear engagement with the literature and has a thorough discussion of findings.

Seventh, your university and the examiners they have appointed to assess your thesis are under an obligation to ensure that you are given enough time and opportunity to respond to questions during your viva. They also have the responsibility to ensure that your viva is fairly conducted, without any bias or prejudice.

Eighth, in the course of your viva and their assessment of your thesis, the examiners are usually required to provide your university with their final reports or recommendations. Many universities also require that PhD candidates are provided with an oral report of the outcome of their viva as soon as the examination is over. The examiners' reports or recommendations are not just limited to their assessment of the thesis being examined in terms of its strengths and weaknesses but usually includes advice on any corrections that need to be made, how to improve the thesis and the duration of time allowed for the amendments to be made.

General factors examiners consider in their assessment

Throughout your viva voce examination, your examiners are most likely to be gradually forming their judgement on your thesis and your performance using a range of criteria or factors. The degree to which you are able to contextualise and explain your study and the original contribution you are making in your field could be critical as a factor. So it is important that you mention specific ways your study has advanced or deepened understanding in the area of your investigation. This could be, for example, in terms of new concepts, models or theories you have developed; new interpretation you have come up with in your study; or a new and innovative way of measuring or analysing a physical or social phenomenon, amongst others.

Another thing that your examiners may be looking out for is how rigorous your work has been in terms of its academic and intellectual content. Not only will they be interested in whether you have done sufficient work to merit an award of a PhD, but they may also want to see how your work compares with other works they may have assessed in other universities. Your research will be expected to have been developed and conducted to a very high PhD standard. So you need to ensure you have enough content in your thesis to meet the requires standard.

Also very important is the degree to which you have demonstrated critical analysis of your data. You need to show a good understanding of the relevant research methodology and the reasons why you've chosen or opted for a particular methodological approach. That means that you need to be aware of several approaches, the strengths and limitations of these approaches and why your approach is preferred.

The level of coherence of your work and your argument could be very critical to how the examiners view your work. You, therefore, need to think carefully about the arguments you are making and how you are making those arguments and the logic and reasoning behind those arguments are well explained.

Your examiners will be looking for confirmatory evidence that the thesis you've submitted is actually your own work. Your viva gives you the opportunity to show that you wrote the thesis and can speak to it and answer questions relating to the work you claimed to have done.

Possible viva voce examination outcomes

After your examination is complete, your examiners may ask you to leave the room for them to privately deliberate on the outcome of your viva and how you have performed during the 3 or more hours of gruelling questioning.

During this period both the internal and external examiners, under the guidance of the chair of the examination, will discuss their views and assessment of your performance. This is usually a critical moment when the examiners need to compare their notes and possibly agree on an outcome that reflects your performance. In most cases, an agreement is usually reached as to whether the examiners think your thesis should pass or fail. This period of deliberation is usually a critical time when the examiners have to fully deploy all the tools required for making an academic judgement as to what constitutes a passing or failed thesis and whether your thesis has met the threshold of a pass. This is also a time when the examiners decide on what corrections or amendments, if any, you may need to make to your thesis before a recommendation of a pass is confirmed or ratified.

This period of post-viva private discussions and deliberations amongst the examiners may take about 2 hours or longer depending on the level of or intensity of discussions, discrepancies or disagreements in opinions between the examiners with regards to your performance. This is usually a very 'long' period of waiting for many PhD candidates who may be extremely nervous and anxious to know about the result of their viva.

As this period is also used by the examiners to deliberate on whether their initial assessments as indicated in their preliminary reports need to be amended, revised or changed in the light of your performance at the viva, the waiting period may be a bit longer than you expected. During this period, the examiners may also need to agree as to any corrections they would like you to make to your thesis and the period they would like you to make the corrections. Usually, during the same meeting, your examiners may be required to write their joint report on your viva to your university, detailing their recommendations. These recommendations may still need to be ratified by your university senate or academic board.

Once a decision has been made about your viva voce examination outcome, you will be invited back into the meeting with your examiners to receive an oral report on your viva. Most universities will, usually, allow supervisors or their representatives to be present and accompany PhD candidate when they receive oral reports on their viva. During this period, you could feel extremely anxious. The advice is to stay calm as much as possible and listen to what the examiners have to report about your viva. If possible, you should try to take notes of what the examiners have to say, although for many students note-taking at this time may not be practicable as a result of the emotions they may go through during the oral report presentation. This is a time when your supervisors could help and take notes on your behalf. In any case, you should and will receive, in writing, the official reports of the examiners on your viva – no matter the outcome.

There are a number of possible outcomes that could be reached by the examiners, following your viva examination. These include the following:

- A pass without any amendments to your thesis
- A pass with minor amendments to your thesis but not requiring resubmission
- A pass with major amendments to your thesis requiring resubmission
- A failed PhD with an offer to transfer to a lower award of a master's/MPhil
- A failed and terminate PhD without any offer to transfer to a lower award of a master's/MPhil
- A failed and terminate PhD after an unsuccessful second attempt at viva (this applies if this is your second viva)

Key features of each of these possible outcomes are summarised in Figure 12.1 and discussed in the following subsections.

A pass without any amendments to your thesis

A pass without any amendments to your thesis is the most desirable outcome you could hope or wish for in a viva. This outcome is often reached by examiners if they think your thesis is excellent and up to the required standards expected for a PhD award. Often, with this outcome, you don't need to make any corrections to your thesis other than some very minor textual or formatting issue. It also means that you don't need to resubmit the thesis for any re-examination. However, you may be required to tidy up the thesis with regards to any formatting or minor textual corrections that may be required. A period of about 4 weeks is usually allowed for you to submit your final revised version.

A pass with minor amendments to your thesis

An outcome of a Pass with minor amendments to your thesis may be reached if your submitted work required some minor revision. What is considered a minor revision may vary from one examiner to another. Generally, a minor amendment would include issues such as minor omissions in your presentation, typographical or grammatical errors in your thesis, minor issues with referencing and citations, the need to redraw or relabel diagrams and the need for further clarification or explanation with regards to an argument, amongst others. All these and other minor changes to your thesis may require some

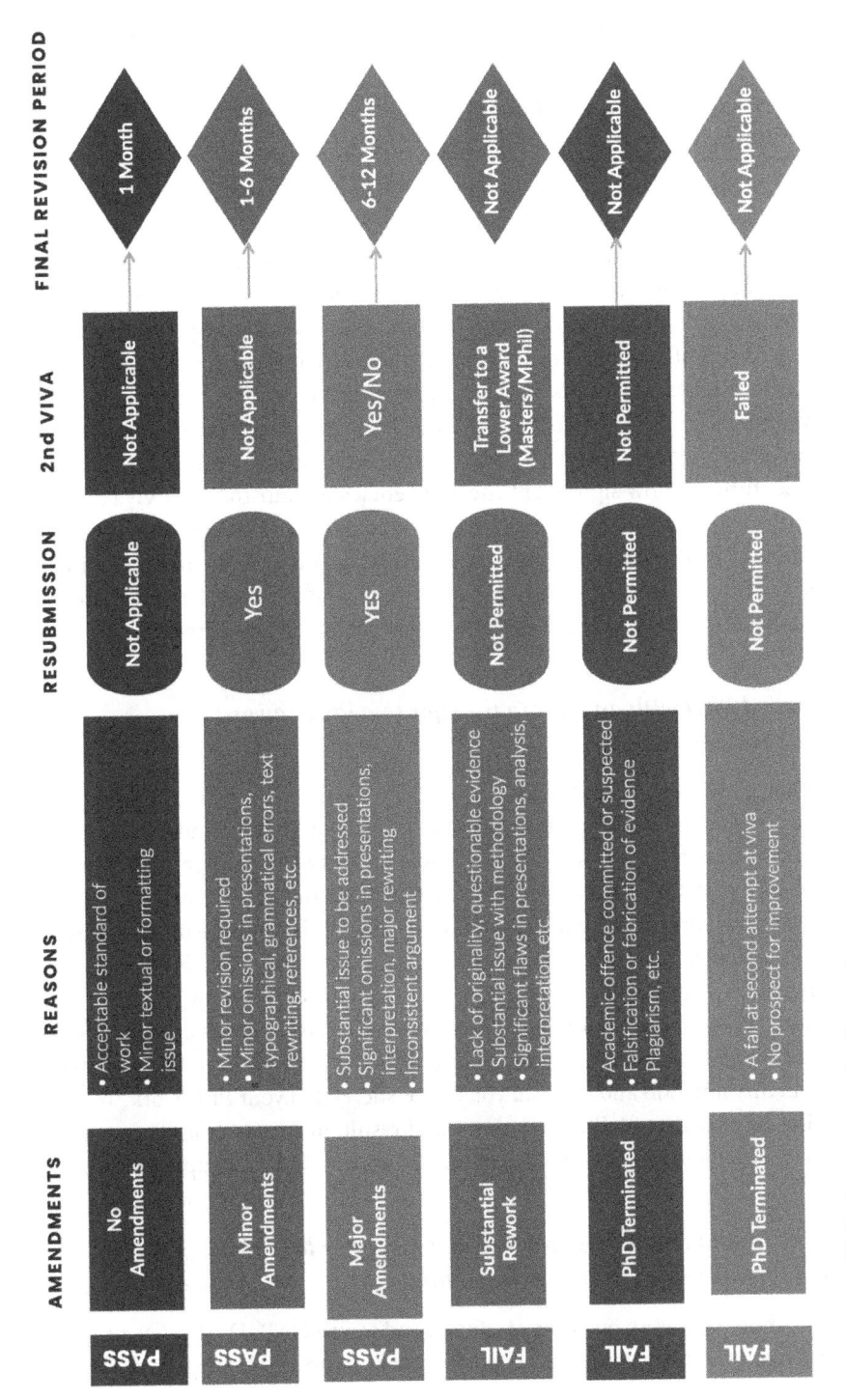

Figure 12.1 PhD viva voce examinations outcomes

rewriting of parts of your thesis. However, the overall standard of your work is still considered good and meets the general requirement for a PhD award.

A pass with major amendments to your thesis (with options for another viva or without a second viva)

If your thesis or submitted work requires that you address a number of substantial issues but it is still good enough to meet the standards of a PhD work, you may get an outcome of a pass with major amendments. Usually, this relates to when your thesis is judged to have significant issues of substance such as omissions in your presentations, errors in your analysis and interpretation, a weak or inconsistent argument or incomplete literature review, amongst others.

This outcome requires that you carry out a major rewrite of parts of your thesis in order to address the issues. It may also require a significant restructuring of your thesis in terms of flow, chapter ordering or formatting. Depending on how significant the deficiencies in your thesis or viva are, you may be asked to resubmit for a second viva voce examination, or your examiners may just be happy to check your resubmission without any further need for them to see you for another viva. A period of between 6 to 12 months is usually allowed for an outcome of a pass with major amendments.

A failed PhD with an offer to transfer to a lower award of a master's/MPhil

Although not very common, it is possible to have an outcome of a failed PhD. This may be the case if your thesis is lacking in originality and there are serious issues with regards to your evidence, methodology, presentation, analysis and interpretation. If the examiners believe that the content of your thesis is inadequate and not up to a PhD standard. Also, if the premise of your research is questionable, your work contains significant errors and you failed to demonstrate any control of your research, then a failed PhD result could be a fair outcome. This could be a devastating experience for anyone who is asked to transfer to a lower award and may cause considerable anguish. It is therefore essential to avoid this situation and to do all you can to succeed in your PhD work. To minimise the chances of failure or suboptimal result, make sure you do not submit your work for examination without the full approval of your supervisor(s).

A failed and terminate PhD without any offer to transfer to a lower award of a master's/MPhil

Even more rare, is an outcome of a failed and terminate PhD. This outcome usually applies when an academic offence has been committed or suspected. This may involve fraudulent activities, such as fabrication of evidence, plagiarism, collusion or identity theft, amongst many academic misdemeanour or infringements.

A failed and terminate PhD after an unsuccessful second attempt at viva

In many universities, a failed and terminate PhD outcome may be reached if a student fails their viva voce examination the second time around. This is an extremely rare situation as many students who failed their viva the first time usually succeed in their second attempt. Again, this is an outcome or a situation to avoid at all costs as this may mean that you have nothing to show for all those many years of working on your PhD.

After your result has been verbally communicated to you, you may be filled with or overcome by great emotions. That is perfectly normal. You may feel exhilarated, deflated, disappointed or any other manner of emotions, depending on your result. Hopefully, you will get the right outcome for your viva and come out of the meeting with some smiles on your face and great joy that you've done it. Your director of studies or supervisors may be able to offer support if your viva didn't go well and the outcome you received is not what you expected. Getting a failed outcome in a viva could be extremely disappointing, devastating and distressing. So, it is important you get support from your supervisors, friends and family and other people close to you to help you through this moment.

Examiners' reports and discrepancies

Most of the time, examiners come to an agreement as to the outcome of a viva. However, there are very rare occasions when an agreement between examiners could not be reached and a unanimous report could not be presented. One examiner may feel that your viva should be passed, and the other examiner may think differently. In such situations in which there are disagreements or discrepancies between the examiners, two separate reports may be submitted to your university. Your university may then make a decision as to whether to get another expert opinion or to go by the report of one of the examiners. Usually, the most senior examiner's report may be considered. Also, the external examiner's report tends to carry more weight in situations like this, if the disagreement is between and internal and external examiners. If there are two external examiners with equal standing, your university may decide to go by the report of any one of the examiners.

Once the outcome of your viva is confirmed, the award of your PhD will then be ratified by your university's academic board or senate, and you will be officially informed of the outcome of your PhD and award.

Disagreeing with and appealing the outcome of your viva voce examination

For many students, viva voce examinations often produce a happy ending not only for the students but also for their supervisors. There are situations in which things don't go well as students may expect and the outcome of a viva is disputed. Many universities have appeals procedures for their students who disagree with the outcome of their viva voce examination. It is essential you understand your university's appeal procedures if you need to raise queries about the outcome of your viva examination. Where official disagreement or complaints are raised, an independent adjudication of academic disputes may be involved to resolve the complaints.

Making corrections to your thesis after your viva voce examination

If the outcome of your viva is a pass with amendments, you will be given a time frame within which to make the corrections and resubmit your thesis. All the necessary corrections need to be made and completed before a pass is confirmed, ratified and a PhD title awarded and conferred on you.

After your viva and you have done all the necessary and required corrections and resubmitted your thesis or done the second viva, if required, the chances are that your PhD journey will come to a successful end. It will feel at this stage that you have come a long way, and the joy of finally getting to the finishing line and passing your viva will have all the feelings of a happy ending.

You must take pride in your achievement knowing that you have come a long away and have achieved your aim in spite of all the odds and challenges you may have faced along the way. You have done very well and you deserve some celebrations. The years of grafting, working and stressing over doing your PhD have now come to an end, and you can have your life back again. Well done!

Key messages

- The viva voce examination is a crucial stage in your PhD journey.
- You need to know and understand the requirements and purpose of the viva voce examination and prepare yourself sufficiently for it.
- Your viva voce examination should be approached with confidence armed with the knowledge and authority to robustly 'defend' your thesis.
- In preparing for your viva, try to anticipate key questions the examiners are likely to ask and think about how you will respond to those questions.
- Developing your communicative skills and your ability to articulate and explaining your research will help you in your viva examination. If possible, do a mock viva and get other people to give you advice as to your level of preparedness.

- A confident and competent oral presentation of your research findings and your contribution to knowledge is critical to your success in your viva voce examination.
- It is essential that the examiners believe in and have confidence that you are the author of your thesis and that you have sufficiently evidenced your knowledge and contribution to knowledge through your viva.
- After the result of your viva is communicated to you verbally, you may be filled with or overcome by great emotions. It is perfectly normal.

Further reading

Golding, C., Sharmini, S., and Lazarovitch, A. (2014). What examiners do: What thesis students should know. *Assessment & Evaluation in Higher Education*, 39(5), pp. 563–576.

Petre, M., and Rugg, G. (2010). *The Unwritten Rules of PhD Research*, 2nd ed. Berkshire, UK: Open University Press. Available at: vbk://0335240267

CHAPTER 13

Making the most of your PhD degree

Introduction

This chapter covers essential information on what comes after a successful viva voce examination and an award of a PhD. To some, getting to the point of completion may seem the end of a long and often tedious PhD journey; to others, it is the beginning of a new venture in their career or professional progression. This chapter explores how getting a PhD may serve as a stepping stone to a new career in academia, publishing and other careers within the social sciences. The chapter underlines the importance of using your PhD experience as a reflective tool for your personal and professional development.

By the end of the chapter, you will have a better understanding of

- talking about and sharing information about your research and what it contributes to knowledge and understanding in your field or profession,
- reflecting on the transferable skills you've acquired doing your PhD,
- how to enhance your personal and professional development through your PhD,
- different career opportunities in academia and non-academic fields that you could pursue and
- publishing your PhD thesis to a wider audience to maximise the benefit of your research to yourself, your community and society at large.

Celebrating your success

Congratulations! You've worked very hard. You've earned your PhD – the highest academic award. This is not a mean feat, given that about a quarter of the people who started a PhD globally never get to the finishing line. So, it is good to celebrate your success given how far you've come. Long hours of literature search, trawling through concepts, theories and which methodology to use to generate those essential data – not to talk about hours of analysis, transcribing, coding and recoding, just to make sense and find meanings in your data. Hours of drafting and redrafting chapters for your supervisors and those sometimes awkward meetings with supervisors. All these show how long the road to your PhD has been and how far you've come.

To help celebrate your success with your friends, family and all those who have played a part in your PhD journey, most universities in the UK have formal award ceremonies to which all graduands are invited. This is usually a very exciting and exhilarating event where you may invite friends, families and loved ones to share with you the joy of getting your PhD. For many graduands, this could be an exceedingly joyful moment and a life-changing experience, at least in having a title *'Dr'* or *'Doctor'* attached to your name. In the midst of all the jubilations and celebrations, it is also necessary to note that for some students, this time can also be a very sad and emotional time for them, especially if they have lost someone dear to them whom they would have loved to be there with them to celebrate their success.

Whatever the situation, graduation and the award ceremony is quite symbolic and has a long tradition. The colourful gowns and the parade of academic staff and university administrators who have helped you on your journey, together with other fellow graduands coming together to celebrate the end of what, to many, have been a long and tedious PhD journey, are all part of the academic tradition. The award ceremony provides you with the opportunity to see other fellow graduands whom you have got to know in the course of your PhD. It is a time you could meet and thank your department or faculty staff, technicians, librarians, IT support staff and others who may have supported you in your PhD. While, for some students, award ceremonies are important and essential events, to others, it is a non-event, and some choose not to attend at all. Whether you join the party or not, there is no doubting the fact that your PhD is an achievement and worthy of celebration.

Making the most of your PhD

As desirable and fulfilling it may be, getting a PhD, should not necessarily be the end of the journey for you. After everything you have been through and worked for since you embarked on your PhD, there are additional opportunities out there to explore which will put your knowledge and skills to good use. So rather than being the *END*, getting your PhD could well mark the *START* or beginning of yet another exciting chapter or phase in your life.

Searching and getting a job

Completing your PhD provides a great opportunity to expand your career choice. It's a perfect time to update your curriculum vitae. Now that you have a PhD and have officially been conferred with the title of Dr, the chances are you may now seriously begin to think about getting a job, if you have not already done so or have a job in your field already. Getting your PhD makes a career in academia sound plausible and realistic. Some people choose to put all the investment and research skills they acquired through doing a PhD into use by opting to work in academia or research-related institutions.

Using your PhD in academia and research-related career

Whether rightly or wrongly, many people associate getting a PhD with careers in academia. This is more so when most universities now insist on having a PhD as a minimum requirement for academic and research-related positions. Unfortunately, it needs to be mentioned that while obtaining a PhD qualifies you to enter the world of academia, there is absolutely no guarantee that you will end up getting an academic position or a job as a lecturer or a professor. It is therefore necessary for you to be realistic and think of what you could do with your PhD if you are unable to get a position in academia.

It has been suggested that only 7 out of every 200 PhD students end up getting a permanent job in academia (Wolf, 2015). There is a chance that you may well be one of the lucky ones who walk straight into an academic position after your PhD. However, there is absolutely no guarantee that will be the case, nor will that necessarily be the best option for you. So keep your options open to include non-academic jobs while searching for work. You may find that many non-academic posts in a wide range of vocations may equally prove rewarding as getting a job as a lecturer if not more rewarding.

Academia and the pressure to publish – making a success of it

If you have chosen or are planning a career in academia, it is important to note that there will be considerable pressure on you to publish. The popular mantra amongst academics, *'publish or perish'*, underlies the enormous pressure on academics to demonstrate their output through research publications. Universities are judged, graded and rewarded on the basis of their research output through schemes such as the REF which places a great deal of pressure on university staff to actively engage in research and to show their research output through publications.

To be successful in academia, you will need to have the interest, drive, skills and tenacity for publishing and doing research. This may require that you develop a special passion for a particular aspect of knowledge, possibly relating to your PhD, that you could develop to form your own niche and chart your own pathway within academia.

As you have just completed your PhD, you may find yourself in a situation in which your progression in an academic career will depend largely on your publications. So obtaining a PhD title and getting an academic position, if you are lucky, may constitute only a starting step in your academic career. The real pressure that lies ahead of you is being able to sustain your interest in research and generate outputs by publishing journal articles that your new academic career demands. It is like charting your career path and finding your own way in what has been described as a crowded academic jungle (Johnson, 2017). Many PhD graduates seeking an academic career strive to publish at least in part, if not all, of their thesis in peer-reviewed academic journals.

It is important to note that becoming a researcher is a way of life. So if you are interested in becoming a career researcher, the chances are that you will need all the skills you've acquired during your PhD if you are to succeed in this career. You may still be interested in working on research problems, gathering data, analysing information and, more important, publishing your results. The experience with your PhD should have equipped and given you the confidence to launch into the world of academia or research if you are so inclined.

No doubt, a PhD offers a great opportunity to use your analytical and critical thinking skills to launch yourself into the world of academia. It gives you the opportunity to further develop yourself as an independent researcher and to engage with knowledge creation and exchange. The contribution to knowledge that you have made through your PhD could form the basis of producing further works and academic papers suitability for publication. The independent research practice and ethos you have developed in the course of doing your PhD can be put to good use. This could help launch you into the world of academic writing.

Although getting into academia, even with your PhD, can be very difficult and competitive, as there are not many academic positions that are readily available, it is still worth considering this as one of your options. With your PhD and with a passion for teaching, learning and researching, you could forge a rewarding and fulfilling career for yourself in academia. If you have already published aspects of your PhD in reputable peer-reviewed journals, this can give you an advantage when it comes to applying for an academic position with your PhD.

Using your PhD in non-academic and non-research-related career

While getting a PhD is usually, associated with careers in academia, there are far more areas of work, professional pursuits and human endeavours to which the skills and knowledge you gained in doing a PhD could be applied. Yes, with your PhD you may choose to go into academic or research-related jobs or whatever career you may decide to go into. Given the growing number of PhDs awarded and the limited number of academic positions worldwide, the chances are that many PhD holders may never have the chance to develop a career in academia, even if they wanted to. While stating this obvious fact may be disappointing to new PhD graduates, who may really want to pursue an academic career, it should, hopefully, be refreshing and reassuring for all newly qualified PhDs to know that there is more to a PhD than just research and academia.

Getting a PhD requires some discipline, training, fortitude, perseverance and a great deal of self-belief and confidence in your own ability. All these virtues could become handy if you decide to go into any career.

Other options you may consider, apart from academia, with your PhD in the social sciences include working in government institutions or civil service jobs, working for international organisations or companies operating across many fields and geographical locations or working for yourself by setting up your own business as an entrepreneur. You may also choose to work as an independent consultant. Even if you don't take any research-related jobs after your PhD, the research skills you've learnt in the course of your PhD could be useful and handy when it comes to developing your career.

Knowledge sharing and publishing your PhD

Whether or not you take up a career in academia/research or you chose to work in other areas of life, there are several ways in which you could share ideas and information about your PhD. The findings of your PhD could be extremely beneficial to organisations outside of academia. Your local community organisations, such as charities, clubs and other public or civil groups within the voluntary sector, would be prime examples. You may want to publish important sections of your thesis that have significant implications for social care, community relations, environmental protection and the like. Your PhD research may have important policy implications that you may want to share with institutions outside of academia such as governmental or NGOs. You may also want to report or publish your own research findings in the form of a book. Reporting your research findings using social media such as Twitter or writing your own blog, Facebook page, amongst others, could also be an option. Your PhD thesis or research findings need not be confined to the academic community. You can make the most of your study and your contribution to knowledge with a wider dissemination of your PhD thesis. The more organisations, institutions, social groups, interest groups and stakeholders can benefit from your study, the greater the real impact of your PhD on society – which is a true mark of success.

Key messages

- Getting a PhD should not necessarily be the end of the journey for you but the beginning of a new chapter.

- A PhD may not necessarily guarantee you a job in the academia. So keep your options open as there are other equally, if not more, rewarding and fulfilling careers you can go into.
- The research skills you've learnt in the course of your PhD could be useful and handy when it comes to developing your career.
- With your PhD you could be self-employed and set yourself up, for example, as consultant.
- The more organisations, institutions, social groups, interest groups and stakeholders can benefit from your study, the greater the real impact of your PhD on society – which is a true mark of success.

Further reading

Caro, S. (2009). *How to Publish Your PhD: A Practical Guide for the Humanities and Social Sciences*. London: Sage.

Dee, P. (2006). The transition to post-doctoral research. In *Building a Successful Career in Scientific Research: A Guide for PhD Students and Postdocs* (pp. 65–66). Cambridge: Cambridge University Press.

Elliot, A. (2016). Doing good by doing good research. In R. Sternberg, S. Fiske, and D. Foss (eds.), *Scientists Making a Difference: One Hundred Eminent Behavioural and Brain Scientists Talk about Their Most Important Contributions* (pp. 351–355). Cambridge: Cambridge University Press. https://doi.org/10.1017/CBO9781316422250.076

Gallagher, P., and Gallagher, A. (2020). *The Portable PhD. Taking Your Psychology Career Beyond Academia*. Washington, DC: American Psychological Association.

Johnson, N. F. (2017). *Publishing from Your PhD: Negotiating a Crowded Jungle*. London: Routledge.

Snieder, R., and Larner, K. (2009a). Publishing a paper. In *The Art of Being a Scientist: A Guide for Graduate Students and their Mentors* (pp. 176–185). Cambridge: Cambridge University Press. https://doi.org/10.1017/CBO978051 1816543.011

Williams, K., Bethell, E., and Lawton, J. (2010). *Planning Your PhD*. Basingstoke, UK: Palgrave Macmillan.

Wolf, J. (2015). Doctor, doctor . . . we're suffering a glut of PhDs who can't find academic jobs. *The Guardian* [Online]. Available at: www.theguardian.com/ education/2015/apr/21/phd-cant-find-academic-job-university. Accessed on 14th April 2020.

Appendix
List of commonly used statistical tests and hypotheses validation techniques in social sciences

N.B. This list is not intended to be exhaustive. Statistical tests should be used based on their appropriateness and relevance to your research question or aim.

Statistical Tests	Main Features
Binomial test	• Predicts the probability with which given conditions occur in a specific number of occurrences • Used to predict the occurrences or events which are mutually exclusive • Uses the relative frequency of mutually exclusive events to work out the probability of an event occurring
Chi-square	• Applies to data expressed as frequencies • Measures the discrepancies between the expected and the observed frequencies • Minimum expected frequencies in any one group must be greater than 5
Cramér's V	• A measure of association for multiple category variables • Based on the phi coefficient
Fisher's Exact Probability Test	• A non-parametric test technique • Used for analysing discrete data (either nominal or ordinal) when the two independent (random) samples are small in size • Test applies to 2×2 contingency tables only
Goodman–Kruskal lambda	• Measures the proportional reduction in the probability of making an error • Test requires categorical data

Goodman–Kruskal Tau Tau Tau	• Similar to Goodman–Kruskal lambda • Uses a different method for minimising the number of possible errors in predicting from one variable to the other
Kolmogrov-Smirnov test	• Tests whether two independent samples have been drawn from the same population, or population with the same or similar distributions • Non-parametric graphical test
Mann-Whitney U test	• Non-parametric test of difference • Tests hypothesis that two independent samples come from populations having the same distribution • Can be used on data measured either on ratio, interval or ordinal scales
McNemar test and significance	• The McNemar test for the significance of changes • Applies to 2×2 tables only • Measurement may be nominal or ordinal
Median test and significance	• Tests whether two independent groups differ in central tendencies • Test evaluates the hypothesis that the groups are drawn from populations having the same median • Dependent variable must be an ordinal measure
Pearson's C	• Contingency coefficient C – a measure of the extent of association or relation between two sets of attributes
Pearson's r and significance	• Measures the amount of spread about the linear least-squares regression line • Variables must be interval measures • Coefficient, r ranges from 1.0 to −1.0, • r = 0 indicates no linear association between the variables
Phi	• A measure of association for 2×2 contingency tables
Sign test and significance	• A non-parametric test used to test the significance of difference between paired variables • Test is applicable to the case of two related samples when a researcher wishes to establish that two conditions are different • Variables must be ordinal measure, and the number of categories in each variable must be equal
Spearman's rho and significance	• Measures degree of association • Requires that both variables be measured in at least an ordinal scale • Objects may be ranked in two ordered series • It is applicable to ranked data on the ordinal scale • Index of correlation (rho) ranges from −1 to +1.
Wald–Wolfowitz Runs Test	• A statistical test of randomness • Useful where a series of observations of recordings are involved • Tests whether the value of one observation influences the values for later observations
Wilcoxon test and significance	• Test applies to the case of two related samples • Test differences between two conditions or variables • Considers the magnitude of differences • Variables must be measured on interval scale • Equal number of categories in the variables required

Adapted from Jegede et al. (2020), Writing Successful Undergraduate Dissertations in Social Sciences. A Student's Handbook. Second Edition. Routledge. London.

References

Agarwal, P. (2020). Tips on working from home with children. *Time Higher Education* [Online]. Available at: www.timeshighereducation.com/blog/tips-working-home-children. Accessed on 7th July 2020.

Atkins, S., Lewin, S., Smith, H., et al. (2008). Conducting a metaethnography of qualitative literature: Lessons learnt. *BMC Medical Research Methodology*, 8, p. 21. https://doi.org/10.1186/1471-2288-8-21.

Bhattacherjee, A. (2012). *Social Science Research: Principles, Methods, and Practices*, 2nd ed. Tampa, FL: University of South Florida.

Bitchener, J. (2017). *A Guide to Supervising Non-native English Writers of Theses and Dissertations: Focusing on the Writing Process*. London: Routledge.

Bogle, D. (2017). *100 Years of the PhD in the UK* [Online]. Available at: www.vitae.ac.uk/news/vitae-blog/100-years-ofthe-phd-by-prof-david-bogle

Brew, A., and Lucas, L. (2009). *Academic Research and Researchers*. Maidenhead, UK: McGraw-Hill Open University Press.

Browne, J., Coffey, B., et al. (2018). A guide to policy analysis as a research method. *Health Promotion International*, 1–13.

Bryman, A. (2004). *Social Science Research Methods*, 2nd ed. Oxford: Oxford University Press.

Bushman, B. J., and Wang, M. C. (2009). Vote-counting procedures in meta-analysis. In H. Cooper, L.v. Hedges and J. C. Valentine (eds.), *The Handbook of Research Synthesis and Meta-analysis* (pp. 207–220). New York, US: Russell Sage Foundation

Cahill, M., Robinson, K., et al. (2017). Qualitative synthesis: A guide to conducting a meta-ethnography. *British Journal of Occupational Therapy*, 81(3), pp. 129–137.

Clark, W. (2006). *Academic Charisma and the Origins of the Research University.* Chicago: University of Chicago Press.

Covey, S. R. (1989). *The 7 Habits of Highly Effective People: Powerful Lessons in Personal Change.* New York: Free Press.

Cox, R. (2020). Mental health and wellbeing – Staying sane when working remotely. *Vita Blog – Realising the Potential of Researchers* [Online]. Available at: www.vitae.ac.uk/news/vitae-blog/mental-health-and-wellbeing-staying-sane-when-working-remotely. Accessed on 7th July 2020.

Cuthbert, D., and Molla, T. (2015). PhD crisis discourse: A critical approach to the framing of the problem and some Australian 'solutions'. *Higher Education,* 69(1), pp. 33–53.

Davies, P. (2000). The relevance of systematic reviews to educational policy and practice. *Oxford Review of Education,* 26(3&4), pp. 365–378.

DeCarlo, M. (2018). Paradigms, theories, and how they shape a researcher's approach. *Open Social Work Education* [Online]. Available at: https://scientificinquiryinsocialwork.pressbooks.com/chapter/6-2-paradigms-theories-and-how-they-shape-a-researchers-approach/. Accessed on 4th August 2020.

Denyer, D., and Tranfield, D. (2009). Producing a sys-tematic review. In D. Buchanan and A. Bryman (eds.), *The Sage Handbook of Organizational Research Methods* (pp. 671–689). London: Sage.

Disability Rights UK. (2020). Funding postgraduate education for disabled students. *Disability Rights UK Factsheet F52* [Online]. Available at: www.disabilityrightsuk.org/funding-postgraduate-education-disabled-students. Accessed on 21st July 2020.

Dupré, B. (2007). *50 Philosophy Ideas You Really Need to Know.* London: Quercus Editions Ltd.

European Union. (2016). *Regulation (EU) 2016/679 of the European Parliament and of the Council of 27 April 2016 on the Protection of Natural Persons with Regard to the Processing of Personal Data and on the Free Movement of Such Data and Repealing Directive 95/46/EC.* General Data Protection Regulation.

European Union. (2018). *General Data Protection Regulation.* Available at: https://gdpr-info.eu/. Accessed on 19th August 2020.

Evans, T., Bira, L., Gastelum, J., et al. (2018). Evidence for a mental health crisis in graduate education. *Nature Biotechnology,* 36, pp. 282–284. https://doi.org/10.1038/nbt.4089

Fazackerley, A. (2019). 'Look at how white the academy is': Why BAME students aren't doing PhDs. *The Guardian.com,* Thursday 12th September 2019 [Online]. Available at: www.theguardian.com/education/2019/sep/12/look-at-how-white-the-academy-is-why-bame-students-arent-doing-phds?CMP=Share_iOSApp_Other. Accessed on 22nd July 2020.

Findaphd.com. (2020). *Writing a Good PhD Research Proposal* [Online]. Available at: www.findaphd.com/advice/finding/writing-phd-research-proposal.aspx. Accessed on 27th April 2020.

Franzke, A. S., Bechmann, A., Zimmer, M., Ess, C. M., and the Association of Internet Researchers. (2020). *Internet Research: Ethical Guidelines 3.0.* Available at: https://aoir.org/reports/e

Fuchs, C. (2020). Everyday life and everyday communication in coronavirus capitalism. *Triple C: Communication, Capitalism & Critique*, 18(1), pp. 375–399.

Fuller, M. (2015). Doctoral education in the UK: Ideal models and the stark reality. *Presentation at the Australian DDOGS Meeting, Sydney, April 19–20* [Online]. Available at: www.researchgate.net/publication/275640304_Doctoral_education_in_the_UK_ideal_models_and_the_stark_reality. Accessed on 21st August 2020.

Giang, V. (2020). The 4 most important relationships you need at work. *Business Insider* [Online]. Available at: www.businessinsider.com/the-4-most-important-relationships-you-need-at-work-2013-3?r=US&IR=T. Accessed on 5th July 2020.

Golde, C. M. (2005). The role of the department and discipline in doctoral student attrition: Lessons from four departments. *The Journal of Higher Education*, 76(6), pp. 669–700.

Gosling, P., and Noordam, B. (2011). *Mastering Your PhD: Survival and Success in the Doctoral Years and Beyond*. London: Springer Heidelberg Dordrecht.

Gov.UK. (2021). *Study in the UK on a Study Visa* [Online]. Available at: https://www.gov.uk/student-visa. Accessed on 27th February 2021.

Hall, S. (2019). *The History of the Doctoral Degree* [Online]. Available at: https://www.theclassroom.com/history-phd-degree-5257288.html

Helmut, L. (2019). *How to Set Goals and Achieve Balance – in and Outside the Classroom: Learn How Solid Goals and Time Management Can Help You Achieve Success* [Online]. Available at: https://blog.dce.harvard.edu/extension/how-set-goals-achieve-balance-outside-classroom. Accessed on 22nd August 2020.

Henderson, T., Hutton, L., and McNeilly, S. (2012). Ethics and online social network research – Developing best practices. *Proceedings of BCS HCI 2012 Workshops HCI Research in Sensitive Contexts: Ethical Considerations* [Online]. Available at: www.scienceopen.com/hosted-document?doi=10.14236/ewic/HCI2012.74. Accessed on 19th August 2020.

HESA. (2020). *Higher Education Statistics Agency*. {[Online}]. Available at: www.universitiesuk.ac.uk/facts-and-stats/Pages/higher-education-data.aspx. Accessed on 18th June 2020.

Higginbotham, D. (2018a). 4 routes to getting doctorate. *Prospects* [Online]. Available at: www.prospects.ac.uk. Accessed on 18th June 2020.

Higginbotham, D. (2018b). 5 challenges faced by PhD students. *Prospects* [Online]. Available at: www.prospects.ac.uk/postgraduate-study/phd-study/5-challenges-faced-by-phd-students

Higginbotham, D. (2019). Research council funding. *Prospects* [Online]. Available at: www.prospects.ac.uk/postgraduate-study/funding-postgraduate-study/research-council-funding. Accessed on 20th July 2020.

Humphrey, R., Marshall, N., and Leonardo, L. (2012). The impact of research training and research codes of practice on submission of doctoral degrees: An exploratory cohort study. *Higher Education Quarterly*, 66(1), pp. 47–64.

Information Commissioner's Office. (2020). *Guide to Data Protection* [Online]. Available at: https://ico.org.uk/for-organisations/guide-to-data-protection/. Accessed on 19th August 2020.

Jegede, F., et al. (2020). *Writing Successful Undergraduate Dissertations in Social Sciences: A Student's Handbook*, 2nd ed. Chapter 8. London: Routledge.

Johnson, N. F. (2017). *Publishing from Your PhD: Negotiating a Crowded Jungle*. London: Routledge.

Jump, P. (2020). PhD completion rates, 2013. *Times Higher Education*. World University Ranking [Online]. Available at: www.timeshighereducation.com/news/phd-completion-rates-2013/2006040.article. Accessed on 20th June 2020.

Koshy, E., Koshy, V., and Waterman, H. (2010). What is action research? In *Action Research in Healthcare*. Sage Books [Online]. Available at: www.sagepub.com/sites/default/files/upm-binaries/36584_01_Koshy_et_al_Ch_01.pdf. Accessed on 5th September 2020.

Kyvik, S., and Olsen, T. B. (2014). Increasing completion rates in Norwegian doctoral training: Multiple causes for efficiency improvements. *Studies in Higher Education*, 39(9), pp. 1668–1682.

Lamont, C. (2015). *Research Methods in International Relations*. London: Sage Publications Ltd.

Lantsoght, E. O. L. (2018). *The A-Z of the PhD Trajectory. A Practical Guide for a Successful Journey*. Springer Texts in Education. Springer International Publishing AG. Springer, 20180525. Vital Book file. Gewerbestrasse 11, 6330 Cham, Switzerland.

Lawrence, C. (2011). *Writing a Literature Review in the Social Sciences* [Online]. Available at: www.academia.edu/2911352/Writing_a_Literature_Review_in_the_Social_Sciences. Accessed on 31st July 2020.

Lawson, A. (2020). Musings on ways of doing research (and socks). *Musings on Methodology: Thoughts, Ideas and Opinions on Research Methods* [Online]. Available at: https://musingsonmethodology.com/tag/methodology/. Accessed on 4th August 2020.

Lee, A. (2019). *Successful Research Supervision: Advising Students Doing Research*, 2nd ed. Abingdon, Oxon, UK: Routledge.

Lindsay, S. (2015). What works for doctoral students in completing their thesis? *Teaching in Higher Education*, 20(2), pp. 183–196.

Lupton, D. (ed.). (2020). *Doing Fieldwork in a Pandemic* (crowd-sourced document) [Online]. Available at: https://docs.google.com/document/d/1clGjGABB2h2qbduTgfqribHmog9B6P0NvMgVuiHZCl8/edit. Accessed on 22nd July 2020.

Mail Online. (2019). Now you need to eat TEN-a-day! Adding more fruit and veg to your diet boosts your mood and emotional wellbeing as much as landing a new job, study finds. *Mail Online*, 5 February 2019 [Online]. Available at: www.dailymail.co.uk/health/article-6669419/Eating-fruit-veg-improves-mood.html

McEwan, C. (2011). Development and fieldwork. *Geography*, 96(1), pp. 22–26.

National Health Service. (2020). Eating more fruit and veg 'improves mental wellbeing' [Online]. Available at: www.nhs.uk/news/food-and-diet/eating-more-fruit-and-veg-improves-mental-wellbeing/. Accessed on 21st July 2020.

Naveed, A., Sakata, N., Kefallinou, A., Young, S., and Anand, K. (2017). Understanding, embracing and reflecting upon the messiness of doctoral fieldwork. *Compare:*

A Journal of Comparative and International Education, 47(5), pp. 773–792. http://doi.org/10.1080/03057925.2017.1344031

Neale, J. (2016). Iterative categorization (IC): A systematic technique for analysing qualitative data. *Addiction*, 111(6), pp. 1096–1106, Published by John Wiley & Sons on behalf of the Society for the Study of Addiction, 9th May 2016.

NHS. (2018). GDPR – Guidance for researchers. Health Research Authority. *National Health Services (NHS)* [Online]. Available at: www.hra.nhs.uk/about-us/news-updates/gdpr-guidance-researchers/. Accessed on 16th August 2020.

Noble, K. A. (1994). Changing Doctoral Degrees: An International Perspective. SRHE and Open University Press Imprint, Society for Research into Higher Education Series, the University of Michigan, USA.

OECD (2019). Education at a Glance 2019. *Organisation for Economic Co-operation and Development* [Online]. Available at: https://www.oecd-ilibrary.org/education/education-at-a-glance-2019_f8d7880d-en. Accessed on 27th February 2021.

OECD (2020). Education at a Glance 2020. *Organisation for Economic Co-operation and Development* [Online]. Available at: https://www.oecd-ilibrary.org/education/education-at-a-glance-2020_69096873-en Accessed on 27th February 2021.

Pauwel, L. (2011). An integrated conceptual framework for visual social research. In Eric Margolis and Luc Pauwels (eds.), *The Sage Handbook of Visual research Methods*. London: Sage.

Pawson, R. (2002). Evidence and policy and naming and shaming. *Policy Studies*, 23(3&4), pp. 211–230.

Pawson, R. (2006). *Evidence-based Policy a Realist Perspective*. London: SAGE.

Peabody, R. (2014). *The Unruly PhD: Doubts, Detours, Departures, and Other Success Stories*. Basingstoke, UK: Palgrave Macmillan.

Phillips, E. M., and Pugh, D. S. (2015). *How to Get a PhD: A Handbook for Students and Their Supervisors*, 6th ed. Maidenhead, Berkshire, UK: McGraw-Hill. Available at: VitalSource Bookshelf.

Quality Assurance Agency (QAA). (2020). Available at: https://www.qaa.ac.uk/ Accessed on 7th June 2020.

QSR International. (2020). Discover how researchers are innovating, rethinking research, and teaching in a remote world. *Remote Research Center* [Online]. Available at: www.qsrinternational.com/nvivo-qualitative-data-analysis-software/resources/remote-research-center. Accessed on 8th June 2020.

Ragin, C. (1994). *Constructing Social Research: The Unity and Diversity of Method* (pp. 31–54). Pine Forge, Thousand Oaks: North-western University [Online]. Available at: http://faculty.uncfsu.edu/hlheem/09-f-420-social%20research.htm. Accessed on 10th August 2020.

Rath, T. (2013). *Eat – Move – Sleep: How Small Choices Lead to Big Changes*. United States: Missionday.

REF. (2014). *Research Excellence Framework* [Online]. Available at: www.ref.ac.uk/2014/. Accessed on 18th June 2020.

Rickinson, M., and May, H. (2009). A comparative study of methodological approaches to reviewing literature. *The Higher Education Academy* [Online]. Available at: www.researchgate.net/profile/Mark_Rickinson/publication/

265008044_A_Comparative_Study_of_Methodological_Approaches_to_Reviewing_Literature/links/56b31d6008aed7ba3fee2f8f/A-Comparative-Study-of-Methodological-Approaches-to-Reviewing-Literature.pdf. Accessed on 26th July 2020.

Ritchie, J., and Spencer, L. (1994). Qualitative data analysis for applied policy research. In A. Bryman and R. G. Burgess (eds.), *Analyzing Qualitative Data* (pp. 173–194). London: Routledge.

Rose, G. (2016). *Visual Methodologies: An Introduction to Researching with Visual Materials*. 4th ed. London: Sage.

Rugg, G., and Petre, M. (2010). *The Unwritten Rules of PhD Research*, 2nd ed. Maidenhead: Open University Press.

Russo, M. W. (2007). How to review a meta-analysis. *Gastroenterology & Hepatology. The Independent Peer-Reviewed Journal*, 3(8), pp. 637–642 [Online]. Available at: www.ncbi.nlm.nih.gov/pmc/articles/PMC3099299/ Accessed on 3rd August 2020.

Scholarship Hub. (2020). What is the difference between a scholarship, grant and bursary? *The Scholarship Bub* [Online]. Available at: www.thescholarshiphub.org.uk/what-difference-between-scholarship-grant-and-bursary/. Accessed on 14th July 2020.

Seagram, B. C., Gould, J., and Pyke, S. W. (1998). An investigation of gender and other variables on time to completion of doctoral degrees. *Research in Higher Education*, 39, pp. 319–335.

Seresin, I. (2019). Withdrawal statement. *Medium.com* [Online]. Available at: https://medium.com/@indianaseresin/withdrawal-statement-56f7411b48b1. Accessed on 6th July 2020.

Shoemaker, P. J., Tankard, J. W., and Lasorsa, D. L. (2004). *How to Build Social Science Theories*. London: Sage Publications.

SleepFoundation.org. (2020). *Common Sleep Disorders* [Online]. Available at: https://www.sleepfoundation.org/. Accessed on 21st July 2020.

Spronken-Smith, R., Cameron, C., and Quigg, R. (2018). Factors contributing to high PhD completion rates: A case study in a research-intensive university in New Zealand. *Assessment & Evaluation in Higher Education*, 43(1), pp. 94–109.

Srivastava, A., and Thomson, S. B. (2009). Framework analysis: A qualitative methodology for applied policy research. Research note. *JOAAG*, 4(2), pp. 72–79.

Student Minds. (2020). *Coronavirus Resource Hub* [Online]. Available at: www.studentminds.org.uk/coronavirus.html. Accessed on 7th July 2020.

Times Higher Education. (2020). PhD completion rates, 2013. *The Times Higher Education*. World University Ranking [Online]. Available at: www.timeshighereducation.com/news/phd-completion-rates-2013/2006040.article. Accessed on 20th June 2020.

Vitae. (2020a). Realising the potentials of researchers. *Careers Research and Advisory Centre (CRAC) Limited* [Online]. Available at: https://resdevportal.uclan.ac.uk/resource/test-vitae-development-framework-online-resource/. Accessed on 1st March 2021.

Vitae. (2020b). Resources and support for researchers with disabilities. *Vitae. ac.uk* [Online]. Available at: https://www.vitae.ac.uk/doing-research/every-researcher-counts-equality-and-diversity-in-researcher-careers/resources-and-support-for-disabled-researchers. Accessed on 21st July 2020.

Vozza, S. (2020). When you should listen to your self-doubt – and when you shouldn't. *Mindfulness at Work* [Online]. Available at: https://www.fastcompany.com/90516081/when-you-should-listen-to-your-self-doubt-and-when-you-shouldnt. Accessed on 7th July 2020.

Walker, M., and Thomson, P. (2010). *The Routledge Doctoral Supervisor's Companion: Supporting Effective Research in Education and the Social Sciences*. London: Routledge.

Warrell, M. (2020). *You've Got This! The Life-changing Power of Trusting Yourself*, 1st ed. Australia: John Wiley & Sons.

The Wellbeing Thesis. (2020). A collaborative open access web-resource to support postgraduate research student mental well-being. *The Wellbeing Thesis*. The University of Derby, King's College London and Student Minds [Online]. Available at: https://thewellbeingthesis.org.uk/. Accessed on 7th July 2020.

Wenger, J. (2020). *Seven Principles to Strengthen Relationships at Work* [Online]. Available at: https://medium.com/@johnqshift/seven-principles-to-strengthen-relationships-at-work-f861b0cbab06. Accessed on 5th July 2020.

Wolf, J. (2015). Doctor, doctor . . . we're suffering a glut of PhDs who can't find academic jobs. *The Guardian* [Online]. Available at: www.theguardian.com/education/2015/apr/21/phd-cant-find-academic-job-university. Accessed on 14th April 2020.

World Economic Forum (2021). These countries have the most doctoral graduates. [Online]. available at; https://www.weforum.org/agenda/2017/02/countries-with-most-doctoral-graduates/. Accessed on 24th March 2021.

World Medical Association (WDA). (2020). World Medical Association declaration of Helsinki ethical principles for medical research involving Human subjects. *Special Communication* [Online]. Available at: www.wma.net/wp-content/uploads/2016/11/DoH-Oct2013-JAMA.pdf. Accessed on 18th August 2020.

Ye, A. (2020). Studying online: Tips and experiences from a student in Singapore. *Time Higher Education* [Online]. Available at: www.timeshighereducation.com/student/blogs/studying-online-tips-and-experiences-student-singapore. Accessed on 7th July 2020.

Recommended further reading

Adcock, R., and Collier, D. (2001). Measurement validity: A shared standard for qualitative and quantitative research. *American Political Science Review*, 95(3), pp. 529–546.

Alderson, P., and Marrow, V. (2011). *The Ethics of Research with Children and Young People: A Practical Handbook*. London: Sage.

American Ethnographic Society. (2020). [Online]. Available at: https://americanethnologist.org/. Accessed on 23rd October 2020.

Aveyard, H. (2018). *Doing a Literature Review in Health and Social Care: A Practical Guide*, 4th ed. Maidenhead, Berkshire, UK: Open University Press.

Aveyard, H., Payne, S., and Preston, N. (2016). *A Post-Graduate's Guide to Doing a Literature Review in Health and Social Care*. Maidenhead, Berkshire, UK: Open University Press.

Badewi, A. (2014). YouTube video – Ontology, epistemology and methodology. *Research Methodology Course (Self-Study) – Session 2* [Online]. Available at: https://youtu.be/kf8wGvunyG8. Accessed on 4th August 2020.

Barron, E. (2014). *The PhD Experience: An Insider's Guide*. Macmillan Education. London: Palgrave.

Beins, B., and McCarthy, M. (2018). Advanced research and data analysis. In *Research Methods and Statistics in Psychology* (pp. 251–252). Cambridge: Cambridge University Press.

Bickerton, P. (2016). 10 things you need to know before starting a PhD degree. *Earlham Institute* [Online]. Available at: www.earlham.ac.uk/articles/10-things-you-need-know-starting-phd-degree. Accessed on 12th April 2020.

Brause, R. (2012). *Writing Your Doctoral Dissertation: Invisible Rules for Success*. London: Routledge.

Brewer, R. (2007). *Your PhD Thesis: How to Plan, Draft, Revise and Edit Your Thesis*. Abergele, UK: GLMP Ltd STUDYMATES.

Briner, R. B., and Denyer, D. (2012). Systematic review and evidence synthesis as a practice and scholarship tool BT. In *The Oxford Handbook of Evidence-Based Management* (pp. 1–47). Oxford: Oxford University Press.

Burton, S., and Steane, P. (2004). *Surviving Your Thesis*. London: Routledge.

Business Research Methodology (BRM). (2020). *Action Research* [Online]. Available at: https://research-methodology.net/research-methods/action-research/. Accessed on 7th August 2020.

Caro, S. (2009). *How to Publish Your PhD: A Practical Guide for the Humanities and Social Sciences*. London: Sage.

Carter, S., Kelly, F., and Brailsford, I. (2012). *Structuring Your Research Thesis*. Basingstoke, UK: Palgrave Macmillan.

Castle, P., and Buckler, S. (2009). *How to Be a Successful Teacher: Strategies for Personal and Professional Development*. London: Sage Publications Ltd.

Castle, P., and Buckler, S. (2018). *Psychology for Teachers*, 2nd ed. London: Sage Publications Ltd.

Chouldhry, I. (2019). I've seen firsthand that academic spaces have a problem with racial slurs – No wonder PhD students are quitting. *Independent*, 8th July 2019 [Online]. Available at: www.independent.co.uk/voices/academic-racism-university-cambridge-n-word-priyamvada-gopal-a8993016.html. Accessed on 6th July 2020.

Churchill, H., and Sanders, T. (2007). *Getting Your PhD: A Practical Insider's Guide*. London: SAGE.

Cole, T., Duval, D. T., and Shaw, G. (2012). *Student's Guide to Writing Dissertations and Theses in Tourism Studies and Related Disciplines*. Oxon, UK: Routledge.

Complete University Guide. (2020). *University League Tables 2020*. https://www.thecompleteuniversityguide.co.uk/league-tables/rankings. Accessed on 19th May 2020. Complete University Guide Limited, Bedford, England.

Creswell, J. W., and Poth, C. N. (2018). *Qualitative Inquiry and Research Design: Choosing Among Five Approaches*, 4th ed. London: Sage.

Dawson, D. C. (2019). *Introduction to Research Methods*, 4th ed. London: Little, Brown Book Group.

Day, T. (2018). *Success in Academic Writing*. Palgrave Study Skills. London: Palgrave Macmillan.

Dee, P. (2006). The transition to post-doctoral research. In *Building a Successful Career in Scientific Research: A Guide for PhD Students and Postdocs* (pp. 65–66). Cambridge: Cambridge University Press.

Denney, A. (2013). How to write a literature review. *Journal of Criminal Justice Education*, 24(2), pp. 218–234.

Denzin, N. K., and Lincoln, Y. S. (2011). *The Sage Handbook of Qualitative Research*, 4th ed. London: Sage.

Dunleavy, P. (2003). *Authoring a PhD: How to Plan, Draft, Write, and Finish a Doctoral Thesis or Dissertation*. Basingstoke, UK: Palgrave Macmillan.

Elliot, A. (2016). Doing good by doing good research. In R. Sternberg, S. Fiske, and D. Foss (eds.), *Scientists Making a Difference: One Hundred Eminent Behavioural and Brain Scientists Talk about Their Most Important Contributions* (pp. 351–355). Cambridge: Cambridge University Press.

Field, A. (2018). *Discovering Statistics Using IBM SPSS Statistics*. London: SAGE Publications Limited.

Finn, J. A. (2005). *Getting a PhD: An Action Plan to Help Manage Your Research, Your Supervisor and Your Project*. London: Routledge.

Gallagher, P., and Gallagher, A. (2020). *The Portable PhD. Taking Your Psychology Career Beyond Academia*. Washington, DC: American Psychological Association.

Gerring, J., and Christenson, D. (2017). *Applied Social Science Methodology: An Introductory Guide*. Cambridge: Cambridge University Press.

Ghauri, P., Grønhaug, K., and Strange, R. (2020). Writing the final report. In *Research Methods in Business Studies* (pp. 276–292). Cambridge: Cambridge University Press.

Gobo, G., and Marciniak, L. (2016). What is ethnography? In David Silverman (ed.), *Qualitative Research*. London: Sage.

Golding, C., Sharmini, S., and Lazarovitch, A. (2014). What examiners do: What thesis students should know. *Assessment & Evaluation in Higher Education*, 39(5), pp. 563–576.

Greenfield, T., and Greener, S. (2016). *Research Methods for Postgraduates*, 3rd ed. Wiley Blackwell.

Gribben, M. (2012). *The Study Skills Toolkit for Students with Dyslexia*. London: Sage Publications Ltd.

Gustavii, B. (2012). *How to Prepare a Scientific Doctoral Dissertation Based on Research Articles*. Cambridge: Cambridge University Press.

Hausman, D., McPherson, M., and Satz, D. (2016). Appendix: How could ethics matter to economics? In *Economic Analysis, Moral Philosophy, and Public Policy* (pp. 337–352). Cambridge: Cambridge University Press.

Hawkins, K. (2017). *A Little Guide to Mindfulness*. London: Sage Publications Ltd.

Hine, C. (2015). *Ethnography for the Internet: Embedded, Embodied and Everyday.* London: Bloomsbury

Holmes, E. (2019). *A Practical Guide to Teacher Wellbeing.* London: Sage Publications Ltd.

Israel, M. (2015). *Research Ethics and Integrity for Social Scientists: Beyond Regulatory Compliance*, 2nd ed. London: Sage.

Kara, H. (2018). *Research Ethics in the Real World.* Bristol: Policy Press.

Kellstedt, P., and Whitten, G. (2018). *The Fundamentals of Political Science Research.* Cambridge: Cambridge University Press.

Kellstedt, P., and Whitten, G. (2020). *An SPSS Companion for the Third Edition of the Fundamentals of Political Science Research.* Cambridge: Cambridge University Press.

Kornuta, H. M., and Germaine, R. W. (2019). *A Concise Guide to Writing a Thesis or Dissertation: Educational Research and Beyond*, 2nd ed. Oxon, UK: Routledge.

Kramer, G., Bernstein, D., and Phares, V. (2019). Getting into graduate school in clinical psychology. In *Introduction to Clinical Psychology* (pp. 415–444). Cambridge: Cambridge University Press.

Krause, C. (2019). *Mindful by Design: A Practical Guide for Cultivating Aware, Advancing, and Authentic Learning Experiences.* Cowin.

Langs, R. (1994). *Doing Supervision and Being Supervised.* London: Routledge.

Lantsoght, E. O. L (2018). *The A-Z of the PhD Trajectory – A Practical Guide for a Successful Journey.* Switzerland: Springer International Publishing AG.

Lee, N. (2009). *Achieving Your Professional Doctorate.* Maidenhead, UK: Open University Press.

Leech, N. L., Barrett, K. C., and Morgan, G. A. (eds.). (2015). *IBM SPSS for Intermediate Statistics: Use and Interpretation*, 5th ed. New York and London: Routledge.

Lemahieu, W., Vanden Broucke, S., and Baesens, B. (2018). Analytics. In *Principles of Database Management: The Practical Guide to Storing, Managing and Analyzing Big and Small Data* (pp. 664–730). Cambridge: Cambridge University Press.

Malone, E. (2020). *Your Booksmart, School-savvy, Stress-Busting Primary Teacher Training Companion.* London: Sage Publications Ltd.

Marchant-Shapiro, T. (2015). *Statistics for Political Analysis.* London: Sage.

Marinac, A., Simpson, B., Hart, C., Chisholm, R., Nielsen, J., and Brogan, M. (2017). Analysing and persuading. In *Learning Law* (pp. 186–208). Cambridge: Cambridge University Press.

McMillan, K. and Weyers, J. (2012). *How To Cite Reference Avoid Plagiarism at University.* Smarter Study Skills. London: Pearson.

Minton, S. J. (2012). *Using Psychology in the Classroom.* London: Sage Publications Ltd.

Moreno, M. A., Fost, N. C., and Christakis, D. A. (2008). Research ethics in the MySpace era. *Pediatrics*, 121, pp. 157–161.

Morris, C., and Murphy, C. (2011). *Getting a PhD in Law.* Oxford and Portland, OR: Hart Publishing Ltd.

Neuhaus, F., and Webmoor, T. (2012). Agile ethics for massified research and visualization. *Information, Communication & Society*, 15, pp. 43–65.

Neuman, W. (2013). *Social Research Methods: Qualitative and Quantitative Approaches*. London: Pearson Education.

Odden, D. (2013). Doing an analysis. In *Introducing Phonology*. Cambridge Introductions to Language and Linguistics (pp. 147–204). Cambridge: Cambridge University Press.

Onwuegbuzie, A., and Frels, R. (2016). *Seven Steps to a Comprehensive Literature Review: A Multimodal & Cultural Approach*. London: SAGE.

Packer, M. (2017). The analysis of qualitative interviews. In *The Science of Qualitative Research* (pp. 71–95). Cambridge: Cambridge University Press.

Patel, S. (2015). The research paradigm – Methodology, epistemology and ontology – Explained in simple language [Online]. *Dr Salma Patel: Research, Digital, UX and a PhD*. Available at: http://salmapatel.co.uk/academia/the-research-paradigm-methodology-epistemology-and-ontology-explained-in-simple-language/. Accessed on 4th August 2020.

Phillips, E. M., and Pugh, D. S. (2015). *How to Get a PhD: A Handbook for Students and their Supervisors*, 6th ed. Berkshire, UK: McGraw-Hill. Available from: VitalSource Bookshelf.

Potter, S. (2006). *Doing Postgraduate Research*, 2nd ed. London: The Open University in association with SAGE Publications.

Pugh, E. P. (2015). *How to Get a PhD: A Handbook for Students and their Supervisors*, 6th ed. London: McGraw-Hill. Available at: VitalSource Bookshelf.

Pyrczak, F. (2017). *Writing Empirical Research Reports: A Basic Guide for Students of the Social and Behavioral Sciences*. Oxon, UK: Routledge.

Ritchie, J., Lewis, J., Nicholls, C. M., and Ormston, R. (2014). *Qualitative Research Practice: A Guide for Social Science Students & Researchers*, 2nd ed. London: Sage.

Rowena, M. (2017). *How to Write a Thesis*. Open University Press.

Russel Group. (2020). *Our Universities* [Online]. Available at: https://russellgroup.ac.uk/about/our-universities. Accessed on 21st August 2020.

Silverman, D. (2014). *Interpreting Qualitative Data*, 5th ed. London: Sage.

Smith, A. (2009). *Interpretative Phenomenological Analysis: Theory, Method and Research*. London: Sage.

Snieder, R., and Larner, K. (2009a). Publishing a paper. In *The Art of Being a Scientist: A Guide for Graduate Students and their Mentors* (pp. 176–185). Cambridge: Cambridge University Press.

Snieder, R., and Larner, K. (2009b). The adviser and thesis committee. In *The Art of Being a Scientist: A Guide for Graduate Students and their Mentors* (pp. 53–64). Cambridge: Cambridge University Press.

Snijders, T. A. B., and Bosker, R. J. (2011). *Multilevel Analysis: An Introduction to Basic and Advanced Multilevel Modelling*, 2nd ed. London: Sage.

Spronken-Smith, R. Cameron, C., and Quigg, R. (2018). Factors contributing to high PhD completion rates: A case study in a research-intensive university in New Zealand. *Assessment & Evaluation in Higher Education*, 43(1), pp. 94–109.

Sturdivant, S., and Relles, N. (2016). Graduate Record Examination (GRE). In *Getting into Graduate School in the Sciences: A Step-by-Step Guide for Students* (pp. 22–37). Cambridge: Cambridge University Press.

Thomas, D. (2016). *The PhD Writing Handbook*. Basingstoke, UK: Palgrave Macmillan.

Thompson, C., and Wolstencroft, P. (2018). *The Trainee Teacher's Handbook: A Companion for Initial Teacher Training*. London: Sage Publications Ltd.

Traer, R. (2008). *Doing Ethics in A Diverse World*. Abingdon, Oxon, UK: Routledge, Taylor & Francis. Available at: VitalSource Bookshelf.

UK Government. (2018). *Data Protection Act 2018*. Available at: www.gov.uk/data-protection. Accessed on 19th August 2020.

UKRI. (2018). *GDPR and Research: An Overview for Researchers*. Available at: https://www.ukri.org/about-us/policies-standards-and-data/gdpr-and-research-an-overview-for-researchers/ Accessed on 16th August 2020.

Universities UK. (2020). Higher education in numbers. *Universities UK* [Online]. Available at: https://www.universitiesuk.ac.uk/facts-and-stats/Pages/higher-education-data.aspx. Accessed on 1st march 2021.

USC Libraries. (2020). Research guides. *University of Southern California* [Online]. Available at: https://libguides.usc.edu/writingguide/theoreticalframework. Accessed on 10th August 2020.

Warne, R. (2017). Applying statistics to research, and advanced statistical methods. In *Statistics for the Social Sciences: A General Linear Model Approach* (pp. 443–484). Cambridge: Cambridge University Press.

Williams, K. (2017). *Referencing and Understanding Plagiarism*. Palgrave.

Williams, K., Bethell, E., and Lawton, J. (2010). *Planning Your PhD*. Basingstoke, UK: Palgrave Macmillan.

World Economic Forum. (2019). Which countries have the most doctoral graduates? Education at a Glance. *World Economic Forum*. Available at: www.weforum.org. Accessed on 20th June 2020.

Zimmer, M. (2010). "But the data is already public": On the ethics of research in Facebook. *Ethics and Information Technology*, 12, pp. 313–325.

Index

Note: Page numbers in italics indicate a figure and page numbers in bold indicate a table on the corresponding page.